Easygoing Guide to Natural Florida

South Florida

Douglas Waitley

Photographs by the Author
Illustrations by Frank Lohan

Pineapple Press, Inc.
Sarasota, Florida

To Mary, wife and traveling buddy for, lo, these many years.

Pineapple Press, Inc.
P.O. Box 3889
Sarasota, Florida 34230

www.pineapplepress.com

Library of Congress Cataloging-in-Publication Data

Waitley, Douglas.
Easygoing guide to natural Florida / Douglas Waitley. — 1st ed.
    v. cm.
Includes bibliographical references and index.
Contents: v. 1. South Florida
ISBN-13: 978-1-56164-371-4 (pbk. : alk. paper)
ISBN-10: 1-56164-371-8 (pbk. : alk. paper)
    1. Florida—Description and travel. 2. Waitley, Douglas—Travel—Florida. 3. Florida—History, Local. 4. Natural history—Florida. 5. Natural areas—Florida. 6. Florida—Guidebooks. 7. Natural areas—Florida—Guidebooks. I. Title.

F316.2.W38 2006
917.5904'64—dc22

2006005112

First Edition
10 9 8 7 6 5 4 3 2 1

Design by Shé Heaton

Contents

Part Two. 'Tween Land and Sea

Preface

Let's start out right. This is an Easygoing Guide.
- Easygoing means no sweat.
- Easygoing means no foot blisters.
- Easygoing means no overnight camping.
- Easygoing means no long, arduous hikes.

These trips are for fun, not exercise.
- Their purpose is to stimulate the mind, not the muscles.
- Appreciating nature does not require dirtying one's hands.
  There are plenty of books for fanatic nature-lovers. This is for more casual nature-lovers.

This is not an encyclopedic listing of Florida's natural places. In order to make this book, a site must meet the following criteria:
- It must be beautiful.
- It must be easy to reach.
- It must not require an inordinate amount of exertion to enjoy.
- It must not cost a lot of money.

Finding natural Florida is not easy, for we do not dwell in the real world. We have made our own reality. An air-conditioned building is not reality. A speeding automobile is not reality. Neat gardens and clipped lawns are not reality. Tanning lotion, sun glasses, and portable radios are not reality. These things were made by humans and will cease to exist when we vanish.

Only nature is real, because only nature is permanent. It's probably the most under-appreciated element in the world, yet it's hiding just behind our false realities.

So one day I made a list of all the natural sights I'd like to see in Florida. The list grew so long that I realized that, if I tried to see them all at once, I'd be doing little more that giving each merely a passing peek. I wanted more. So, after dividing Florida into sectors, I decided to concentrate first on the southern portion. But I quickly discovered that even within this region there were two distinct geographic units. One involved the ridge country and the Kissimmee and St. Johns River systems and the other the swampy lowlands dominated by the Everglades.

Therefore I separated my explorations into two sections: "Ascending the Spine" and "'Tween Land and Sea".

This done, I gathered my notes, started my engine, and headed south. Why not follow me? Check the maps included here, and the roads traveled are in bold in the text. Be sure to follow my motto:

Be easygoing.

Let events flow as they will.

There are many things to be enjoying

If I'm just thoughtful and still.

Part One
Ascending the Spine

N

Tampa

Atlantic
Ocean

① Sunrise
Beaches

③ The
Vast
Marsh

② The
Fascinating
Lagoon

Ft. Pierce

④ The
Great
Prairie

⑤ Forests of
the Spine

Lake Wales Ridge

*Lake
Okeechobee*

Ft. Myers

Part Two
'Tween Land and Sea

⑥ Swamp
Worlds

⑦ Sunset
Beaches

⑧ The
Mysterious
Mangroves

Miami

⑨ Roaming the
Everglades

**Gulf of
Mexico**

⑩ Adrift in
the Keys

General Setting

Part One

Ascending the Spine

Introduction

The landscape of peninsular Florida is mainly the creation of a succession of Ice Ages that began two million years ago. They influenced Florida, not in the form of massive glaciers, but as tremendous fluctuations in the sea level.

One hundred thousand years ago the tepid seas around Florida stood 170 feet above the modern level. This meant that only the highest part of the state remained above water. Waves deposited large sand dunes on these beaches, which thereby became the spine of Florida.

Then the weather turned cold as the last of the four major ice ages began. Northern glaciers grew up to three miles thick, capturing such tremendous amounts of water that the ocean began receding. This recession was not a steady process. Sometimes the cold weather diminished and the glaciers stabilized. Then the ocean would remain at the same level for thousands of years, allowing the waves to create semi-permanant beaches, with a ridge of dunes behind them and open water or marshy flatlands farther back. But the cold would return and the ocean would fall again, leaving the former beach and flatland as a terrace.

There are many such terraces in Florida. Highest is the Lake Wales Ridge, which many call Florida's spine. Eastward from the spine each successive terrace is slightly lower than the one preceding it. Many of these terraces support quite different ecosystems. For example, the south-flowing Kissimmee River, with its wide prairie, occupies one such terrace. And the north-flowing St. Johns River, with its vast marshland, occupies another.

The last glacial age continued for ninety thousand years, until the ocean had fallen far below the modern level.

Finally the climate entered the long warming cycle that we are still in today. The glaciers began to melt, causing the ocean to start rising once more. And the ocean continues to rise, as we see by our eroding beaches. And, according to scientists, we are encouraging this warming with our emissions of greenhouse gases.

So where will the rising ocean stop? Since there is much more ice to melt, particularly in Alaska and Antarctica, perhaps not until most of peninsular Florida is under water once more and all that remains is the sandy spine.

It was my plan to explore the ecosystems of four of the most pronounced of these ancient terraces; I would begin at the Atlantic barrier islands, the most recently formed of the terraces. Then I would drive westward, ascending each slightly higher, more ancient, terrace until I ended in the world of 100,000 B.C. atop the spine of Florida.

Easygoing Guide to

Natural Florida

South Florida

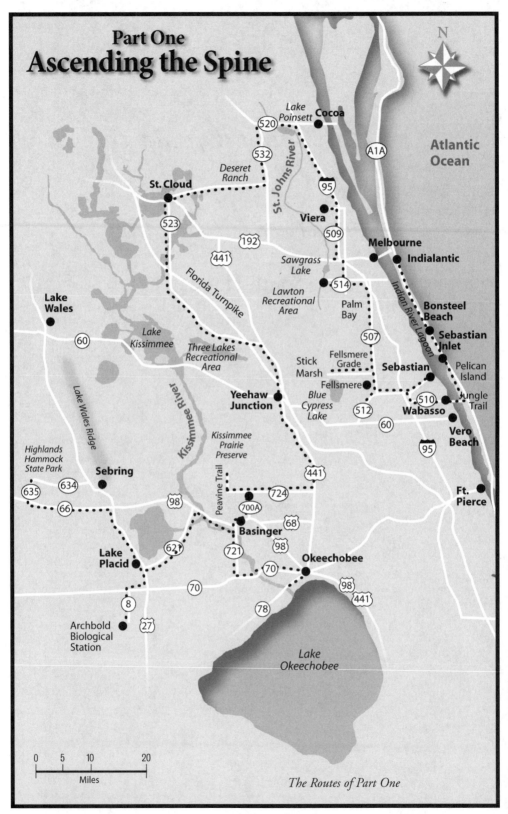

Part One
Ascending the Spine

The Routes of Part One

1

Sunrise Beaches

Facing the ocean at the Indialantic beach seemed to be a strange way to begin my ascent of the spine. Tumultuous breakers rumbled onto the shore, stubborn remnants of the fierce Atlantic nor'easter that had shattered the coast during the night. A gritty wind huffed along the sand. Storm clouds, outlined in the pre-dawn skeletal gray, rolled over the eastern horizon.

Standing on the shore, I had the unmistakable sensation that an elemental force prowled the beachfront. It was the same force that had created the low hills of Florida's spine, as well as the dunes, marshes, and sandy terraces that I would explore as I made my way up to the spine. This barrier island was merely the first of these landscapes.

Sunrise at Indialantic Beach
This beach is part of the narrow string of barrier islands that stretch along most of Florida's Atlantic coast. They formed as sandbars when the water was higher, but were exposed when the ocean fell during the depths of the last glacial age. Now the dying glaciers are releasing their hoard of water and the ocean is rising again. I could feel the ocean's return in the waves rumbling at my feet

Walking the shore, I noticed that the fringes of the storm clouds were assuming a reddish tint that grew ever more intense. Soon I could see the cloud-folds billowing like the sails of the Spanish galleons that once cruised these waters. Then, as the first sunlight glinted on the waves, the entire ocean turned wine-red.

The windsurfer reemerged, tired, but laughing and excited.

Now the wind began to die down and the waves became somewhat less violent. As the sun rose higher, a few people began coming to the beach. I met a couple of college-age kids carrying surfboards. The waves were still thunderous, so I expected they were going to wait for calmer conditions. "No way!" they exclaimed.

I watched them put their surfboards into the water. They had hardly paddled more than a few feet when I lost them amid the swells. It was easier to follow the bright sail of a windsurfer. He sped through the wave troughs, creating a magnificent silver spray. Later I met him as he emerged, tired, but laughing and excited. He paused for a moment to tell me of the exhilaration he experienced amid the dashing water. "You should try it!" he told me, with enthusiasm radiating like an aura. But I don't think I will.

Sea Foam

After the windsurfer left, I stood for a while watching the waves crash to shore, then slide up the sand as if they could go on forever. Where did such energy come from? I wondered. The world has been around for more than four billion years. Wouldn't you think things would begin slowing down?

The tumbling waves left foam on the sand. I knelt down, listening to the bubbles sputter and pop. Soon valleys and pocked plains appeared, leaving white ridges high enough to be mountains in this miniature sea-foam world. Then a second wave rolled in. The old foam-scape vanished, replaced by new valleys, new ridges, new mountains in entirely different configurations. Then they, too, gave way to yet another exotic landscape.

A Little Girl and Her Dog

As I was engrossed in my bubble-universe, I heard a little girl squeal with delight as she and her puppy reached the sand. She whipped off her shoes and socks, and, before her mother could stop her, dashed across the sand to where the wind had blown numerous cakes of foam. She attempted to grab one, but it floated out of her reach. Then more foam-cakes blew her way and she ran after them as if they had been prize balloons at a circus. The dog, having as much fun as she, barked in squeaky puppy tones as he stuck his nose into the foam and tried to bite off chunks.

The tumbling waves left foam on the sand. I knelt down, listening to the bubbles sputter and pop.

"Jennifer!" called her mother, a smooth-looking young woman who I sensed had come to the beach to enhance her already gorgeous tan. "Jennifer, come back. I have your favorite coloring book." But the little girl played like she didn't hear, for she was having too much fun dashing after the foam. "If I have to call again, we won't go to McDonald's!" That did it. Jennifer shambled to where her mother was laying a blanket on the sand. The puppy, as subdued as his mistress, followed. Although Jennifer dutifully picked up her coloring book, I noticed her eyes were following a foam-island that hovered nearby just waiting to be cupped in a little girl's hands.

An Egret's Game

Inspired by the little girl, I removed my shoes and socks, rolled up my pants, and sloshed through the wavelets and the foam. The sun reflected brightly on the water, causing a large egret down the beach to appear like a mahogany carving. Suddenly, more than anything else, I wanted to get a photograph of the bird. I walked slowly and stealthily toward him, hardy moving the upper part of my body. But just as I raised my camera, the skittish bird glided a few hundred feet farther down the beach, where a couple of shell-hunters passed within several feet of him—he never moved. Encouraged, I carefully approached him once more, trying to act with complete nonchalance. But again, as I raised my camera, he flew a few hundred feet further down the beach. I tried twice after that, with the same results. Finally I concluded that he was just toying with me. Who says birds don't have a sense of humor?

The Beginning

Refusing to give the bird further satisfaction, I occupied myself by looking out over the ocean. The storm clouds were mere lumps on the horizon, resembling the headlands of a distant continent. Once there had actually been a continent out there, for during the eons before the Atlantic formed, North America's east coast had been welded to Africa. But, eventually, North America began breaking away from Africa, taking Florida with it. As the drift began, a deep chasm opened between the two continents. Water rushed into this chasm and gradually the Atlantic Ocean formed.

Imagination can do strange things. I saw myself standing here as the chasm that became the Atlantic opened up. Earthquakes rattled the land—not every day, not every year, not even every century, for geological processes occur very slowly in human terms. But my imagination does not involve ordinary time. I felt the earth wrench apart. I heard water cascading into the Atlantic chasm. I watched Africa drifting away. Even today the Atlantic is getting wider—an inch a year. In imagination-time that's very fast.

Sweet Yesterday

The past hovers over Florida's Atlantic beaches. As I walked along the shore, I came upon a man with an electronic metal detector. It reminded me of a hand-held floor scrubbing machine. He slowly waved the detector just above the sand.

"Are you getting anything?" I asked.

When he turned to answer, he blinked, and I got the impression he had been so absorbed that for a moment he had forgotten where he was. "Oh," he answered, "not so far. But just after a storm is the best time. The waves expose things that might have lain undiscovered for years." As he spoke, he kept waving his detector over the sand.

"Last month a guy working the beach just to the south found one hundred eighty Spanish coins worth more than forty thousand dollars," he continued. "A hurricane had washed away enough sand to bring the beach back to where it was in seventeen-fifteen, when a big Spanish fleet was wrecked near here. The following high tide covered the site and now it's lost once more. But they're still buried coins up and down the beach. Metal detectors like mine keep turning them up."

"Have you found any?" I asked.

"A few. But I usually get old U.S. dimes and quarters. Once I found an engagement ring. It was a false diamond, so it's probably lucky it got lost. Some gal was going to get a rude awakening."

He stopped and looked wistfully up the beach to where a large group of gulls and terns were fluttering about. "I did find a treasure many years ago," he said softly. "It was the girl who became my wife." He paused. Reflecting. "We had a lot of happy years together." His voice trailed off and I knew he was back in a yesterday that would never return.

I watched him for a while as he made his careful way down the beach. His head was down and he was deep in nostalgia. I saw him stop twice to pick up an item from the sand. The first time he tossed it into the waves. But the second time he brushed it against his pants leg and put it into his pocket. Was it an ancient Spanish doubloon? Was it just a weathered quarter? Or could it have been a lady's earring with a design that was familiar and dear?

Messengers from Other Continents

As I watched the dream-hunter grow smaller down the beach, I noticed the line of sea wrack that the high storm-tide had left. In a curious mood, I knelt beside a portion for a closer look. Most was sargassum weed wrenched from the Sargasso Sea and dispatched to Florida by the recent storm. Sargassum is kept afloat by multitudes of air sacs that resemble miniature balloons. Some of these had already broken loose and were skittering along the beach. When I separated the mass of sargassum, I found embedded in it the remains of all sorts of sea life. There were shell pieces, egg cases, barnacles, coral fragments, fish bones, and bird feathers. And there was a good assortment of the globules called sea beans.

I picked up a half dozen sea beans and held them in my hand. These were seeds of land plants that had dropped into rivers or onto tropical beaches, where currents or tides had carried them out to sea. Here, encased in their tough, waterproof shells, they had probably drifted for months, even years. The sea beans around me may have come from a hundred different plants. They appeared in many different shapes. Their names reflected these shapes: sea hearts, sea purses, starnut palms—one type of sea bean is even called a hamburger.

I couldn't tell much about my own beans, encrusted as they were with sand and salt. Most were also outfitted with algae, barnacles, or even colonies of the coral-like bryozoans called sea lace. What they wore depended on how long they had been at sea and in what currents they had traveled. I've seen photos of the sea beans after they were cleaned up that show them in reds, purples, oranges, grays, and other colors. It takes six weeks in a rock tumbler, then a good polish to bring out their luster. Since I had neither a tumbler nor six weeks to spare, I contented myself with the magazine photos.

Some people take the sea beans home to plant. Before putting them in the ground, they gently crack their tough shells. Once in a while a few sprout. You never know what will emerge. One lady reported a monstrous vine that would have taken over her house had she let it. An archeologist discovered a sea bean in an Egyptian tomb, planted it, and found he had an orchid that was thought to be extinct. If this seems farfetched, take your complaints to Cathie Katz, for I got this story from her excellent book *The Nature of Florida's Beaches.*

But I'm not a bean nut and could appreciate sea beans without disturbing what's inside. The fascinating thing was to imagine them falling off some tree or vine and into, say, the Amazon River, then sailing off on a long voyage that ended in my palm. In a way they were envoys from foreign lands telling me that the earth recognizes no barriers; that even the ocean is a highway along which life flows as it communicates with the rest of the world. And, just as all living things are related, so are all the regions and environments. We're all part of life's great mystery. Such was the message I received from the little beans resting so quietly in my hand.

Backward Tracks
Now I realized I had walked far down the beach and it was time to head back. It was odd returning, for the tide was going out and most of my outward-bound footsteps remained in the wet sand. I found the place where I had turned to face the waves and speculate on the Atlantic chasm—the line of dark clouds that reminded me of Africa had been replaced by limitless blue. Farther along I saw where the space between my footsteps narrowed as I slowed to get a picture of the obstreperous egret—it had long since flown to another portion of the beach to frustrate some other camera bug. Then I came to the little girl. The coloring book lay in her lap as she stared at the ocean. Her mother was dozing and she could have played in the foam—but the foam was gone. Farther on, my footsteps led to a piece of driftwood from which I had photographed the windsurfer. He had left the beach, for the waves were leveling out.

It was strange to realize that the events that happened such a short time ago were over and could never be replayed except in my mind. I guess that's why the past is called the past.

Sand Plants

It was still early in the morning when I left Indialantic on **Wavecrest Avenue,** which edged south along the dunes. There were parking places and boardwalks over the dunes to the beach. Natural vegetation had been left in place: sea grapes, sea oats, saw palmettos, beach beans, even some prickly pear cactus, for sand makes very dry soil. There were also railroad vines with a few large purple flowers as well as some beach sunflowers with yellow petals clustered around brown cores.

These hardy plants provide vital stabilizing elements against the storm waves that threaten this and the other barrier islands that separate the Atlantic Ocean from the Indian River Lagoon immediately west.

Soon Wavecrest joined **A1A,** upon which I continued south. Now the dunes had clusters of private homes. It would seem only a matter of time until the entire coast will be developed. But just beyond the Spessard Holland Beach something quite unusual is happening. This is the growing network of lands forming the Archie Carr National Wildlife Refuge.

A Patchwork Wilderness: The Archie Carr National Wildlife Refuge

The Archie Carr National Wildlife Refuge extends south along the Atlantic for twenty miles to the Wabasso bridge (SR 510). The impetus for such a refuge originated with Archie Carr, a professor of zoology at the University of Florida. He had done considerable research on sea turtles and was greatly concerned that they might be facing extinction. Although they spend most of their lives in the ocean, they must come ashore to lay their eggs. At this time they need long stretches of undisturbed sandy beaches in which to dig their nests. Because Florida was one of North America's most important sea turtle nesting sites, and because the state's beaches were rapidly succumbing to homes and resorts, Carr emphasized the need for quick action to secure proper nesting areas. Thus, in 1991 Congress created the refuge, named in honor of Carr, who had died four years earlier.

Unfortunately, it was already too late to accumulate a continuous strip of unbroken wilderness, for private homes were scattered throughout the selected area. So the government had no choice except to purchase whatever was offered. What evolved were four major segments along this part of the coast. As more parcels become available, they will be added to the refuge, and perhaps one day it will run uninterrupted for the entire twenty miles.

Because the refuge is designed to remain as wild as possible, there are not many public access points. One is Bonsteel Park a few miles south of Holland Beach.

Turtle Tracks on Bonsteel Beach

I parked at Bonsteel and crossed over the coastal dune, capped with saw palmettos and sea grapes and brightened by golden beach sunflowers. The waves had lessened and now played a quiet serenade on the sand. On a whim I recorded a few minutes of the sound on my pocket recorder and they have given me considerable pleasure whenever I replay them.

Although this was nesting time, I hadn't expected to find any turtles, for the females emerge from the sea in the darkness. They lumber up the sand, dig their nests, deposit their eggs, and return to the water while it's still dark. What I hoped for was to find some of the tracks left by the turtles.

Bonsteel Beach was a long and lonely expanse where only a single fisherman was casting his line into the surf.

The beach was a long, lonely expanse on which a single fisherman was casting his line into the surf. Although it was not as wide as I had expected, it is one of the best places to find sea turtles. Refuge guides conduct turtle-viewing night expeditions from here during the nesting and hatching season, which lasts from May 1, when the first females begin laying their eggs, until to the end of October, when the last babies hatch. Since I was here in early May, I had reasonable expectations of finding turtle tracks. But you can never be sure, for markings in the sand are among nature's most fragile phenomena.

I walked far down the beach, past the fisherman, who had caught nothing and was not in a chatty mood. I had begun to suspect that the wind and showers of the previous night had obliterated the tracks. But then I came upon them. They were unmistakable, resembling three-foot wide tire marks. They began at the high tide seawrack and ran for several yards to where the female had reentered the ocean. In the center of the track was a narrow, flattened groove where her tail dragged in the sand. On each side, like tire treads, were the marks of her flippers. If this were a loggerhead turtle, she would have weighed more than three hundred pounds and looked like the top half of a three-foot-wide boulder. The energy expended must have exhausted a creature used to the weightlessness of the ocean.

Motherhood Comes Lucy Loggerhead

Loggerheads are by far the most frequent sea turtle visitors to Florida beaches. It's estimated that each year nine thousand loggerhead nests are dug in the Carr Refuge alone. That compares to three thousand nests of green turtles, the second most common. Leatherbacks also come to the refuge, but they are too few to be significant.

A loggerhead turtle will hollow out a two-foot-deep excavation in the sand, into which she will deposit around one hundred eggs. Then, after refilling it with sand, she will ruffle the surface to disguise the nest. Her mission is then over and she returns to the ocean. She will never see her young. Does she care?

Thereupon her mission is over and she returns to the ocean. She will never see her young.

No, the job nature conditioned her for has been accomplished. The ocean calls.

It's a Tough World above the Sand

It takes two months for the eggs to develop into babies an inch or so long. The nest is a cozy place, heated by the sun and protected from most enemies by the sand. But the time comes when the babies break through their shells. Then, when coolness indicates night has fallen, they dig to the surface and run pell-mell toward the ocean, which they discern by its reflection of the stars or moon. Waiting for them is a hungry army of raccoons, ghost crabs, and birds. It is mayhem. When a few turtles make it to the water, they are greeted by delegations of equally voracious fish. Out of the two million hatchlings born in the Carr Refuge during the birthing season, the barest few will survive. Common estimates are one in a thousand, but this is probably far too optimistic.

The Odyssey of a Loggerhead Sea Turtle

So what happens to the lucky hatchlings that survive the slaughter of the first few hours? They paddle out to the Gulf Stream, from which they eventually reach the Sargasso Sea, that weedy lens of listless water more than a thousand miles wide that begins just east of the Gulf Stream. Here they hide out amid the sargassum weeds for ten years while they grow and their shells harden. Then they migrate to reefs and warm water lagoons, where they become predators themselves. Their main food is conchs, mollusks, and crabs, which they crush with the massive jaws from which they receive their "loggerhead" name. Twenty-five years after fleeing from their birthing beach, they reach sexual maturity. They then swim back to the very coast they fled in such haste so many years earlier. After mating in the water, the female emerges from the ocean and ascends the beach—perhaps the one at Bonsteel. Here she digs her nest, deposits her eggs, and once more vanishes into the sea.

Instinct

How do the turtles find their way from the Sargasso Sea to the beach where they were born? Scientists still do not know. Some believe they possess a sense whereby they can orient themselves by the magnetic stripes on the ocean floor that are left as the Atlantic Ocean widens. Others believe it may be from a sense that lets them discern the particular chemical composition of the water they seek. Others believe it is a combination of these and of a multitude of other factors not yet discovered.

Whatever it is, apparently the turtles' nesting routine has been programmed in advance. Something is ingrained in their physical makeup impelling them to return to the beaches where they hatched. We call that something instinct.

That made me wonder how many human actions are also governed by instinct. Is there a "group instinct" in humans? Is it based on the fact that primitive humans were basically defenseless against wild animals, and only those humans that combined into groups survived? And, to carry it further, since larger groups were more effective than smaller ones, did those that combined into nations fare better? Are nations basically aggressive hunting groups based on the need for survival? Is a group instinct the basis for our wars? Can we ever surmount this instinct, if indeed it exists?

I knelt down and asked the turtle tracks, "Are you trying to tell us something?" But there was no answer.

Sanderlings: The Champion Wave-runners

By now it was ten o'clock. The air had calmed and the waves had modified into rolling mounds of water. This was perfect sanderling weather.

Sanderlings are plump birds, pale gray above and sugar white below. The are so small that one would almost fit in the palm of a person's hand. During the winter they are on most every Florida beach. But the cutest sanderling, I'm sure, was the one scurrying among the waves near my feet. I named him Rat-a-tat and I enjoyed some time watching him.

As each spent wave nudged the beach, little Rat-a-tat would run along it pecking the sand for invertebrates that had ridden in with the flow. And as the water receded, Rat-a-tat would dash seaward hunting whatever goodies the undertow had uncovered. His stubby legs moved so fast that I could hardly see them.

The longer I watched, the more I was caught up in Rat-a-tat's dance with the waves. Had I been a drummer, I could have given the world a rhythm it had never heard before. Here's the way part of it went: run, run, run, up, up, up, stop . . . peck, peck, peck . . . run, run, run, down, down, down . . . stop . . . peck . . . peck . . . run, sideways, sideways, stop . . . peck, back, back, peck, peck . . . down, down, peck. . . .

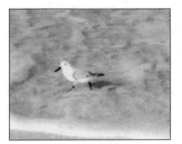

As each spent wave rustled onto the beach, little Rat-a-tat would run along it pecking into the sand for invertebrates that had ridden in with the flow.

Meanwhile his brain must have been aquiver with instructions: "watch that wave, relax—it's little, no it isn't—run toward shore, stop and get that shell, watch that wave, water going out, run with it, no—turn, run toward shore, be quick, stop, get that shell, oh, oh here's a new wave, run, be quick, quick, don't let it catch you, get that shell, run. . . ." Sometimes a wave rolled over Rat-a-tat's feet. If it was larger than he could handle, he'd flutter a foot into the air until it passed. This was a dangerous game, for it he got caught off guard, a big wave could carry him out to sea.

I got out my binoculars and lay on the sand in order to see the world as Rat-a-tat experienced it. Now the little bird was as large as a pelican. I saw his feathers fuzz in the wind. I saw his head dart this way and that. I saw waves as large as waterfalls rumbling toward him. But most of all I saw his legs. Ah, those amazing legs. They moved like loose pistons, like blades of lightning, like, well you get the idea.

The more I watched, the more I felt a paradox. Such a little bird. He seemed so frail that I almost wanted to carry him off and release him beside some fair-weather brook with ripples instead of brutal ocean waves. Yet this would be to misread what sanderlings are all about. They are about the toughest little critters imaginable. Most of the time they live and breed in the Arctic! Some sanderlings fly all the way north from Argentina to get to this beloved refrigerator. Here they no longer eat the soft parts of sea animals, but shift to tough-bodied insects and gritty plant material. When it comes time to nest, they simply scrape up debris from the tundra and lay their eggs on the ground.

I rose from the warm sand and saluted Rat-a-tat, who I hope appreciated my gesture, for I don't give it to just every animal.

The Great Atlantic Flyway

Migratory birds, like Rat-a-tat, are common at Bonsteel Beach, for it is on the great avian skyway used by northern birds each fall to escape the winter, then taken again each spring as these same birds flock back north. A single barrier island may provide a stopover for two hundred or more species. Florida's Fish and Wildlife Conservation Commission publishes *The Great Florida Birding Trail,* a booklet in which the Atlantic coast receives considerable mention. The booklet highlights birds that can be sighted along the ocean. Among them are gannets, jaegers, shearwaters, and petrels, which, I must admit, are not birds familiar to me. But there were plenty of gulls, terns, and pelicans. They may be common, but at least I can recognize them.

The Lovable Killers

Walking back to the parking lot, I came upon a white cat sitting calmly beneath a sea grape. Although she had no collar, apparently she had been the pet of someone who had tired of her. She was obviously used to people, for she did not move as she regarded me with a benign look. Her eyes, large and unblinking, seemed to be questioning me. Would you like to stroke me? Would you like to feed me? Would you like to take me home? Those luminous eyes told me she would be a nice pet. But, they also told of independence—and that, if I did not want her, that was all right, too. She could do just fine without me.

Aware that I had no place for a cat, I turned to go when I noticed in the shadows three little kittens watching me just as intently as their mother.

Seeing the cats made me sad. They all looked well fed, so mama must have been catching something. That something probably included song birds—one study estimates that feral cats kill around one hundred million song birds each year. It also estimates that in one single Midwestern state there are more than two million homeless cats on the loose. Now there is agitation to legalize the killing of many of these cats in order to save the birds. Two states already allow it.

The white cat and I looked at each other. What a beautiful animal, I thought. Far too beautiful to be hunted. But birds are beautiful too. Who is not thrilled by their lilting serenades at springtime! Shouldn't they be protected from feral cats?

The world is a complicated place.

Three Generations at the Sebastian Inlet State Park

Continuing south on **A1A**, I passed the Inlet Marina, then came to the main entrance of Sebastian Inlet State Park. The park's chief attractions are its spacious three-mile beach and the inlet itself, through which tides constantly carry water between the Atlantic Ocean and the Indian River Lagoon. This watery interchange is a vital component in maintaining

One popular fishing location is the catwalk beneath the A1A bridge.

the lagoon's unique blend of salt and fresh water so important to the various organisms living in it. Many types of sea creatures ride in and out on the tides. This makes for exceptionally good fishing. Among the fish caught at or around the inlet, depending on the time of year, are redfish, trout, amberjack, sea bass, and even tarpon. Tackle can be rented within the park. Bait and fishing licenses are also available. One popular fishing location is the catwalk beneath the **A1A bridge.**

There was only one family on the catwalk when I arrived, but it was still before noon on a weekday. A middle-aged man had two poles angled over the railing, his wife sat in a lawn chair, and his young son was busy tossing pebbles into the water gushing through the inlet. A row of pelicans sat on the wooden pilings that protected the bridge's supports. A few steps away the grandfather was baiting his line while humming a tune he must have brought over from the old country. "We're getting snook," the boy told me, as he ran down the catwalk toward the parking lot for more pebbles. "They're coming through like crazy on the tide!"

I watched the family. There was unity here: three generations enjoying being together. Once a common scene, nowadays it was unusual. When gramps hooked a fish, I heard the woman shriek, "You got him!"

It was big. The pole bent and Gramps strained at the reel. "Let me help," the man said. Gramps simply muttered, "Mind your own business." But there was good humor in his voice. It was slow going and soon I found myself rooting for him. When the fish got away, I was almost as disappointed as the rest of them. The father, noticing me for the first time, smiled and shrugged. A conversation had passed between us, although not a word was said.

After a while, I strolled back down the catwalk to where a man was cleaning his catch on a cutting board supplied by the park especially for that purpose. Squatting almost at his elbow were three pelicans expectantly waiting for the leavings. I wondered if pelicans' mouths watered.

From there I ambled along the walkway beside the inlet. The inlet is very wide and it was difficult to believe that originally a thick mound of sand separated the Atlantic from Indian River at this point. The first channel was dug by hand more than a hundred years ago. But winds and waves quickly filled it, as well as two subsequent channels. It wasn't until after World War II that the present channel was put into operation.

The World of the Pier

I continued along the breakwater to the great pier, which is the park's main attraction. Protruding 440 feet into the Atlantic, it offers thrilling seascapes as well as opportunities for good fishing.

The pier is a little world all its own. I had hardly taken more than a few dozen steps on it, before a salty mist diminished contact with the shore. The air had an unusual fragrance, like a combination of sea plants and watermelons. Waves rumbled against the jagged stone boulders that protected the pier's footings.

I leaned over the railing and regarded the boulders as the waves washed over them. Some were composed of the blend of limestone and coquina shells that is so common in Florida. Others were of granite, with flecks of mica giving off sparkles. They had been formed in mountains and trucked here to give the rocky barrier a toughness that the coquina lacked. I also saw schist and gneiss boulders—banded rocks altered from their natural state by the heat and weight of great depths and later exposed by erosion or by earth upheavals. The boulders were actually a geological museum.

As I stood regarding the rocks, a little brown bird strutted almost

The Pier is a little world all its own.

under my feet. He had a tan head with a streak of white around the eyes and a long, thin beak. It was a dunlin, which is a type of sandpiper. Oblivious to me, he was busy pecking at the pier's surface. I wondered what he was after, for concrete slabs are hardly known for their seafood. More dunlins nearby were just as happily pecking at the concrete. I guessed there were fish remains that I couldn't see. Anyway, they'd all soon be flying back to their beloved homes in the Arctic tundra.

The further I walked out on the pier, the more fishermen I encountered. They were a special breed, a kind of inbred community. They were here not only to catch fish, but for comradeship and to share a way of life. Out on the pier there was no difference between CEOs and machinists. The dress for everyone was casual-grubby. Nor was there expensive equipment—just a fishing rod, a fish bucket, a bait bucket, and a thermos with coffee or other beverages of choice. Most of the anglers had small ground-level carts that they used to move their supplies. Special holders in the carts stored the rods in an upright position. Many fishermen had folding chairs and some had radios. But I didn't hear loud music. This was fishville, not Woodstock.

The Code of the Pier

There was constant chatter among the citizens of fishville. "What'd you catch?" "What's a good bait today?" "Are the mullet runnin'?" Baseball and football were also good topics. So was NASCAR. Man talk. If anyone had mentioned how pretty the waves looked, he'd probably get tossed over the rail. Sissy conversation was not allowed. That was the Code of the Pier.

As I made my way through the fishermen (and a few fisher-ladies), my main concern was not getting hooked myself. For once in a while someone forgot that, when he cast his hook forward into the ocean, he first made a backward movement. It was like a game of dodgeball. My goal was to reach the end of the pier, which I managed to do.

At the Pier's End

The view from the end was appealing. To the north I saw white-capped waves rolling against a broad, golden-hued beach that reached beyond imagination. To the south was the inlet, with tidal currents creating ever-changing water swirls. Across the inlet was a shorter jetty, with its own row of fishermen, and beyond that more of the wild, limitless beach. Looking east out to sea, I viewed a line of cascading breakers. Buzzing around these breakers were a trio of fast-moving jet skiers. Heading at full speed into a wave, they'd slam over its crest, where the

Looking east, out to sea, I viewed a line of cascading breakers.

force of the wave would fling them through the air. Most times the skier could stay aboard his craft and come out flat on the surface. But sometimes his jet ski would fly off in one direction and he in another.

A guy standing next to me was also watching. "That's some skill out there," he said with admiration. Then he turned to me. "You've never had excitement until you've jet skied! You should try it."

That was my second offer of reckless adventure that day. Evidently word had not made it to the pier that I was an Easygoing Traveler and such exertion was not part of my agenda.

Surfing at the Inlet

Far more popular at the inlet than jet skiing is surfing. Around the beginning of April each year the East Coast Surfing Championships are held here. At this time around four hundred of the area's top surfers, plus a large audience, gather for the four-day competition. At a recent championship, a storm the day before had left the ocean "pumping" (to use their lingo) with head-high surf. And a brisk offshore wind created clean-breaking waves. It was an ideal venue for the contestants to demonstrate their surfing skill.

On this day just getting out to the waves could be nearly as difficult as successfully riding them. As the surfers paddled out to the line-up area, they had to "duck dive" through the oncoming breakers. Those that did not do this successfully were caught in the waves and rolled violently toward shore. "When you go under you're completely helpless," remarked one surfer. "All you hear and all you feel is the ocean thrashing about you." Once the surfers were lined up beyond the breaking waves, the first in line caught his wave. It was his alone. No one else could take that particular wave with him. "To ride a heavy, 'pipeline' wave," one surfer recalled, "it's like, man . . . imagine that a runaway freight train is beneath your board and you can't get off. The roar of the churning water is terrific. But you don't really hear it. All you know is that you gotta stand on your board and guide it by shifting your weight and position. A false move and you're gone."

There are various stunts that the competitors must perform, for which they are given points by the judges. In one of the most spectacular the surfer and his board jump out of the top of the wave and fly through the air. The winner of one year's competition was a seventeen-year-old who grabbed onto a monster wave and, with the crowd and the judges gasping, maneuvered himself into a daring high, then shot over the crest in what a commentator described as an "electrifying" air show. When the youngster came to shore, he exclaimed exuberantly, "It was my biggest thrill ever! It was totally epic!"

While out at the end of the pier, I heard several tales of the glories of surfing. But I'm still resisting the sport. Maybe I'll try my luck sometime later.

Or maybe not.

2

The Fascinating
Indian River Lagoon

The Setting

The Indian River Lagoon was formed from flooded lowland between the barrier islands along the Atlantic and a line of mainland dunes, call the Silver Bluff, formed during an earlier period when the ocean was higher. The lagoon runs north and south for 156 miles. It is a unique blend of salt water from the Atlantic and fresh water from streams and rain. The lagoon supports 2,200 species of animals—more than any other lagoon or estuary in North America. These include 310 species of birds and 700 species of fish—four of which breed nowhere else. Over a third of the nation's manatees live or find winter shelter in the lagoon. It is also home to the Pelican Island National Wildlife Refuge, the very first in the nation's wildlife refuge system.

For these reasons I wanted to explore not only the lagoon but one of the streams that empties into it from the Silver Bluff country.

Getting There

On this trip I intended to explore the lee side of the barrier island as well as the lagoon and the Silver Bluff country beyond. So I started on the barrier island at the Sebastian Inlet State Park.

I began my exploration at Sebastian Inlet State Park's marina. I reached the marina by driving north on **SR A1A** about a mile from the park's main entrance, where I had ended my travels last chapter. Upon reaching the marina's entry road, I turned left and soon came to the docking area.

I was now on the interior side of the barrier island. The sea oats and other plants of the frontal zone were gone. In their place was lush vegetation dominated by mangroves, where the land was wet and brackish, and by cabbage palms and live oaks, where the land was slightly higher and drier. Although the soil was still predominantly sand, it was darkened by the mulch of decayed leaves.

live oak

Off into the Lagoon

At the marina I boarded a tour boat for a two-hour voyage on the Indian River Lagoon. As the boat headed slowly south through the marina cove, the calm water was only slightly ruffled by a gentle breeze. On my left the shore made an easy southward arch. The engine hummed as the scenery began gliding past. I rested my arm on a wooden sill and watched some egrets vying for a place atop a piling. The cruise promised not only a pleasant tour of the lagoon, but a visit to the Pelican Island National Wildlife Refuge, a highly prized refuge for many types of birds.

Our captain was a long-time park ranger who had been called from other duties to pilot the boat. "It's been a while since I've been out on the lagoon," he told us, "and I've missed it." He adjusted a nautical cap that had just been given to him and was a size too small. "My name's Captain Nemo," he said in a semi-serious tone. "I know just about everything there is about the Indian River Lagoon. And what I don't know I'll make up." He liked to joke, but I found him to be well informed, and I don't think he made very much up.

Out on the Mainstream

We cruised southward to the Sebastian Inlet, where, from a score of fishing boats rocking with the tide, fishermen were hoping to catch grouper, flounder, and other fish. More anglers were standing on the A1A bridge catwalk letting their lines ride the current. "Earlier this week," Nemo said, "there was a major run of shrimp on the outgoing nighttime tide. People on the catwalk caught a bonanza of redfish and sea trout feeding on the shrimp."

As we turned into the mainstream, almost immediately we encountered a brisk wind, not cold, but stiff enough to cause some of the passengers to don their jackets and others to wrap their shoulders with beach towels. Although the boat did not pitch, it did vibrate. And once in a while the bow split a wave, sending a spray over one portion of the craft. Captain Nemo, tanned and hardy, laughed. "You can expect some ruffles. The lagoon averages only three feet in depth, so whenever the wind kicks up we have a little fun."

It's Not a River, It's a Lagoon

Out in the middle I could understand why some persons call this a river, for it ran north and south farther than I could see. "In pioneer days," Nemo said, "people loaded their household goods onto boats at Titusville and made the easy cruise down to land vacated by the Seminoles, who the U.S. Army had persuaded to leave—that or die," Nemo added. "Before them, the Spanish sailed the lagoon."

As the engine droned on, Nemo continued. "There's a no-no on this boat. You can't call it a river. It might look like a river, but it doesn't flow anywhere. Neither does it have a mouth or a source. Its only outlets are six widely spaced channels to the Atlantic. That's why it's a lagoon. But more than that, its connection with the ocean makes it also an estuary. The proper name of the whole thing should be the Indian River Lagoon Estuary. That's too long, so many people still call it the Indian River. Just the same, it's not a river, it's a lagoon."

By now we were in the middle of the lagoon. The lagoon's ruffled surface was pale blue—reflecting the sky and the hazy clouds drifting across it. The wind tossed fine spray around us. The soft splash of the water against the hull almost made me imagine I was riding the clouds themselves.

The Lure of the Spoil Islands

The lagoon was two miles across at this point, although in some sections of its long route it widens to three miles and in others it becomes very narrow. When we reached the opposite shore, we turned south once more, passing the tossing masts and weathered docks of Captain Hiram's marina, which I would visit later in the day. There were many pleasure craft out on the water—everything from humble motorboats to luxury schooners.

"You may wonder how the larger boats can travel the lagoon,"

At one spoil island there was even a houseboat.

Nemo continued, "when they obviously require greater depth than the lagoon's three feet? The answer is that now we're on the Intracoastal Waterway where a channel has been dug to a depth of twelve feet. The Waterway runs all the way down the East Coast from Chesapeake Bay to Key West. That's nearly a thousand miles. Digging it took a lot of dredging, as you might imagine. The dredgings, called spoils, were deposited in mounds beside the Waterway. At first they were ugly, barren things. But gradually they attracted mangroves and other plants, and soon became ideal sites for picnics and overnight camping. These pretty little islands in a row are spoil islands."

We cruised close to several of these islands. Small vessels were anchored at many, and at one I noticed there was even was a houseboat. "These spoil islands are also popular with large numbers of birds," Nemo said, "for we're also on the Great Atlantic Flyway." He pointed to our left. "Those white birds are egrets. The dark ones are cormorants. And look over there! See the blue herons? Beyond them are a couple of wood storks. Don't worry, folks, only the European storks deliver babies." There were some chuckles, but I think he expected more.

Knockout Lunches

Eventually we cut back across to the eastern side of the lagoon where there was a cluster of natural, not man-made, islands. About that time we saw a dozen or so brown pelicans that were plummeting headfirst into the water. The velocity with which they smacked into the lagoon would have knocked out the toughest human boxer. "They're snacking on a school of fish," Captain Nemo shouted above the throb of the engine, which he then cut so we could observe them. I watched one bird circle from a height of forty or fifty feet until he drew his bead on a fish. Then he folded his wings and hurled himself toward his prey. Hitting the water with a violent splash, he scooped up the fish, as well as several others. Then he took to the air once more, none the worse for his knockout experience.

"Enough of the preliminaries," the Nemo called, as he hit the throttle. "Now on to the wildlife refuge!" He was having as much fun as the rest of us.

The Wonders of Pelican Island

Ahead was a lump of land famous among conservationists as the Pelican Island National Wildlife Preserve. For some unknown reason this particular island is populated by birds in almost unbelievable numbers. Though humans are prohibited from setting foot on it for fear of disrupting the birds, boats are permitted to hover a hundred or so yards offshore, which is close enough for binoculars to provide excellent views. For those who did not have them, the captain handed out loaners.

I was eager to see the island, for I had read numerous articles about it. Many of the passengers were as excited as I. One middle-aged couple told me they had come all the way from England with a visit to Pelican Island as one of their major goals. When I asked them if Disney World was another goal, the man answered, "Oh, does Disney have a world?" His wife grinned. This was their thirtieth wedding anniversary and they were strictly eco-touring.

Although Pelican Island was small and just one of many, it was easily distinguished by the horde of pelicans roosting in the low mangroves that covered most of it. From a distance they reminded me of ornaments on Christmas trees. Soon we came to a buoy with a marker indicating further advance was prohibited. So we hovered here for a half hour, let-

I turned my attention to the brown pelicans, who prefer to rest in the mangroves rather than on the sandbars like their white cousins.

ting our binoculars bring the birds almost within stroking range.

The most spectacular were the white pelicans that had congregated on a narrow sandbar between two portions of the island. There must have been two dozen of them standing almost wing to wing. They were so large and so pure white that they could have been mistaken for swans. Some were always taking off or landing. In the air their eight-foot-long snowy wings tipped with black presented a memorable sight. These birds just had just arrived, possibly from as far as Manitoba. Being tourists, like we humans on the boat, they planned to spend the winter in balmy Florida, then take the sky road back north when spring came.

I watched one white pelican as it took wing and soared upwards on an invisible updraft until he was just a moving white dot. I wondered if he might dive from there, but I learned from Nemo that white pelicans do not indulge in such brain-addling meal-gathering tactics. Instead they feed on the surface by scooping up small fish in their pouches as they swim.

Then I turned my attention to the brown pelicans, who prefer to rest in the mangroves rather than on the sandbars like their white cousins. Although they are called brown pelicans, only the young are truly brown. The adults are grayish, with long, white necks and white faces topped by what looked like glowing yellow skull caps. They sat quietly on the mangroves, as if in deep contemplation. Some could even have been asleep, for flock birds can rely on their comrades to give alarms.

The Hero of Pelican Island

Today brown pelicans are very common along the Florida coasts. But this wasn't always so. At the end of the nineteenth century hunters who sought them for their feathers, which were popular adornments on the ladies' hats, had almost wiped them out. Indeed, Pelican Island was almost one of the last refuges for these beleaguered birds. They were saved mainly by the efforts of an unlikely hero, Paul Kroegel, an immigrant bean farmer and accordion player.

Kroegel lived on the family homestead across the water in the town of Sebastian. He loved the Indian River Lagoon and often sailed among its islands. He was especially fascinated by one special island that had an overpowering attraction for pelicans. Whenever an influential person passed through the region, Kroegel saw to it that he became aware of the plight of Florida's birds.

Through his activities, Kroegel gained the attention of Frank Chapman, who had founded the Audubon Society in 1899. The Society successfully urged Congress to prohibit interstate transportation of illegally killed birds. This was a vital step in diminishing the plume trade. Another step was taken in 1903, when President Theodore Roosevelt declared Pelican Island a National Wildlife Preserve, the very first in a series of such preserves that now total well over five hundred. Although Kroegel was made the warden, oddly, no provision was made for his salary. Again the Audubon Society took action, providing for an initial pay of $7.00 per month.

In the days when Kroegel patrolled the waters in his own boat with a double-barrel shotgun to enforce his authority, Pelican Island was more than double its current size. But over the years waves from storms and motor boats dislodged much of its sandy base. The island may have been on its way to oblivion if the federal government had not recently begun to build it up again with tons of sand and oyster shells dredged from the Intracoastal Waterway.

Extinction is Forever

The boat rocked gently as I watched the pelicans. Pleasant as it was, I felt a little uneasy thinking how close these birds had come to vanishing as others already have. I remember reading from John Burroughs, one of my favorite nineteenth-century nature writers:

> In my boyhood the vast armies of the passenger pigeons were one of the most notable spring tokens. . . . the naked beechwoods would suddenly become blue with them. . . . What man now in his old age who witnessed in youth that spring and fall festival and migration of the passenger pigeons would not hail it as one of the gladdest hours of his life if he could be permitted to witness it once more.

Thank you, Paul Kroegel.

Mermaids They're Not

It seemed as if we had just arrived when Nemo revved up the engine and we headed homeward. Often we passed strange floating objects resembling oversized cigars. "These pods are young mangroves out to seek their fortunes," Nemo said. "Some people think they are seeds, but before they fall off the adult trees they already have miniature leaves sprouting from one end. When a pod strikes a bit of muck, it will take root and pretty soon a red mangrove will appear."

For a while I watched a group of dolphins leap and frolic beside the boat. But they soon bounded off to some new playground. Then I noticed a dark shape about ten-foot long lumber away from the boat. "That's a manatee," Nemo said. "They're mammals and have to come to the surface to breathe. To me they resemble big globs of fat. But in the days of wooden sailing vessels sailors, long at sea, wanted to believe they were beautiful mermaids. Imagination does strange things, for a manatee can weigh up to a ton! Today we just call them sea cows. And nobody wants to date 'em."

Since we were not going very fast, the manatee had heard us in time to swim out of our way. That's not always true, for speeding boats can catch the animals off guard. Because manatees like to feed near the surface, some of them are killed each year by the propeller blades on motorboats. Even more have the scars on their backs that result from such encounters. Ironically, the shapes of these scars help scientists to keep track of particular manatees and thereby determine their survival rates and migration routes. The scars also enable environmentalists to not only identify them, but assign them folksy names. To help the manatees avoid dangerous encounters with boats, speed limits have been established throughout much of the lagoon, to the resentment of many boaters, who protest that the manatee population has stabilized and no longer needs protection.

Watery Meadows

Manatees are most frequent during the winter, when the lagoon is warmer than the Atlantic. Learning that one of their favorite foods is seagrass, I began watching for it. The grasses were easy to distinguish in shallow water. There are seven species in the lagoon. They are not primitive plants, for they have flowers, shed pollen, and bear seeds, just the way their land-based cousins do. "Seagrasses are known as an indicator species," Nemo said, "for their health indicates the general health of the lagoon. We're concerned about them, for they are dying in many places. And, when they die, many other creatures go with them. Here's a statistic for you. A single acre of seagrass provides food for forty thousand fish

I watched a fisherman cast his line as a wood stork hovered overhead, ready to share his catch.

and fifty million small invertebrates. Ponder that!"

As I pondered, I found such figures almost incredible. Since an acre is only about seventy yards on each side, that meant that, as the boat moved forward, I was passing over hundreds of thousands of fish and smaller animals. I tried to picture them living out their lives in the dense meadows beneath the boat. To them nothing existed except the grass, the water, and danger. The boat itself was just an inconsequential passing shadow.

The main factor affecting seagrass growth is the amount of sunlight each plant receives. This depends on the clarity of the water as well as its freedom from pollutants and sediments entering the lagoon from rivers and canals and from storm sewer runoffs. Over a fifty-year period the lagoon's seagrasses have declined almost twenty percent. Although they seem to be recovering, scientists still consider the lagoon to be in a state of stress.

Upon rounding Roseate Island, we sailed parallel to the long sliver of the barrier island dividing the lagoon from the Atlantic. At Coconut Point I watched a fishermen cast his line as a wood stork hovered overhead hoping to snare his catch. Passing the Sebastian Inlet, we soon reached the state park marina. Here Nemo made a rather bumpy landing and left us with his final comment: "Don't forget, it's a lagoon, not a river."

On the Road Again

From the marina I headed south on **A1A,** enjoying a good view of the state park's spectacular jetty pier from the **Sebastian Inlet bridge.** Beyond the bridge, vegetation coated the low dunes along the Atlantic side of the road. There were places to park and paths that led over the dunes to protected beaches where on summer nights sea turtles lay their eggs and, later, the young scamper into the ocean. On the lagoon side of the road were cabbage palms, sea grapes, and a long sidewalk for scenic strolls.

I stopped briefly at the McLarty Treasure Museum, which specializes in relics of a Spanish fleet that was wrecked off this coast while loaded with plunder from Inca and Aztec lands, scattering gold and silver in the shallows and along the shore. Even today treasure hunters with magnetic search devices find valuable coins hidden in the sand.

Today the sandy byway is wide and graded, but the jungle is there.

Then I continued along the narrow strip of land that I had seen from the boat. The homes occupying the dune crests had wonderful views of the ocean, but their location exposed them to the hurricane winds that destroyed or severely damaged many a few years ago.

The Jungle Trail

The land widened as I passed onto Orchid Island, where I found the entrance to the **Historic Jungle Trail,** as the sign read. The trail is five miles long and, although composed only of hard-packed sand, it is easily passable for cars, except after heavy rains. Upon turning onto the entry road, I quickly came to the Welcome and Orientation Building with informational display boards. From there I drove south through what was once a 150-acre grapefruit grove. Today it is an overgrown hodgepodge of palmettos and abandoned citrus trees that are gradually being replaced with native plants. In a mile I came to a short turnoff where a circular extension culminated at a boardwalk called the Centennial Trail, which led a few hundred yards to an elevated platform with a good view of Pelican Island.

Strolling along the boardwalk, I discovered that each plank is dedicated to a specific wildlife refuge (the nation has more than five hundred), starting with the most recent and continuing to the earliest, which was Pelican Island.

Then I ascended the eighteen-foot high platform. There, about a quarter mile away, was Pelican Island. Having been much closer by boat, I was surprised how small it was—just a low mound covered with mangroves. Then I reflected how the word "small" is relative. True, two acres is insignificant as far as an island's size goes. But if you multiply that by the island's influence in establishing the national wildlife refuge system, it expands to impressive proportions.

The Civilized Wilderness

Continuing south on the **Jungle Trail,** I was carried back to the era when grapefruit wagons groaned along its narrow, rutted confines. Dense vegetation would scrape the wagons' sides and dripping fronds would douse the drivers. Although the sandy byway was wide and graded when I passed over it, live oaks still overhung the road. Their limbs were gnarled and gracefully misshapen and exuded mystery. Mingling with the oaks were cabbage palms, their fronds as ragged as in the old days. At ground level was a matting of saw palmettos and rank grasses.

Today I could see that the trail has a precarious existence, for developers have lopped off large acreages along its route. Indeed, the lower two-thirds of the trail barely survives as a dusty ribbon edged on each side by a mere twenty feet or so of wilderness, behind which I could clearly see modern homes and a neatly manicured golf course. I even heard cries of "fore!" riding on the wind. No, this was not the jungle trail of old. But it's the best we can do. The past can never be recreated.

Sails in the Afternoon

The northern portion of the Jungle Trail ended at the **Wabasso Causeway (SR 510).** Although the southern portion of the Trail continued across the road, it was not on my route. Instead, I turned west on the causeway and ascended the arched bridge over the Indian River Lagoon. At the top I caught a magnificent view of the lengthy waterway shimmering in the sun. Just over the bridge I came to the sign for the Environmental Learning Center. The Center is on a largely unpopulated island in the lagoon and the short road leading to it is much like the Jungle Trail.

I stopped for a while to watch a boat pass under the **Wabasso bridge.** With its sail cupped in the wind, there was something incredi-

With its sail cupped in the wind, there was something incredibly romantic about it.

bly romantic about it. I could imagine the hull jammed with stolen treasure, with rollicking pirates on deck, and maidens aboard, too. I heard female laughter echoing across the water. Was I missing a good party? In a few moments the boat slipped out of sight. But the laughter lingered.

The Environmental Learning Center

I continued down the narrow road and in a moment arrived at the Learning Center. It consists of a modern central building with a gift shop and enough literature on environmental matters to fill a wheelbarrow, or so it seemed. There are several satellite buildings devoted to research and the activities of students exploring the natural world. And there is an elevated walkway through the mangroves that dominate the island.

Leaving the central building, I headed for the boardwalk. I had never actually strolled through a mangrove forest. Not many people have, for the ground is always mushy and the tangle of branches, roots, and vines make it all but impassable without a machete. I had to admire the workers who installed the elevated boardwalk. The mangroves engulfed me. Where the ground was slightly higher were white mangroves, somewhat larger than the others. Farther on, I encountered black mangroves, each surrounded with its miniature legion of fingerlike growths. But the red mangroves, with their bizarre jumble of prop roots, were dominant. Although the mangroves are denoted as white or black or red, one would have to use one's imagination to see those colors—just the way the persons who named them did.

red mangrove

Even with the elevated boardwalk, the way was not what I would call a stroll in the park. Although the day was not hot, the mangroves were so dense that no breeze freshened the heavy atmosphere. Moisture from the sodden earth made the air sticky. In the summer this would be a perfect breeding ground for mosquitoes, and even today, in late winter, a few dined on my arm. The only thing good I can say about them is that the greedy little bugs stayed around long enough for me to give them a satisfying swat.

The boardwalk ended at a branch of the lagoon, where a short pier reached far enough into the water for me to observe the seagrasses. Watching them sway in the opaque water, I thought they looked like discards from an unkempt aquarium. It was difficult to believe that the health of the lagoon depended on such humble plants.

On the way back I stopped at the students' laboratory. There were only a few young people there. One future scientist was peering into a microscope so intently that, when I asked him a question, he didn't even hear me. There were numerous nature displays, including a bird exhibit that attracted several girls. "They are *so* pretty," one remarked. Wouldn't these youngsters be horrified at the ladies a hundred years ago who adorned their hats with their plumes. At another large table was an assortment of seashells. This was not a formal display—they were just lying around for anyone to pick up and examine. One was a conch that a boy had just put up to his ear. "Hey, Joey," he shouted excitedly to a friend across the room, "listen to this. You can really hear the sea!"

I left feeling good.

Caring for the Lagoon

Residing along the lagoon's 156 miles are some one million people. To them a healthy lagoon means jobs, recreation, tourist income, and higher property values. This economic impact is estimated at more than a billion dollars annually. So it's not surprising that volunteers are usually readily available for lagoon cleanups. Some groups go on regular "trash-bash" expeditions to the spoil islands to remove debris from around the fire pits, picnic tables, and benches. Helping finance their efforts is the sale of auto licenses displaying the Indian River Lagoon logo. These popular plates raise around $300,000 annually for the lagoon, an amount that is almost tripled by matching contributions from state and other sources.

You Can't Make a Sandwich without a Computer

Continuing west on the **Wabasso Causeway,** I passed a parking area from where there was a good view of the lagoon. Several miles farther on I came to **US 1,** where I turned north toward the town of Sebastian. Reaching **Indian River Boulevard,** I veered right on it. This road led along the lagoon and was bordered on the land side by well-maintained parks. In a few miles I reached Captain Hiram's Restaurant, directly on the water.

I had chosen Captain Hiram's not only for its appealing setting, but for the adjoining marina, from where I could take the *River Queen* for a three-hour cruise up the St. Sebastian River. The St. Sebastian supplies an important portion of the fresh water that merges with the salty influx from the Sebastian Inlet to form the Indian River Lagoon's brackish mixture so vital to the plants and animals that depend on it.

Having time for lunch, I gave the waitress, a sprightly teenager, my order. However, she returned in a moment saying my sandwich would be delayed because the computer was down. When I asked her if the computer did the cooking, she answered that all orders to the kitchen were placed through it. When I asked her if she couldn't just hand the order to the cook, she answered rather brusquely, "That's just not the way it's done," as if everyone should know this. Well, when she finally brought my lunch, she had an excited look on her face. "I gave the order directly to the cook," she said. "I've never done that before!"

Chalk up one for humans over machines. We don't win very many.

Voyage on the St. Sebastian River

After the excitement of lunch, a ride on the *River Queen* could have been anticlimactic, but it wasn't. The boat was a spacious catamaran that

Our captain was a youngish miss with long blond hair and a cheerful disposition. She was helped by a retired merchant mariner, who spotted birds and knew a lot of good stories.

could seat about thirty people. Our captain was a youngish miss with long blond hair and a cheerful disposition. She was helped by a retired merchant mariner, who spotted birds and knew a lot of good stories. All in all they made a nice combination.

To reach the St. Sebastian River we first sailed north up the Indian River Lagoon, defined on the left by a low sand ridge. We passed several spoil islands, on each of which were a few Australian pines that had been uprooted by hurricanes. But most of these tall trees had weathered the storms even though they were anchored in nothing more than wet sand.

"The Indian River is commercially rich in crabs," our stalwart captain said, pointing out softball-size buoys of various colors that indicated the locations of crab traps.

After a half hour, we came to the low **US 1 bridge** across the mouth of the St. Sebastian River. As we inched under the bridge, the captain told us that one of the two spans had been built in the 1920s and the other in the 1950s. I don't usually take pleasure in inspecting the underside of bridges, but I found that the supports of the older span were rather graceful arches similar to those used in the Keys, whereas the newer bridge was supported by simple four-sided posts. I'd select the old arches for my Eye-Pleasing Award, if I had such an award to give.

The Dolphins of the St. Sebastian River

The St. Sebastian River, where it cuts through the bluff, is several hundred yards wide. The water was dark, but clear enough near the shore that I could see the bottom. The clarity is from the springs that make the water fresh. This freshness attracted Spanish sailors, who came here to fill their casks. It was they who named the river in honor of St. Sebastian.

The river was alive with striped mullet, which attracted dolphins. Almost immediately a pod of dolphins began swimming along with our boat. They moved with a rolling glide that exposed their dorsal fins and then their backs, which glistened silver in the sunshine. As cameras began clicking, the captain came on the microphone: "People who take pictures of dolphins get a lot of water," she chuckled, "for the full animal rarely appears."

"I've gotten to know this pod fairly well," the captain continued. "My boyfriend is that one with a handsome white spot on his head. At least I think it's a boy." She cut the engine. "Aren't they graceful! Let's watch for a couple of minutes."

The dolphins milled around the boat. Some came as close as four feet. Then one must have spotted a school of mullet, for they were off in a silver flash. "Wow! There they go! Their normal speed is about seventeen miles an hour. But when they really want to get somewhere, they can rev up to nearly forty. And that's moving! Even sharks steer shy of them, wary of being butted silly."

The Great Vulture War

As the captain resumed our voyage, she gave the microphone to her salty mate, the merchant mariner who had plowed the ocean lanes when the captain was still a tow-headed schoolgirl. Their styles were definitely different.

"The former US 1 bridge was near here," came his sandpaper voice. "This is where the Ashley gang was shot up. A mean bunch they were. Scared 'most everyone. Good riddance." He waited for the boat to move farther up the river. "See those two houses over there? The first one belongs to a lady who loves to feed vultures. They're ugly birds with horrible habits. Nevertheless, the lady loves 'em. But that's not the case with the guy next door. He hates vultures and even went so far as to secure a permit to kill up to forty-five of them each year. So the lady feeds them and the man pops them off. The local newspaper calls it the Great St. Sebastian River Vulture War."

He was just getting started. "The guy the river was named after lived during Roman days. He got himself killed because he was a Christian. It was a gruesome thing. I'll tell you about it . . ."

"No thanks, Sinbad," the captain interrupted pleasantly, for "gruesome" was not part of a pleasure cruise. "I want the folks to watch that osprey flying past. Such a beautiful bird! Look at those huge, creamy white wings with dark bands. He can actually hover over the water while he watches for fish. See, folks, he has a fish in his talons."

Along a Mystic River

We had not gone very far before the river broke into three segments. This was caused by the Silver Bluff, hidden from view a few miles to the west. The Silver Bluff is a geological formation that can be traced the entire length of Florida's Atlantic seaboard. It marks the seashore as it was four thousand years ago when the ocean was higher. At that time the Indian River Lagoon was part of the Atlantic and the barrier islands beyond were just sandbars.

One prong of the Sebastian River ran north for a short distance. Another continued west and connected with Canal 54, which leads into the St. Johns Marsh—I intended to visit that on a later day. The main portion of the river turned abruptly south—it was this that we followed.

Now the river narrowed and there was almost no sign of civilization. The banks were clothed by tall cabbage palms mixed with red maples and laurel oaks. Tumbling down to the shore were leather ferns, water willows, and wax myrtles. In the shallows were cattails and water lilies. At one point we saw a great blue heron standing in the shallows watching us. He was as still as a marble carving. A little later we came upon a cormorant sitting on a limb with its wings extended.

Great Blue Heron

"Once I was snorkeling near here," the captain said. "Imagine my surprise as I looked underwater to see a bird chasing a fish! " She laughed softly. "It was a cormorant. They have no oil in their wings so they can swim under water. But when they emerge, they are soaked, so they spread their wings to let them dry."

The Lazy Gator

Although the captain had confidently predicted we'd see alligators, we were nearing the place where the river became too shallow for the catamaran to continue before she spotted old Ramses dozing among the water willows. She cut back on the throttle so everyone could take pictures and generally gawk. Ramses, for his part, had seen this catamaran and the strange critters within it many times. Since the boat was too big to eat, he wasn't much interested in it. As for the critters, they always seemed to be clicking away with their black boxes and Ramses sensed that for some reason that pleased them. So he didn't swim off, but posed patiently. At last the noisy thing moved away and Ramses resumed his afternoon nap. This was the good life.

A Glimpse of Genesis

As the boat proceeded slowly up the river, the captain and the mate became involved in a private conversation that involved a lot of subdued levity. That left us passengers with the quiet that beauty of this kind deserved. Rounding one bend, we came to a section where the river's

We had almost reached the point where the river became too shallow and narrow for the catamaran to continue when the captain spotted old Ramses dozing among the water willows.

It was like a scene that might have come from Genesis before the sky and the earth and the waters had been quite separated.

ripples were caught by sunbeams at a precise angle that caused them to reflect on the undersides of the palm canopy. As the boat glided past, the reflections flowed and flickered as they lit folds in the fronds, then disappeared to illuminate other folds that also vanished. Intricate and delicate designs danced everywhere. It was as if another river was flowing upside down through the trees. There was magic here.

It was like a scene that might have come from Genesis before the sky and the earth and the waters had been quite separated. There was no sound, except in my mind, where a great symphony seemed to be playing. I felt that if the captain would let me disembark briefly, I could immerse myself in this workshop of creation and emerge a new person.

But we did not stop, and I'm almost certain that no other person on board even noticed the enchanted landscape. Another bend and it was gone. Soon the captain and the mate rejoined the group. Then the boat headed back down the river and eventually chugged under the US 1 bridge. Once out in the Indian River Lagoon, we encountered a brisk wind that buffeted us until we reached Captain Hiram's, where I managed to buy a Coke even though the computer still wasn't working.

3

The Vast
St. Johns Marsh

The Setting

The western limit of the Silver Bluff Terrace is marked by the Ten Mile Ridge, once a line of sand dunes, now the elevation upon which **Interstate 95** runs. Although the Ten Mile Ridge is low, it is sufficient to prevent water from draining from the interior into the Indian River Lagoon. The result is the formation of a marsh west of the ridge that is some twenty miles wide and thirty miles long. This marsh gives birth to the St. Johns River, Florida's longest stream. The land here is part of the Pamlico Terrace, the second of the four terraces I would encounter as I gradually ascended Florida's spine. It was formed when the Atlantic was higher than the Silver Bluff Terrace, at an earlier time.

The predominant vegetation of the St. Johns Marsh has nothing in common with the sea oats and sea grapes of the beaches, nor with the salt-loving mangroves of the brackish lagoon. The water here is fresh and slow-moving—the type sawgrass loves. So do pickerelweeds and cattails.

Getting There

From the town of Sebastian I headed west on **CR 512.** I crossed the little bridge over the St. Sebastian River, here not much more than a creek, and in a half dozen miles came to the Ten Mile Ridge.

Passing **Interstate 95,** I continued on **CR 512** through a rural area where a sign informed me that this section of the road was cared for by the Indian River Swine Club. Soon I passed the small community of Fellsmere and in eight more miles came to the Blue Cypress Conservation Area, where I turned in.

Blue Cypress Conservation Area

The Blue Cypress Conservation Area is part of the Upper St. Johns River Basin Project whereby more than fifty thousand acres of marsh has been restored by the Army Corps of Engineers. This is a welcome reversal of its role in the 1950s and 60s of virtually destroying the marsh with a series of dikes and canals. Large as Blue Cypress is, it is just one of the four conservation areas in the project, which is managed by the state's St. Johns River Water Management District. This project extends northwest for some thirty-five miles and I intended to explore much of it.

Out on the Levee

I began by walking slowly out on the broad levee that leads into the St. Johns Marsh. Wax myrtle bushes grew where the levee was dry, but gave way abruptly to grasses closer to the water. Cattails thrived where the pond was shallow, with lily pad islands replacing them farther out. Many lilies had buds that would soon grace the marsh with flowers. In the distance a row of tall cypress showed the fuzz of new-growth needles. A large flock of ducks sailed overhead, then I heard them splash into the water just out of sight.

I walked slowly along the broad levee that leads into the St. Johns Marsh.

Everywhere the juices of early spring were flowing into billions of plant cells around me. Roots were fingering ever deeper into the mud. Leaves were transpiring moisture into the pungent atmosphere. I could see clouds forming along the distant rim of the marsh. Eventually showers would refresh the marsh as part of the cycle that has repeated itself for as long as the marsh existed.

Three Vignettes

Returning from my levee walk, I spent some time strolling around the recreation area. There were picnic tables, a fishing pier, and a boat launch.

At the far end of the park there was a small pavilion overlooking a boat trail. An older couple were there with binoculars. "Almost always we see some ospreys here," the man told me. "And usually blue herons and snowy egrets," his wife added. "Once we even spotted a snail kite," the man continued. "It's endangered, you know."

Excitement played in his voice. Tall, with white hair and a thin moustache, he appeared distinguished enough to have been a bank president before he retired. Once he may have been responsible for millions of dollars. That may account for the network of lines around his eyes. Now that was past and he could thrill to the sight of a small bird. I left the pair scanning the marsh for birds.

The fishing pier was nearby. There I found a man and his son casting lines into the water. The boy was about ten. They were too far away for me to hear what they were saying. But I could tell by their gestures that the father was pointing something out to his son, who apparently would rather have been playing baseball with his friends. I walked on. There's a time for nature and a time for baseball.

On my way to the boat launch area I met a member of the cleanup crew. "It's quiet today," he said. "But if you were here on a weekend you'd find the parking lot filled with cars and airboat trailers. Most of the airboaters take the water trail out to Blue Cypress Lake, which is about five miles west of here. Good fishing. Largemouth bass, crappies, bluegills, shellcrackers—you name 'em. Other folks bring their canoes or kayaks and paddle the marked trails. As for me, I go over to Middleton's Fish Camp on the far shore of Blue Cypress Lake. They have the latest reports on where the best fishing is." I saw a sort of dreamy look play over his face. "That's where I'm going when I get off today." He seemed to be about to relate some good fish stories, but the truck honked and he had to leave.

Yesterday or Tomorrow?

I left the recreation area and drove north on **CR 512.** For a while the marsh accompanied me. But, when I crossed a narrow waterway known as Canal 34, the marsh was replaced by a citrus grove that extended as far as I could see. It was obvious that I had left the conservation area.

As I drove along the grove, I noticed rows of ditches that reached into the distance. These ditches were separated from the canal that ran along the road by an earthen embankment. Every so often there were hand-adjusted valves that controlled the flow of water into or out of the grove depending on the weather conditions.

In three miles I came to the grove's entrance. I pulled over to the side of the road across from the entry. I hadn't expected to see such a large agricultural operation in the midst of what my maps referred to as

The marsh was replaced by a citrus grove. It was obvious that I had left the conservation area.

the St. Johns Marsh. The sign atop the gatehouse said Fellsmere Farms in letters that were both large and authoritative. Beside it a large American flag fluttering proudly and commandingly. I watched a truck as long as a railroad flat car exit the farm, its deck piled high with layers of bright green sod. Obviously Fellsmere Farms was growing a variety of products.

The Saga of Fellsmere Farms

The story of Fellsmere Farms makes an interesting comment on how marshlands have been viewed. From Richard and Juanita Baker's beautifully illustrated book *Reflections of Blue Cypress,* I learned that back in 1910, when people believed wetlands existed to be drained and converted into farmland, E. Nelson Fell, a retired English expert in water management, purchased a hundred square miles of wetland running from the shore of Blue Cypress Lake east to Ten Mile Ridge. Fell was convinced that by lacing this area with drainage canals the no-account marsh could be made available for farms. Then the land prices would soar from the paltry $1.35 an acre that he had paid to $50 or even $100 an acre. With this in mind Fell formed the Fellsmere Farms Company, combining his name with "mere," the Old English word for marsh.

Fell brought in dredges and steam shovels, and soon sixty-seven miles of canal were completed. The most important was the Main Canal that flowed into the Indian River Lagoon by way of the St. Sebastian River. It was fed by five north-south lateral canals two miles apart. One of these is the canal that still runs beside **CR 512.**

Settlers arrived almost right away. Many took up residence in the newly laid out village of Fellsmere, which by 1912 had a population of six hundred. Cotton and sugarcane were planted and plans were made to construct a large syrup mill. For a few years things went well. Then heavy rains came, the canals overflowed, and water surged over everything. Some families had to be rescued by boat. Fellsmere was all but abandoned and the company fell upon hard times. But it managed to survive and today is a major presence in the area.

The Town in the Marsh: Fellsmere

I left Fellsmere Farms on **CR 512.** Driving northeast, I found the land to be marshy at first, but it soon became drier and turned into pine woods. In three miles I came to the town of Fellsmere, population under four thousand. Here I turned due north on **CR 507,** which is Fellsmere's main street. I passed the community center, the fire station, a feed and farm-supply business, a small grocery story, a barnlike building selling antiques, and the Marsh Landing Restaurant, specializing in gator tail and occupying the building that was once the land sales office for the Fellsmere Estates Corporation. There were also a slew of vacant lots and several decrepit buildings with "For Sale" signs.

Too Successful: Canal 54

Once back in the country, I skirted a few large citrus groves and some cattle pastures. In five miles I came to Canal 54, which occupies the route of Nelson Fell's Main Canal, but was greatly widened by the Army Corps of Engineers in the 1950s and 60s. Canal 54 was a centerpiece in the Corps' plan to control flooding while at the same time dry out the marsh for farming.

There was a place to park nearby, so I left my car and walked up the bridge, from where I gazed down Canal 54's long, broad channel leading eastward to the St. Sebastian River and the Indian River Lagoon beyond.

Canal 54 not only did what it was supposed to do, it did far more. As floods were controlled, the water table dropped, thus permitting the expansion of citrus farms. Yet the marsh lakes also shrank, causing largemouth bass and other game fish to become scarce. At the same time the numbers of wading birds and waterfowl plummeted. Wood storks almost vanished Meanwhile, the flow from the canal changed the delicate salt water–fresh water balance in the Indian River Lagoon, thereby damaging the fishing industry.

By the 1970s, it became clear that the Corps' project was an ill-planned failure. So a new program was formulated whereby, instead of sending runoffs coursing down Canal 54, they would be rerouted into four large reservoirs where the water would be stored until the dry season, when it would be released slowly down the St. Johns River. This would not only serve to control flooding, largely replacing Canal 54, but the reservoirs would purify by natural processes the polluted runoffs from nearby citrus and cattle farms. Furthermore, the reservoirs would be be stocked with fish and thereby would become magnets for birds. Thus they would also serve as recreational attractions.

One of the most important reservoirs is Stick Marsh, six miles west of the Canal 54 bridge. So it was to here that I now headed.

The Road West

My map indicated that the road to Stick Marsh ran along the south side of Canal 54 and was called the Fellsmere Grade—the bed was composed of material excavated from Fell's old Main Canal. But the road I found before me didn't have any marker, so I waited until I saw a car turn onto it. The driver was proceeding at a good clip, so I surmised he knew where he was going.

After the dust drifted away, I started westward. In about a third of a mile I came to a turnoff where there was a picnic table overlooking Canal 54. It was a minimal setup, but at least it indicated persons besides canal workmen were using the area. So I continued.

The road was embraced by a heavy growth of cabbage palms. Although an embankment prevented me from seeing much of Canal 54, Nelson Fell's old canal accompanied me on the left. A booklet said I might see swallow-tailed kites, bobwhites, and caracaras along here, but I encountered none.

After two miles I spied a waterway leading south. This was Fell's U-Canal, the same one that paralleled the road I had taken through Fellsmere Farms. I crossed the small bridge by means of which the U-Canal connected with Canal 54.

Stick Marsh

When I reached the end of the road, having been dusted by several cars along the way, I found a good-sized public area with picnic facilities and a boat launch. To the south was a most unusual vista. The park occupies a thumb of elevated land that juts into a narrow bay. In the southern distance was the huge expanse of open water known as Stick Marsh—the "sticks" referred to are the few dead trees protruding from it. Between the bay and the lake was a long row of cabbage palm trees growing on a thin strip of land that must be all that remains of Fell's old levee.

Stick Marsh occupies a rectangular enclosure four miles long and a

The road was embraced by a heavy growth of cabbage palms.

Between the bay and the lake was a long row of cabbage palms growing on a thin strip of land that must be all that remains of Fell's old levee.

couple miles wide. Although it is not deep, it is reputedly among the top bass fishing locations in the entire United States. As a result, on the weekends the boat launch is in constant use.

On the north side of the parking lot was a two-gate dam controlling the flow of reservoir water into Canal 54. When I was there, the water on the reservoir side was about six feet higher than on the canal side. So, if the gates had been fully opened, a six-foot wall of water would have cascaded down the canal and out into the Indian River Lagoon. Then not only would Stick Marsh have been drained, but the marshland all the way down to Blue Cypress would have dried up. Thus the dam is a vital key to the health of the marsh.

The current policy is to divert water into Canal 54 only when the reservoirs are close to overflowing. Even then the release can be a touchy issue. During recent hurricane deluges, portions of the city of Palm Bay, unwisely built in the former marsh, suffered flooding. Concerned property owners clamored to open the Canal 54 dam to bring the water level down. But officials of the St. Johns River Water Management District, in charge of water control, held firm until Stick Marsh and other reservoirs were filled to the limit. Then, the dam gates were opened and for several days waters gushed down Canal 54. Although this was a rare worst-case scenario, Canal 54 is there and ready when another inevitable emergency arises.

The T. M. Goodwin Waterfowl Management Area

On the other side of the dam is the T. M. Goodwin Waterfowl Management Area. In the 1960s this area had been drained, replanted with grass, and turned into pasture. But when the marsh was restored, it was converted into ten water impoundments designed to attract waterfowl as well as wading birds. Since the levees that set off the impoundments are open to hikers, I set out on one.

Dawdling

I must admit I am not a great hiker. Hikers have urgent, fixed destinations. They maintain a brisk pace. They become irritated if something unexpected interferes with their stride. They particularly abhor persons who dawdle on the path.

I am one of those dawdlers—or, as I prefer to call myself, a stroller.

What hikers don't understand is that strollers are not going anywhere in particular. Every distraction is a goal. I have a friend who hikes diligently each morning, yet he never stops to listen to the mockingbirds.

As a practiced dawdler, I didn't intend to walk very far along the levee. I was looking for the distractions that the hikers disdained.

The Duck Circus

One of the distractions was the ducks. I stopped to watch them. There were so many of various sizes and colors that it was almost like a circus. The males were decked out in their breeding finery, which they sported dur-

Blue-winged Teal

ing the winter and spring. I consulted my trusty copy of *Florida's Birds, 2nd Edition* to identify them. There were names I seldom heard. Like shovelers, the males with iridescent green heads and bright white chests. And wigeons, modest brown birds with faint orange hues. And blue-winged teals, with white crescents around the males' eyes.

The ducks seemed to glide through the placid water without the slightest effort. But I knew that beneath the surface their little webbed feet were paddling furiously. They were all so cute, almost like the battery-driven toys one might give a child for his birthday. But these were wild animals used to defending themselves.

A Kite and a Kid

Resuming my stroll along the levee, I soon became aware of an unusual bird circling not far above me. Its body was so white it could have been made of talcum. Its wings, outstretched to a width of four feet, were edged with a black as deep as obsidian. Even more notable was its tail, the feathers of which forked out in a "V" form. This was a swallow-tailed kite. The bird was so striking that I lay on my back at the side of the dike the better to watch it.

The bird floating majestically above reminded me of a paper kite that I flew in childhood. For a moment I was back in the vacant lot behind my house. It was a day in early March with a fresh breeze blowing in from Lake Michigan. The other kids had kites in the air, but mine was the finest. It tugged on my string as if it were alive. Yes, it wanted to fly off and take me with it. We'd cruise the skies together.

People would gape at us as we hovered above them. "How'd that kid get up there?" they'd gasp. Then we'd be off again, leaving them to wonder, my kite and I.

It was a fine daydream until one of those pesky hikers stopped and asked if I was all right. Just because I was lying on my back he thought I was ill. He obviously didn't know that the art of dawdling involves a certain amount of time for aimless musings.

A Strange Place for a City

Leaving the impoundments with their bounty of ducks and daydreams, I took the Fellsmere Grade back to **CR 507,** also called **Babcock Road.** I paused here, for I was tempted to continue east by following a sandy road called Buffer Preserve Drive, which led along the north side of Canal 54 into the St. Sebastian River State Park. This road runs for four miles through land that is mostly scrubby flatwoods. There are visitors center and many hiking trails. But my interest was in the resurrected St. Johns Marsh, so I resumed my northward trek on CR 507.

I passed citrus groves, potato fields, cattle spreads, and patches of beautiful pine flatwoods. The land drained into the St. Johns Marsh, which paralleled the road a few miles west. There was still an aspect of the wild about this loosely populated area. Thus some neighborhoods are bothered by wild hogs, many as heavy as four hundred pounds. They roam in packs of up to twenty animals and rut up the neat suburban lawns with ease.

In fourteen miles I came to **CR 514, Malabar Road,** which is at **Exit 173** of **Interstate 95.** I turned west on Malabar. A major canal paralleled the road and smaller canals periodically crossed beneath the road to feed into the main canal. Much of this former marsh has been converted into homes and incorporated into the city of Palm Bay, population more than eighty thousand. During heavy rains large portions are subject to flooding due to the fact that the excess water is usually prevented from being dispersed down Canal 54, as was originally planned.

Continuing farther west, I reached the Malabar Lakes West subdivision. It seems almost incredible that homes continue to be built this far out into the former marsh. Yet here they are, and more are planned. Perhaps prospective buyers should heed the word "lakes" in the subdivision's name.

After I passed the Palm Bay Regional Park, the pavement ended and the road turned to sand and gravel. A little farther on was a broad pasture where black angus cattle grazed on bahia grass, which must be fertilized. The runoff from these and nearby fields pollutes both the Indian River Lagoon and the St. Johns Marsh, of which they are geographically a part. Nine miles from where I started on CR 514 the road ended at the C-1 Retention Area, the name referring to Canal 1 a mile north.

The Thomas O. Lawton Recreation Area

Now I was back in the reclaimed area that is part of the extensive Upper St. Johns River Basin Project. I followed the road as it turned south and ran along the base of a levee to a boat launch. At this point the road ascended the levee to a park overlooking a spacious reservoir some two and a half miles long and a mile wide. There was a wonderful view on all sides from the twenty-foot-high levee. The only trouble was somebody had forgotten to fill the reservoir with water.

Well, the water had not exactly been forgotten, it just hadn't gotten there yet. The problem was that Canal 1, which is supposed to fill the reservoir, happens to flow the wrong direction—that is, east into the

There was a wonderful view on all sides from the twenty-foot-high dike. The only trouble was that somebody had forgotten the water.

Indian River Lagoon instead of west into the retention area. Of course it wasn't planned like this, for the canal was scheduled to be turned around by the Army Corps of Engineers several years ago. But funds were lacking, so nothing was done. Now, at last, a new money source has been found and work is beginning on a small dam across Canal 1, near the Indian River Lagoon. When completed, storm water flow will be reversed, and the Lawton retention area will fill.

Without the water the most I could do was watch cloud-shadows drift over the meadow that should have been a lake. It took them five minutes and twenty-five seconds to cross the wide expanse. Upon reaching the opposite shore, they darkened the thin line of trees along the levee before vanishing into the marsh beyond my vision. In this marsh meander the three little creeks that form the first recognizable channels of the St. Johns River. From here the St. Johns wends slowly north for 310 miles as it matures into the formidable river that surges into the Atlantic just beyond Jacksonville.

At Last: the Culprit! Canal Number One

Despite the fun with the clouds, the C-1 Retention Area failed to hold my interest. So I drove back on **CR 514** to **CR 509 (Minton Road)**, where I turned north. In a mile I came to Canal 1, more popularly known as the Melbourne-Tillman Canal. It didn't rate much compared to Canal 54. The water was almost stagnant, but during heavy rains it swells as it is fed by other canals, including those I crossed on the way to the C-1 Retention Area. Then the waters rumble east to Turkey Creek, and from there into the Indian River Lagoon. The C-1 Retention Area was designed to prevent this, but, of course, Canal 1 will have to be turned around first.

The Joy of Distance

After passing through semi-forested land for a few more miles, I came to **US 192 (Kissimmee Highway),** upon which I turned west. Three miles after passing **Interstate 95,** I reached the **St. Johns River bridge.** Parking on the west side of the river in the Camp Holly lot, I walked up the bridge and from there I took a photo looking south. I was standing at the northern head of the great wetland restoration project. Its success was very important, for, when it was begun, there was considerable

Below me the St. Johns was running fresh and unpolluted. Beyond were no signs of human habitation.

doubt that it would succeed. The fact that the use of reservoirs proved successful helped determine the plan for the subsequent restoration of the Everglades.

I was viewing a masterpiece. Below me the St. Johns was running fresh and unpolluted. Southward there was no sign of human habitation. Native marsh plants dominated the landscape, with the only trees being a faint row in the distance along the ridge marking the course of Canal 40. This is all government land that will remain in this condition for the foreseeable future. Seldom these days, especially in Florida, is one able to enjoy such a vista. I stood there for some time drinking in the scene.

Wild Bill Rides Again: Camp Holly Airboat Rides

Descending the bridge, I went to Camp Holly, which consisted mainly of a stubby airboat dock and a restaurant-bar that some persons might call quaint, but others call rundown. Inside was an oldtime fishermen's lair replete with the odor of grilled burgers and yesterday's beer. I was greeted by a large, genial lady with tattooed arms. After buying a ticket for an airboat tour up the river to Sawgrass Lake, I ambled down to the dock, where the captain and several other passengers were waiting. The captain was a lanky Cracker with unruly brown hair that tumbled down to his shoulders. He had several front teeth missing—how he lost them I decided it was best not to ask. He was all in all a rough-looking hombre, not the kind you'd ordinarily pick to escort you into the wilderness. But first impressions are often wrong. He proved to be a well-mannered fellow. However he was also a rambunctious driver who earned the name I was to award him: Wild Bill.

The airboat had only two narrow bench seats. "It's small," Wild Bill said, as he passed out earmuffs, "but it's a real cutter." I was soon to learn what the word "cutter" meant.

Then we were off. Not directly up the river, which would have given us a smooth ride, but to the left into a melange of grass, sticks, muck, and an occasional trace of water. It was no use asking Bill if he knew where he was going—not with the roar of the gasoline engine and the throb of the airplane propeller at head level.

Wild Bill found a ditch and for a while we zipped along it. Then he apparently wearied of the ditch and swerved once more across the leafy green tangle of brush and six-foot maiden cane bedecked with tan seed spikes. At last we reached Canal 40, to which he could have taken us right off, for it was clearly marked by the long row of trees growing on the embankment. Seeing Wild Bill lean back in his driver's seat, I hoped a less energetic segment of the ride was at hand.

The Beautiful Relic: Canal 40

Canal 40 was a broad waterway dating back to the 1920s and 30s, when agricultural concerns dug it in order to pile the muck into a levee to protect their farms from flooding. This earthen embankment had now accumulated a colorful assembly of cabbage palms and other plants. But the canal itself serves no purpose in the regeneration of the St. Johns Basin, and there has been talk of filling it in.

We cruised leisurely down this beautiful relic. The water was mirrorlike, although closer to shore soft ripples created a mosaic of changing reflections. On our left was the embankment with its jade wall of palms, their shaggy tops fluttering in the gentle breeze. If we had the time, we could have continued on Canal 40 for its total length of about twenty miles, past the Canal 1 Retention Area and on to the Goodwin Waterfowl Area. Instead we turned into Sawgrass Lake, slowing as we bounced across the wake of a small fishing boat. The air was filled with the fragrance of fresh water and growing things.

Sawgrass Lake: Gators but No Sawgrass

Sawgrass Lake proved to be merely a wide place in the St. Johns. It was barely a mile in diameter and not much more than six feet deep. Large rafts of water lilies, their leaves large and flat, floated across the surface. They would be beautiful later on, but for now they had only the buds of future flowers. There were also clusters of water hyacinths. Sometimes they are so numerous as to nearly choke the lake. But today they were few due to recent sprayings.

"The water's not too low today," Wild Bill shouted to us. "I don't see any sandbars. So I'm gonna open her up, okay?" Not waiting for an answer, which he couldn't have heard anyway, he turned her loose. We skirted one relatively large island, and probably more, but, with the wind in my eyes and all the zigging and zagging, I'm not sure.

Wild Bill was apparently beguiled by alligators, and wanted to

We cruised leisurely down this beautiful relic. The water was mirrorlike, although closer to shore soft ripples caused the reflections to flutter.

show us every one. So he sped close to shore, blithely assuming there would be no hidden snags. When he saw a gator, he would hurriedly point to it, unaware that by the time we focused on the location, we'd be beyond a good view, and sometimes beyond any view at all.

Wild Bill slowed briefly as we went between the barely protruding posts of a former railroad trestle. He told us that the railroad once hauled cypress out of a now-vanished forest. But my attention was on the posts and all I could think of was what if the lake had been a little higher and Wild Bill had rocketed into an unseen post! I wondered what other hidden obstructions were waiting for us.

Now at full throttle again, we shot past the place where the St. Johns entered Sawgrass from the south. Four miles upriver was a lake called Hell 'n Blazes, the last of the little lakes at the river's source. That name had tradition and tang. Too bad some prissy folks have recently pressured map-makers into mellowing it into Hellen Blazes.

Sawgrass Lake likewise has trouble with its name, for the shore is mostly scrubby water willows and wax myrtle bushes, with ferns often forming miniature groves beneath them. As for sawgrass, I saw none. The reason, I learned later, was that unfiltered runoffs of farm fertilizers in the past have been detrimental to the sawgrass while, at the same time, encouraging the willows, wax myrtles, and other such plants. With runoff water now being filtered through impoundments, it's hoped the sawgrass will return, but this is far from certain.

Wild Bill stopped once to give us a brief spiel. "It was near here," he recalled, "on a windy day that my engine cut out. We drifted to shore at the exact place where a gator was snoozin'. Well, that critter was so startled he jumped right into the boat. Before we could even react, he ran to the opposite rail, leaped over the side, and kept right on goin'!" Bill chuckled at the recollection. "That'll git yer skin pricklin'!" He paused. "Don't worry, folks. If the engine quits today, I got my cell phone handy."

"Over there," he continued, "I saw a panther. Only one I ever saw. They're really rare, you know. The passengers saw him too. Yeah!"

With that Bill was apparently palavered out. He throttled up and shot past a lot of flapping wings that could have been egrets, herons, and ducks. Homeward bound, Wild Bill rejected the detour along Canal 40 and the joys of the trackless marsh. Instead he stayed on the river and within five minutes we were back at Camp Holly.

"There ya are, folks," Wild Bill said as we debarked. "I gave ya a full day's tour in a half-hour."

If that were true, perhaps he could have slowed a little and given us just a half-day's tour.

A Foreboding Success: the Viera Development

Leaving the "Sawgrass Speedway," I took **US 192** back east to **Interstate 95,** upon which I turned north. In eleven miles I came to **Wickham Road (Exit 191),** upon which I headed west once more toward the St. Johns wetlands. But first I had to go through the Viera development.

Viera is a community-in-the-making. Just a few years ago this area was a rustic ranch belonging for more than six decades to Duda & Sons. Duda is the world's largest producer of celery as well as an important grower of sweet corn, citrus, sugar cane, and other crops. In addition, the company has large cattle ranches in Texas as well as in Florida.

In the 1980s the Duda Company, with its considerable resources, decided to convert their 38,000-acre ranch into a city to be called Viera, after the Slovak word for "faith." The plan called for the eventual erection of 17,000 homes as well as shopping centers and governmental and business buildings. In addition, ample space would be set aside for parks and miles of nature trails. There would even be a quality golf course with gently rolling land, courtesy of a chain of dump trucks hauling in over a million cubic yards of soil. The fact that the water table here was only a foot or two below the surface did not deter the planners. Far from it. As backhoes scooped up the sandy topsoil to form home sites, the little lakes that appeared became part of the picturesque landscape.

Although much of Viera is still in the construction stage, it is already a popular place. The shopping center, called The Avenue, has been built along a crescent-shaped street. It boasts up-scale fashion stores as well as a sixteen-screen movie theater. There are also excellent restaurants on The Avenue. I enjoyed lunch at one.

Mitigation Magic

Before Viera could be built, the plans were subjected to close scrutiny by a host of local, regional, and state agencies as well as by the St. Johns River Water Management District. The result was that Duda agreed to a program called "mitigation," whereby they would restore wetlands in other parts of the region to compensate for the environmental damage caused by the Viera development.

Although Viera is a quality enterprise built with adherence to the strictest environmental regulations, it made me sad. One would think that such a waterlogged environment would be among the last places of interest to developers. Yet this is not the case. It demonstrates how, with the proper equipment and sufficient financing, there is hardly anywhere in Florida that can not be transformed into sprawl.

The Other Side of Town

After lunch I continued west on **Wickham Road.** On my right was the Four Mile Canal bordered by the fourteenth and fifteenth fairways of the Duran Golf Club. A quaint arched bridge spanned the canal as it led to an exclusive gated community beyond. On my left was a wild grassland studded with palmettos. The difference between the two sides of the road was stark.

Wickham Road ended at the Brevard County Wastewater Treatment Plant, a new facility built to handle the sewage issuing from fancy-dancy Viera. The operation is in two parts. The first is the actual physical plant where sewage is converted into water of suitable quality to irrigate Viera's lawns, road medians, and golf course. The second is man-made Viera Wetlands, where surplus water is refined to a higher degree so that it can be released into the St. Johns River, which is a few miles further west.

After registering at the office (as required) and picking up a wetlands map, I stopped briefly at the sewage plant's large, circular clarifying tank. Climbing up the ladder, I peered across the open top where water stood placidly as the sludge settled to the bottom. In subsequent operations air would be pumped through the wastewater, enabling bacteria to help cleanse it. Finally, just before the water is routed back to the city, chlorine and other chemicals would be added to it.

But I had not driven out here merely to inspect the sewage plant. Immediately beyond the plant was a sign announcing entry into the Viera Wetlands. With that the roadway ascended a berm—and there before me was a marsh as unusual as any on earth.

As I followed the berm road along Cell 2, I passed bunches of cordgrass and sawgrass. There were also soft-rushes, each plant sporting prominent tannish seed balls.

A Soggy Success: the Viera Wetlands

The Viera Wetlands is a 240-acre, L-shaped series of four water cells grouped around a central lake. The part of the reclaimed water not needed for irrigation is directed into these cells by way of a gate at the southeast corner of cells 1 and 2. From there the water passes into the lake and into cells 3 and 4. During circulation various plants in each cell rid the water of the nutrients which, although they may be welcomed by lawns, are out of place in a river environment. This accomplished, the water is available to be dispatched into the Four Mile Canal via a gate at the northwest corner of the wetlands. From there it flows into the St. Johns River.

Oddly, the Viera Wetlands has now taken on a function that was not its primary one. The reclaimed waters have become favored destinations for thousands of birds, so school children, nature groups, and everyday folks who enjoy watching flying creatures find the place rewarding. That was why I was here.

Along the Berm

Once on top of the berm, I came on a couple of display boards. Both prohibited swimming, one because the water was reclaimed sewage and the other because of alligators. The narrow Berm Trail was one-way only. As I followed it along cell 2, I passed bunches of cordgrass and sawgrass. There were also soft rushes, each plant sporting prominent, tannish seed balls. Although they were distinctive, they were not particularly pretty. At one point I saw water spouting up from a large black pipe. This was being pumped back from cells 3 and 4 to circulate once more through the marshes. Nearby I drove past one of the cement culvert pipes used to direct water from the higher cells, numbers 1 or 2, to the lower cells, 3 or 4.

This Is for the Birds

Rounding the northeast corner of the wetlands, I quickly came to a split in the road. Leaving the outer Berm Trail, I headed into the interior of the marsh. On one side was the body of water called simply The Lake. The Lake has a depth of thirty feet. It is so deep because it was dredged to obtain material to build the berms.

The Lake was alive with birds. Many were the same type of ducks that I had seen earlier at the Goodwin Waterfowl Area: teals, wigeons, and shovelers. There were also coots, egrets, herons, and birds that I couldn't identify and whose names I probably wouldn't have remembered anyway. They were constantly diving and soaring and fluttering about, seemingly aimlessly. The birds were so numerous that I could follow the passage of other drivers on the berms by the updraft of wings.

Then my attention was attracted by a bright sulfur butterfly that had apparently taken a liking to me. She cruised past my window and seemed to be showing off. Then she coquettishly changed her mind, flicked her yellow wings, and abruptly darted away. But a few seconds later she was back, coyly drifting past my window. Just when I thought we were going to strike up a meaningful relationship, something distracted her and she darted off once more leaving me with just a memory. Alas!

The Pickerel Party

But I had my birds. Driving slowly among them, I soon arrived at another fork in the berm road. This was the site of a two-story observation deck. I pulled to the side of the road and climbed the wooden steps. To my surprise, at the top I found three young women in their early twenties dancing to light rock music. At one side were their deck chairs and a jug with mysterious contents. Although they asked me to join them, I felt their invitation was not all that sincere, and, besides, my wife was waiting in the car below. So I descended to the lower observation level and, while the frivolities continued above, gazed out over cell 3.

This cell was mainly a jade meadow of pickerelweed. Sunlight sparkled on their lanceolate leaves. In the middle distance, where the land was slightly higher, a platoon of cabbage palms seemed to stand guard. Small pools of water, ever so blue, appeared here and there. A slight current must have been present, although it wasn't apparent to me, for the wetlands had been constructed for water to slide through the pickerelweeds, which absorbed the unwanted nutrients. I was told later that on an average day nearly a million and a half gallons of reconditioned water moves through the wetlands.

Cell 3 was mainly a jade meadow of pickerelweed. Where the land was higher, a platoon of cabbage palms guarded the cell. On my right was a berm upon which the narrow roadway ran.

What Can Top This?

As I continued along the berms, I was impressed not only by the lush growths on the wetland side, but by the pasture on the other side of the berm. The wetlands had been constructed on top of a portion of this pasture, which itself existed over some prior landscape—perhaps sand dunes that existed when the Atlantic reached this far inland. And there were other former landscapes even farther below. Maybe lava beds from the days of the dinosaurs. Ever deeper there could be deserts formed when Florida was part of North Africa. Continuing into the past were the eons when this was the floor of an ocean that existed long before the Atlantic. Here sea animals had lived their brief lives, then their shells had sunk to the bottom, where they were compressed into the limestone that today forms the bedrock of the Florida Platform.

The saga of the ages was beneath my feet.

And around me were the birds and the pickerelweeds and the berm with my car resting on it. It was weird to realize that one day another landscape would cover where I now stood.

I could have spent the entire day meandering along the nearly four miles of dreamy berm byways. Each cell, each vista, was so different from the others. And maybe I'd link up with my flirty butterfly! But the day was fleeting. So I took **Wickham Road** back to **Interstate 95** and headed north toward Lake Poinsett, a watery dip in the St. Johns River.

On the Road to Lake Poinsett

The Interstate runs on the top of the Ten Mile Ridge, which, although it is low, provided me with a wonderful view of the St. Johns wetlands. Then I skirted Lake Florence, a wide place in a murky creek that connects with Lake Poinsett a half-mile west. In steamboat days Lake Poinsett was the farthest up the St. Johns that could be traveled on a regular schedule. So the paddle-wheelers turned east through Lake Florence to Rockledge, where a rocky outcropping offered a dry landing. During droughts, Lake Florence virtually dried up, so wagons had to slosh far out into the Lake Poinsett shallows to pick up passengers.

I turned off **I-95** at **SR 520 (Exit 201)** and drove west. On my left was an appealing marshy vista and on my right a series of housing developments. Years ago, when I first traveled this road, it was a quiet short-cut between I-95 and SR 50 to Orlando. Now it is a main thoroughfare widened to four lanes. In five miles I approached the bridge over the St. Johns. Here was the turnoff to the Lone Cabbage Fish Camp.

The Lone Cabbage Fish Camp

On my visit to Lone Cabbage many years ago, it was a solitary place patronized almost exclusively by fishermen. Today the appropriately grubby atmosphere is still there—the beat-up bar, the bluegrass dance floor, the weathered walls, the odor of a thousand fried feasts. Gator tail is still served, and so are frog legs, catfish, and chicken wings. Fishermen still guzzle beer and exchange lies. But nowadays, during favorable weather, moms, dads, and kids crowd into the place, which is less than an hour's drive from Orlando. There's excitement here. They like the novelty of eating at picnic tables on the long, open-air deck beside the river where they can watch the airboats cruising past. Most of the airboats are small contraptions transporting just a couple of fishermen. But large airboats, their motors rumbling and propellers flashing, also pull in and out of the docking area beside the deck.

The highlight of a visit to Lone Cabbage, if you discount the gator tail, which, of course, tastes like chicken, is an airboat excursion up the river to nearby Lake Poinsett. These airboats are not the rambunctious

Large airboats, their motors rumbling and propellers flashing, pull into and out of the docking area beside the deck. There's excitement here.

little broncos like that favored by Wild Bill. They are broad vehicles with many tiers of seats. Although they make a great deal of noise, the captain stops often to disperse information and answer questions.

Into Lake Poinsett

I boarded one of these airboats and in a few minutes was headed upriver. Reaching Lake Poinsett, we moved into sawgrass and cattails, for the lake had no clear shoreline—it simply merged with the marsh. We slowed when we came upon two men casting fish lines from the deck of their airboat. "They'll probably catch sunfish and bluegills," the captain said. "But we do have some nice size bass in the lake. Also catfish. They're all mighty fine eating." He spoke with the air of a college instructor turned river rat.

Yesterday's World

We continued along the side of the lake. Maidencane, tall and scruffy, dominated the landscape. It rustled against the side of the boat as if it were trying to keep us in the marsh forever. We spied a gator some distance off sunning himself on a tiny hump of land. When we approached, he glided soundlessly into the water. Nearby a great blue heron regarded us with a wary attitude, ready to soar off should we come much closer. Ducks honked in the distance. I felt as if we were in yesterday's world and that at any moment a Timucuan dugout might materialize out of the cane.

Clouds passed over the sun and it grew darker. ""What happens if it rains?" someone asked. "Is there a shelter close by?"

"If it rains, you just get wet," was the captain's reply. "What's a little water anyway? It's warm today. There used to be quite a few private fishermen's shacks around the lake that we could use in emergencies, but the state forced them to be demolished. Said they were eyesores. As for rainstorms, don't knock them. We need the water to keep the river up. Once in a while it's so dry that the St. Johns actually runs backwards. On the other hand, there's flood times when all you can see is water for miles."

We paused to watch some egrets. But most of the passengers were anxious to see alligators, so the captain nosed out into the open part of the lake. The water was as placid as sheet of plastic. Far out we spotted three small lumps that were a gator's eyebrows and nose—nothing more was visible. We moved slowly toward him. "You can tell how long he is by the distance from his nose to his brows," the captain told us. "This guy's is about ten inches. That means there's ten feet of hungry gator beneath the water."

The captain slowed to let us look at the gator, who was undoubtedly watching us with those malicious eyes that never blinked.

"At night," the captain continued, "gators' eyes catch the light of a flashlight or even that of the moon. Then they glow with red devil's fire. There could be a hundred pairs around the lake. It'll unnerve you the first time."

The Alligator and the Baby Raccoon

The captain shut off the motor. "I'll tell you folks a little story," he said. "A month ago I was near here when a raccoon family came down to the shore. For no reason a baby raccoon started swimming across the lake. He hadn't seen the gator that was watching him with just his eyes above the water. 'That little feller's not going to make it,' I told my passengers. Well, we saw the gator's eyebrows disappear and knew he was on his way. For a little bit all was quiet. Suddenly a huge pair of jaws broke the water and in a split second the baby raccoon vanished."

We saw other gators after that, most of them fully exposed as they lay in the sun. Many had their jaws open, exposing teeth lined up like knife blades.

The excursion was a half hour. When we got back, I stopped for a drink at the riverside deck. With people laughing and kids darting here and there, it didn't seem possible that just around the river bend was a quite different place—one of beauty, but also of savagery. I thought of the alligators sunning themselves with their fearsome jaws open. But what I remembered most vividly was the gator with just his eyes above the water and a baby raccoon about to go for a swim.

4
The Great Kissimmee Prairie

The Setting

The Great Kissimmee Prairie is located on the Penholoway Terrace, which is twenty-five or thirty feet above the St. Johns Marsh. Superficially the marsh and the prairie appear similar. They are both extensive grasslands. But in the marsh the drainage is sluggish—at times nonexistent. This gives rise to plants like sawgrass. On the other hand, the prairie has better drainage and the predominant plant has traditionally been wiregrass.

The reason for the difference in drainage is that the Pamlico plain has hardly recovered from Ice Age flooding. It is nearly as flat as when it emerged from the Atlantic. Although the Penholoway plain may appear just as flat to the naked eye, it tilts southward sufficiently to support enough current on the Kissimmee River to transport rainwater to Lake Okeechobee.

Today the bahia grass that has replaced the wiregrass on much of the Kissimmee Prairie supports a large cattle industry. But the native wiregrass, along with the birds and other creatures of the original prairie, can be found in an offbeat corner of the prairie, and that was my ultimate goal.

Getting There

From the Lone Cabbage Fish Camp, where I ended my exploration of the St. Johns Marsh, I drove west on **SR 520**. The road was through a second-growth pine forest—that on my right was part of the extensive Tosohatchee State Preserve. In three miles I reached **CR 532,** upon which I turned south. I had not gone many miles before I went up a rise to the Penholoway Terrace. At this point I passed over Taylor Creek on a bridge with no name.

Taylor Creek Reservoir/Deseret Ranch

The region hereabouts is favorable cattle country and has long been part of the Mormon-owned Deseret Ranch—at 300,000 acres one of the largest spreads east of the Mississippi.

For the next four miles the road followed the embankment of the Taylor Creek Reservoir. Behind the embankment is a large impoundment of potential drinking water sought by Orlando and other central Florida cities. But, because the reservoir is on Deseret's land and because the ranch may need it to supply the subdivisions it might build, this reservoir will undoubtedly become an object of dispute in the near future.

Soon the highway turned due west and I continued for a half dozen more miles through Deseret property. The road was straight and there were almost no cars. The extensive pasture through which I passed was mostly bahia grass. Groups of cattle appeared periodically. One count has the herd, which is mostly calves to be fattened and sold to other ranchers, at 44,000 head.

Eventually I left the ranch land and passed up another almost invisible ridge. This ridge was a sandbar when the Atlantic was forty or fifty feet higher than at present. As the ocean retreated, the sandbar changed into a barrier island and eventually into a dry ridge. The land west of the ridge is part of the Kissimmee Valley.

Three Lakes Wildlife Management Area/Parker's Slough

Reaching the town of St. Cloud, I turned south on **CR 523,** also called **Canoe Creek Road.** In twenty-five miles I reached the Three Lakes Wildlife Management Area. I took the second turnoff where I saw the sign for the Prairie Lakes Unit. In a moment I reached a kiosk displaying a map and offering some informative leaflets. Then I continued along a sand and gravel road marked **Route 16** a short distance to Parker's Slough. I parked here and walked to the rustic bridge over the soggy morass.

I watched a pair of ibis poke their saber-bills at prey in the water.

I stood on the bridge for a while and watched a pair of ibis stab their saber-bills at quarries in the murky water, which was high due to recent heavy rains. Although a sign pointed to a footpath that leads through the lush, semi-tropical growth to an observation platform overlooking Lake Marian, the path was soupy and partially blocked by fallen, rotting trees. Moisture was everywhere, opening even the resurrection ferns that usually hugged the live oak limbs. Surrounded by a wall of vegetation, this hardly seemed a likely place for me to begin my exploration of the Kissimmee Prairie. But it was, for the great prairie was created by the Kissimmee River, which has multiple sources—among them the swamps and bogs of the Three Lakes Wildlife Management Area.

The Birth of the Prairie

During the thousands of years before the advent of white men the river twisted sluggishly across a flatland that extended south to Lake Okeechobee. When the summer rains came, uncountable gallons of water gushed into the river, causing it to flood, killing all plants not able to exist under such watery conditions. But during the dry winter months, the Kissimmee shrank until its floodplain was almost desert-

In the midst of that wide saw palmetto plain was the humped mass of a large cypress dome.

dry, wiping out any plants that needed constant moisture. One of the few plants to thrive under such severe extremes was wiregrass. Thus the Great Kissimmee Prairie was born.

Tough Yet Fragile

Parker's Slough is just a small part of the Three Lakes Wildlife Management Area. Continuing on **Route 16,** I quickly I came to **Boat Ramp Road,** upon which I turned right. This road led along the margin of Parker's Slough, which was clothed with trees. The land on the other side was almost entirely covered with the dagger blades of saw palmettos. Yet in the midst of that wide palmetto plain was the rounded mass of a large cypress dome.

I stopped my car to appreciate what I was seeing. Here were three completely different ecosystems. Each was a self-contained biological unit, friendly to certain plants and hostile to others. The saw palmetto, so overwhelming in the drier flats, could not grow in the slow-moving slough that was so agreeable to the live oaks. The cypress were emperors in the still-water depression that nurtured the dome. But their seedlings were unable to grow in the slough or in the saw palmetto plain. Thus, because each plant had adapted so thoroughly to certain soil and water conditions, in a way each was living a precarious existence, for environmental change is part of nature's eternal rhythm.

The Prairie Lakes

In a mile **Boat Ramp Road** ended at Lake Jackson, the second of the three lakes (the third being Lake Kissimmee, which has its own state park). A purple gallinule was bobbing along the shore until I approached for a photo, when he flew off in a huff. There was a boat launch beside the lake, which is frequented by fishermen who catch blue gills, sunfish, speckled perch, catfish, and, if they're lucky, large-mouth bass. Some of the fishermen had left mementos in the form of empty beer bottles and bottle caps. I've read that by bending beer bottle caps just right they make wonderful fishing lures. And there is a proposal to grind glass bottles into fine, rounded grains and use them as artificial beach sand. So maybe someday fishermen will reconsider discarding such valuable items.

Three miles west of here, a short canal connects Lake Jackson with Lake Kissimmee. This is where the Kissimmee River formally begins its long journey south to Lake Okeechobee. The Kissimmee has had a strange career, for in the 1960s the river was straightened, broadened, deepened, and shortened as the U.S. Army Corps of Engineers transformed it into Canal 38. Now much of Canal 38 is being converted back into the river. But more on that later.

An Interpretive Trail at Sunset Ranch

I returned to **CR 523,** locally known as **Canoe Creek Road,** and drove south through a protected wilderness that is part of the Three Lakes Wildlife Management Area. Shortly I came to an inconspicuous marker on the right for the Sunset Ranch Interpretive Trail. A plaque in the small parking area indicated that this was a two-mile trail with frequent signs describing the plants and animals that might be encountered on the way. The trail was an appealing footpath that leads to Lake Marian. The way was through saw palmetto and scrub oaks, with large patches of wiregrass, aglow in its mid-autumn pale-bronze hue. I had hardly gone more than a few yards before a white-tailed deer bounded past me and into the trees.

Soon I came to a viewing blind, which was a small, wooden structure with long, narrow windows looking out over a small wiregrass prairie. As I watched, a group of bucks, does, and fawns walked slowly across my line of vision. They moved with grace, as lightly as smoke. The adults were alert, watching for danger. The fawns scampered here and there. But they were cautious, and when a strange noise startled them, they dashed for the security of their mothers. Apparently there were several families here and they reminded me of humans out for a picnic. It seemed incredible that anyone would want to injure them.

However, in nature things are not always as represented. "The white-tailed deer is denuding forests," declared an alarmed writer in a recent issue of the *Nature Conservancy* magazine. His complaint was that, with the elimination of such natural enemies as wolves and cougars, the deer population had exploded beyond the ability of forests to support them. Now in some places across the nation the hungry deer are killing the trees by stripping their bark as food. They are also eating such a significant amount of understory plants that many ground-nesting birds are suffering. The damage is most severe where deer hunting isn't allowed. This makes it easier to understand why the Three Lakes Wildlife Management Area allows hunting during certain times of the year in much of the park (but not here). Nevertheless, it did not make it easier to think of little Bambi trying to comprehend why his mother lay dying in the grass.

Whooping in the Wild

Eagles are plentiful at Three Lakes. Indeed, this region is in the heart of Florida's most populous eagle area. But I had especially hoped to see a whooping crane or two. On land they are striking birds that stand five feet tall with white bodies, long black legs, and black markings on their faces. In the air they are magnificent, with white wings tipped with black that spread seven feet wide. There are not many of these protected birds, but they are out there. However, I didn't see any of them.

These whoopers are part of a successful effort to save the species from extinction. Only a few years ago the world population of migrating whoopers had been reduced to barely nineteen. To try to bring them back, in 1993 a flock raised in captivity was released in the Three Lakes Wildlife Management Area. Although this was a start, the birds were non-migratory and at peril from hurricanes. What was needed was a flock that would fly north in the spring, then return in late fall, after the hurricane season. Thus in 2001 fourteen whoopers, guided by an ultra-light plane that was crudely but effectively disguised as a whooper, flew down from Wisconsin, where they had been raised, to the Chassahowitzka Wildlife Management Area on Florida's west coast. When these same birds flew unescorted back to Wisconsin the follow-ing spring, a true migratory flock was established to match another migrating out of Texas. During each of the following years more young birds have been escorted to Florida. Now the flock numbers in the dozens and is growing.

The Hidden Glen

Beyond the viewing blind I entered a beautiful oak hammock. The trees were widely spaced, allowing sunlight to prance on the forest floor. The tree limbs rose all about me in the weird patterns so appealing in live oaks. I felt as if I were in some sacred glen in ancient Greece and that Pan would soon appear playing his pipes. But even without Pan, the glen was pleasant. I wished I had brought my lunch to enjoy at one of the picnic tables scattered among the trees.

Canoe Creek Road

Once more I continued south on **Canoe Creek Road (CR 523).** Although I was beyond Three Rivers' protected territory, the wayside was virtually unpopulated. I passed through a landscape of pastures and second-growth timber, with a scattering of cypress domes. There were no tract homes or strip shops. There were not even advertising signs—why should there be? The road only went to Yeehaw Junction. I passed only one settlement along the way. This consisted of a café/grocery, a few mobile homes, and a house on stilts. Otherwise the highway was pretty much deserted. In other words, **Canoe Creek Road** was a delight.

After passing over the **Florida Turnpike,** I saw a diamond-shaped sign with a figure of a cow, thereby warning drivers to watch for live-stock out for a stroll. Just beyond the sign was the Heartbreak Hotel, an apparently remodeled structure that may have accommodated horse travelers in the days when Canoe Creek Road went someplace.

Regretfully Canoe Creek Road ended at **US 441,** where my map insisted I'd come to the town of Kenansville. What I found was just a country store specializing in bait and tackle. It also boasted gas pumps, a rare commodity in this semi-wilderness.

Kenansville originated as a watering stop on the branch of Henry Flagler's East Coast Railroad that left the main line near Titusville and ran down the Kissimmee Valley to the town of Okeechobee. Flagler named the place in honor of his third wife, Mary Lily Kenan. But the stop never was much, and, when the branch line died, Kenansville all but vanished.

Entering Cattle Country

Happily **US 441** was almost as serene as Canoe Creek Road, for nearly all the traffic was using the nearby Florida Turnpike.

As I continued south, I encountered ever more cattle pastures. Soon I passed a sign announcing bulls for sale. Then came an ad proclaiming, "Beef. It's What's for Dinner." Next I passed a horse farm enclosed by a white board fence reminiscent of such farms in Kentucky. Then I came to the Capital Ranch, where grazing cattle studded the bright green pasture. After crossing the Turnpike once more, I entered Yeehaw Junction.

Yeehaw Junction: Gateway to the Prairie

"Yeehaw Junction." I love the name. It rings like an Indian war cry, and is Seminole for the wolf packs that once frequented the Kissimmee Prairie. After Americans eliminated the wolves, the settlement's name was changed, perhaps in frontier humor, to Jackass Junction. This, apparently, did not suit Henry Flagler, so after he built a locomotive watering station near here, the name reverted to Yeehaw. As the years passed, a paved road finally reached settlement. Then a modest restaurant/motel was constructed. Called the Desert Inn because of its location amid the dry grassland, today it is not only still serving food, but has made the National Register of Historic Places.

Yeehaw Junction is the epitome of Old Florida, but big changes are probably in the wind, for more than 27,000 acres have recently been sold to a developer. This great parcel runs eight miles west from Yeehaw along SR 60 and nearly six miles south along US 441. A whole new city could go up here: homes, schools, parks, hospitals, shopping centers—the works. Long range plans may even include an east-west, coast-to-coast expressway. But I don't want to think about it.

The New Prairie

From Yeehaw Junction I continued south on **US 441.** The pastures were broad and often dotted with cattle or horses. I could make out occasional ranch houses in the distance. All this land was originally covered with native wiregrass. But after World War II, the wiregrass was plowed under and replaced with bahia grass, the seeds of which had been imported from the Argentine pampas. Bahia is far more tender and nourishing to cattle, but it requires fertilizer to make it suitable for pasture.

Signs continued to reminded me that "beef is what's for dinner." I went through Fort Drum, a minor post during the Second Seminole War, which began in 1835 and ended seven years later with most of the Indians killed, herded off to Oklahoma, or driven into the Everglades. Fort Drum is still minor, and the fort has long since vanished.

Bulls and Birds

Beyond Fort Drum I passed a sign for the Rollins Ranch. Then I came to **Old Eagle Island Road (CR 724),** where a small sign pointed west toward the Kissimmee Prairie Preserve, one of Florida's newest state parks. It is designed to protect one of the last segments of the original wiregrass prairie. Eagle Island Road was paved but narrow. The land was

Entrances to ranches appeared every so often. One was decorated with bright yellow, cast iron wheels from old horse wagons.

very flat and reached out as far as I could see. All around me was grass, grass, grass—bahia, of course, but beautiful nonetheless. Periodically the vista was punctuated by a few sabal palms. Entrances to ranches appeared every so often. One was decorated with bright yellow, cast-iron wheels from old horse wagons. It was so unique that I paused to take a photo.

Often I passed large herds of cattle. On one occasion, when I stopped for a photo, a bull turned toward me, his brows beetling and his sharp horns looking as dangerous as a pair of lances. Only the barbed-wire fence between us made me brave enough to come close for the picture. Nevertheless, I was uneasy, for, if he had charged, I'm sure those barbed wires would have given way like cloth ribbons.

Oddly, the bull's ferocity had no effect on the small, white bird that hopped along the ground beside him. It was a cattle egret, happily snatching up the bugs that flitted up from the grass as the bull stomped past. As for the bull, he was hardly even aware of the egret. Two species living in complete harmony.

The Old Peavine Railroad
After fourteen miles, I came to a stop sign where County Road 700A

If he had charged, I'm sure those barbed wires would have given way like cloth ribbons.

headed off to the south. Although there were probably no active autos within cowbell distance, I dutifully kind of slowed before continuing west on **CR 724.** Shortly the road ended at **Peavine Trail,** bearing the name of the old Peavine Railroad, which once ran south to the town of Okeechobee and north to Kenansville. The line itself may have been named for partridge peas, a vine with yellow flowers that often grow along railroad embankments. **The Peavine Trail** is also denominated **NW 192 Avenue,** indicating its inclusion in the street numbering system of distant Okeechobee.

I turned north on **Peavine Trail** and continued through the grasslands. At some time or other this area had been marked for development, for a sign from the Coquina Water Control District gave restrictions for prospective builders. Numerous side streets, most deserted and overgrown, shot out from Peavine. I passed NW 272 Street, identified by a small hand-painted sign. Farther on, a street sign was nailed onto a telephone pole. Somewhere I passed an ad for American Dream Properties, certainly an overstatement for offerings in this isolated, almost deserted, region. But changes may soon come, for the area is zoned for development.

Out on the Prairie: Kissimmee Prairie Preserve State Park
After six miles on **Peavine** I came to the Kissimmee Prairie Preserve, hosting a lonely kiosk with an informative display board. "This tract," said the display, "is likely the largest and best example of dry prairie in the world." Inspired, I walked out on the prairie. Ahead were limitless miles of grass. This was not that tame bahia with its munchy greenness. This was wiregrass, brown and tough. And the cattle that once chomped it were half-wild critters leftover from the Spanish era.

Being on the original prairie was an awesome experience. As I looked over the immense distance, I let myself merge with the landscape. I drifted over the grass in its autumn dress—all shades of browns and tans, with patches of olives and fragile grays created by passing cloud-shadows. I felt exhilarated, as if I could roam forever across that vast grassland. Yes, there is unbounded freedom out on the prairie.

Then the vision vanished. But I was not ready to let go of the prairie. So I stood quietly and simply listened to the overpowering sound of silence. It was a strange experience to hear nothing. Oddly, nothing can be loud. For a moment this nothing was broken by the sweet call of a meadowlark. Then the silence returned louder than ever. Being in a noiseless place was a pleasure, yet it was also disquieting. Yes, that's how it is sometimes out on the prairie.

But one can listen to silence only briefly. Soon I found my mind wandered upwards toward the cup of sky that was so brimming with blue it seemed about to spill. I imagined I had a magic ladle and scooped a dipperfull of that wonderful blue. When I sipped it, the taste was of fresh mint, chilled ether, and the essence of turquoise. I licked my lips. Yes, strange sensations come to one out on the prairie.

The Birds of the Prairie

For a while I watched the gliding birds. I followed an eagle riding a high thermal current until he vanished from sight. Then, closer to earth, I observed a coasting hawk scanning for careless muskrats or unwary snakes. I searched for caracaras. They are good-sized birds, about two feet long. With their black head-crests and ruddy faces, caracaras are among the most colorful members of the falcon family. I had been told they were fairly common out here, but evidently they were busy some-where else on this particular occasion. Neither did I spot a whooping crane, but I'll keep watching and maybe someday I will.

Oddly, one of my greatest pleasures was watching the buzzards. Don't knock them. They are among the most graceful of the gliders. Their wings are large and they flew low enough for me to see them adjust to every puff of wind, every wayward current, every unexpected updraft. I watched one cut endless figure-eights high above me for more than five minutes without once flapping his wings. Buzzards get a bad rap because they eat roadkill. But would you rather have it rot? "Sure I'd prefer sirloin," the buzzard seemed to say, "but carrion is what's being served."

The Cattle Frontier

I continued driving north on **Peavine Trail,** which became gravel, but was in good shape. This was once ranching country. Florida had its own cattle frontier, as rough, rugged, and cruel as any. There were range wars and rustlers and murderers. There were cattle barons who lived lives of luxury. And there were small farmers who couldn't make it. The classic

Some rancher had once called this forlorn structure home.

account of the cattle frontier has been vividly told in Patrick D. Smith's award-winning novel *A Land Remembered.* In this story a frontier family on the Kissimmee Prairie rises from abject poverty to great wealth in three generations. But it was otherwise with most of the early settlers.

I came to a dwelling in which one of these failures may have lived. The windows were gone and the rusted tin roof had caved in. Nearby was a live oak, its grotesque branches hung with a ghostly drapery of Spanish moss. Someone must have planted this tree, and a few others closer to the house, for live oaks do not normally thrive on the prairie. Someone had brought it water, and watched it grow, and, as it flourished, lounged beneath its welcomed shade. But that someone is long gone and the tree is dead.

My imagination continued. Once a ranching family may have called this forlorn structure home. A young man and his bride, perhaps. If so, they probably had a small herd of cattle that brought them a pitiful income. And they may have grubbed in a tiny garden where they raised corn and beans. Over the years they may have had a slew of kids, all of whom grew up as wild and unruly as the prairie itself. One died of a rattlesnake bite, another from the milk-sick. A third was gored by a bull. The others ran away as soon as they were old enough and were not heard from again. Then the drought came. The cattle died and the garden withered. Destitute and despairing, the man and wife, old now, hitched their creaky wagon to their remaining ox and abandoned the homestead they had built with such high hopes so long ago.

Maybe it didn't happen like this, but it could have. Such events were commonplace on Florida's prairie frontier.

The Mystery of Wiregrass

For untold centuries wiregrass had been an awesome, even fearsome presence on the Kissimmee Prairie. It reached unbroken from the gates of Orlando to the shores of Lake Okeechobee. Now barely eighty-four square miles of the original prairie remains huddled in an offbeat corner of a deserted countryside.

Wiregrass is a strange, poorly understood plant. Where it occurs, its growth is vigorous and dense. Yet its rate of growth is so slow that it seldom penetrates into cleared areas. It produces many seeds, yet it is almost impossible to grow the grass from seed. Once wiregrass has been eliminated from a field, it almost never returns. So how is it that wiregrass dominated not only the Kissimmee Prairie, but a grand swath of land reaching from the plains of North Carolina to the Mississippi River?

One theory is that it was spread by grazing animals such as the buffalo that formerly roamed these prairies, presumably in as large numbers as on the Great Plains. It wasn't that the grazers liked the wiregrass. As a matter of fact, they found it tough and all but unpalatable. So they feasted on other plants, which allowed wiregrass to take their place.

Another factor allowing wiregrass to increase was that individual specimens could live for an astonishing several hundred years. At that rate, the plant didn't have to spread very fast to eventually take over a very large area.

Entranced by the wiregrass, I pulled to the side of the road and picked a frond. From out of the central spike grew long, thin branches. Along these branches sprouted short, even thinner subsidiary branches, each bearing a series of pods. From those pods emerged miniature stalks onto which seeds clung like tiny popcorn kernels. Surrounding each seed was a bevy of hairs as soft as strands of the finest cotton. When I held the wiregrass against the sky, it appeared so beautiful, so intricately

In the distance, beyond the wax myrtle, a lone cabbage palm and a bristling mound of saw palmetto rose like some tropical island amid the boundless sea of wiregrass.

crafted, that it was difficult to believe that the fields surrounding me had countless millions of these same masterpieces.

Besides the dominant wiregrass, the prairie supported many separate mini-ecosystems. Wax myrtle bushes grew in the small, damp depressions. Crushing some of their leaves, I smelled a sharp, pleasing odor similar to that issuing from bayberry candles, which actually get their fragrance from wax myrtle berries. Low spears of pickerelweed also relished the dampness, as well as the myrtles' shade. Their dark green, upright stalks were covered with purplish-blue flowers.

Where the land was ever so slightly higher I found broom sedge, also known as bluestem. Their tall stalks ended in a mass of whitish-gray seeds. These plants had actually been used as brooms by the pioneers. Attached to each seed was a silken threat that served as a parachute. I plucked a few seeds and launched them into a winnowing wind. "Good luck," I wished them, as they drifted out of sight.

In the distance, beyond the wax myrtle, a lone cabbage palm and a bristling mound of saw palmetto rose like some tropical island amid the boundless sea of wiregrass. A hawk surveyed the landscape from atop the foremost palmetto. But he flew off just as I pointed my camera his way.

I felt quite distant from civilization. I spied no houses, no advertising signs, no evidence of human beings, aside from the road, which was deserted. There were not even utility poles to puncture the sky. But then my eyes fell upon a hardly noticeable three-foot-high cylinder painted green to match the surroundings. And there on the side was the word "Sprint." So just below the wiregrass and broom sedge were cables carrying thousands of conversations. To such an extent has humanity intruded on nature.

The Camper

Three miles farther down **Peavine,** I came to a road called **Military Grade,** originally laid out by American soldiers during the Second Seminole War to connect Fort Drum with the Kissimmee River, down which supplies came by boat. I turned west on **Military Grade** and soon came to a grove where there was an area for campers. A middle-aged man saw me and came out to my car. He had a slouch hat with a few dry-fly fish hooks attached. His face bristled from several razorless days, but his skin was not lined from outdoor exposure, so I surmised that he made his living from a white collar job.

We got to talking. From him I learned that, since the park is on the Great Florida Birding Trail, bird-watching was one of the main activities. Hiking is also popular. The easiest trail is a circular path near the entry kiosk. Another easy one is north along Peavine Trail beyond Military Grade. In about a mile this reaches Dead Pine Island Marsh, usually active with wading birds.

I also learned that the campers have electricity—the cable must run along the Sprint line. They also have fresh water from a well. When I mentioned that camping here didn't seem so tough, the man pointed west down the road. "People looking for a more primitive experience can get it a mile and a half farther down Military Grade. You have to bring your own water. And there's no electricity."

"Do you mean there's not even TV?" I said with a smile.

"Yeah," he smiled back. "Now that's *really* primitive."

As we conversed, we found we had many things in common. We ended up sitting in portable chairs beside his tent.

"The nights are some of the best times to be out here," he said. "You should see the stars! This is one of the few places in Florida where you can see them without electric lights interfering. Astronomy clubs come here. The Milky Way is, like, paved with pearls. You should see it!"

He waved his arms about him. "And the prairie at moonrise! There're not many places more beautiful. That's when the coyotes begin to howl."

"Coyotes?" I asked.

"Yeah, there's not a lot of them. But they're out there. There should be wolves, too. But they were wiped out long ago. I wish they'd bring them back the way they have in some western states. They should be here. So should the panthers."

He wanted to tell me more, but I couldn't stay. We parted good friends. Only when I was back on the road did I realize we had not even exchanged names.

The Underground Owl

I drove slowly back down **Peavine** hoping to come across some of the rare creatures inhabiting this special environment. Among them are grasshopper sparrows and burrowing owls. The sparrows are only five inches long and have chestnut and black stripes. According to one bird book, their songs are "a thin buzzy tumble of notes." I listened for this buzzy tumble, but didn't hear it—at least, I don't think I did.

The burrowing owl makes his home year-round in Florida and no other state east of the Mississippi River. My Roger Tory Peterson bird guide said the owl chatters during the day and "mellow-coos" during the night. Colonies of these unusual birds actually live in burrows they dig in the ground. I think I spotted one of these cute little nine-inch birds perched on a fence post near the derelict cracker house. He wasn't chattering, but I guess he had no fellow owl to chatter with.

Friendly Fires

Now I began smelling the delicious odor of burning grass. Such a fragrance! The smoke was probably from a burn purposely set by rangers. Oddly, fires do not destroy the prairie, but preserve it. More than that, fires are what created prairies in the first place.

Traditionally fires have been the result of lightning. At those times the flames swept over the prairie burning not only the grass but the bushes and saplings that had taken hold. The wiregrass, with root systems that reached deep into the earth, survived while the other plants were consumed. Hence the prairie flourished.

Today fires started by lightning strikes are put out, for such uncontrolled fires can kill cattle and destroy homes. Instead, in order to preserve the prairie, the government sets fires on days when the wind is gentle and from the right direction. Fortunately, I was there at one of those special times.

Canal 38

I left the preserve reluctantly and arrived once more at the lonely stop sign, where I turned south on **CR 700A.** In five miles I reached **US 98,** upon which I headed west. In several minutes I passed through a map-dot called Basinger, honoring Lt. William Basinger, killed during the Second Seminole War. Then I crossed the Kissimmee River on a good-sized bridge. Surprised that the river was far broader than I had imagined, I realized that this was not the Kissimmee at all but Canal 38, which the Army Corps of Engineers had constructed to replace the river in the 1960s. The purpose was to control flooding in the Kissimmee Prairie and thereby help dry it out so ranchers could convert it from

This was not the Kissimmee at all but Canal 38, which the Army Corps of Engineers had constructed to replace the river in the 1960s.

what they regarded as no-account wiregrass into cattle-friendly bahia.

But times change and what was approved yesterday is considered a disaster today. For it was soon apparent that Canal 38 was dousing Lake Okeechobee with pollutants that had formerly been strained out in the Kissimmee floodplain. Environmentalists began calling for the revival of the river. Although it was deemed impractical to bring back the entire 103-mile channel, forty-three miles could be resurrected by back-filling nearly half of Canal 38. This would result in the restoration of much of the floodplain.

This is now an ongoing project. Ironically, the Army Corps will be able to use most of the material it had removed to dig the canal, for they had piled it up along the canal banks. Nevertheless, it is a major undertaking. The cost has been projected to exceed half a billion dollars, with a completion date of around 2010.

As I looked at a map furnished by the South Florida Water Management District, the state agency directing the operation, I realized that the portion of Canal 38 over which I was passing on US 98 was due to be filled in. This meant that what is now a broad waterway will become a historical oddity. Future travelers will undoubtedly wonder why such a large bridge had been constructed merely to cross a grassy plain.

The Reluctant Cranes

Just over the bridge I turned south on **CR 721.** For four miles I drove through pastures and citrus groves, then turned east on the entry road to the R.K. Butler Boat Launch and Camp Ground County Park. On the way I came to a group of sandhill cranes standing in a field. I stopped my car, got out my camera, and approached the barbed wire fence enclosing the field. Wanting to get a photo of the large birds spreading their wings as they took off, I aimed my camera and waved my free hand. No flight. So I whistled. They barely took notice. Finally I took off my hat, threw it in the air, and shouted loudly. No flight. Instead the cranes began to strut away, muttering something among themselves, presumably disgusted at such ridiculous antics.

The Kissimmee River at Last

Entering Butler Park, I drove down to the Kissimmee. For all the news

I took off my hat, threw it in the air, and shouted loudly. No flight—instead they began to strut away, muttering something among themselves, presumably in disgust at such ridiculous antics.

it has engendered in the press, the river was an unassuming little thing. The current hardly moved, allowing beautiful reflections of cabbage palms and other vegetation along its banks. The river's languor was not surprising, since most of its flow had been captured by Canal 38. When this portion of the canal is filled in, the sleepy river will spring to life.

As I stood by the river, a fisherman guided his motor boat to shore. He was a talkative fellow. "I been coming here for years," he told me. "I usually get me blue gills and speckled trout." Occasionally bass found his lure, but they were less than a couple of pounds. He loved the river with its bends and bars and ever-changing vistas. As for Canal 38, he'd be glad when it's gone. "It's just a sewer for the ranchers," was his comment.

The Kissimmee River vs. the St. Johns River

At this point I found myself comparing the Kissimmee with the St. Johns, only thirty miles east. They are as different as two rivers can be. The Kissimmee begins in a series of large lakes from which it flows south, while the St. Johns begins in an extensive, ill-defined marsh and flows north. The Kissimmee, in its meandering, creates a wide prairie,

The river was an unassuming little thing. The current hardly moved, allowing beautiful reflections of cabbage palms and other vegetation along its banks.

then a massive lake (Okeechobee) from which it traditionally overflowed in a broad sheet that gave birth to the Everglades. On the other hand, once the St. Johns leaves its marshy source, it flows down a deep channel that empties into the Atlantic Ocean. The Kissimmee is a shallow river, whose snags and sandbars make it suitable only for motorboats and other small craft. The St. Johns, for most of its course, is deep enough for good-sized ships to travel. The Kissimmee flows past no large commercial centers. The St. Johns has Jacksonville, with its extensive docks and commercial buildings.

So which river is the more important? Economically it is the St. Johns. Environmentally? That depends on how great a value one places on Lake Okeechobee, on the Everglades, and, of course, on the Great Kissimmee Prairie.

The Hunters

Returning to **CR 721,** I continued south across large expanses of bronze-tinted wiregrass. In a few miles I reached **SR 70,** where I turned east. Soon I passed the impressive double archways of a prosperous sod farm. Then I came to a sign for Out West Farms, which offers opportunities for wild animal hunting. Later, when I looked at their website, I learned that there are plenty of wild creatures to kill on the prairie. There are feral hogs. There are wild turkeys. There are white-tailed deer. And there is a bonanza of quail, although, regretfully (for the hunters), there is a limit of twelve per person.

Canal 38 Again

Soon I came to Canal 38 once more. After driving down the access road to the canal bank, I stood for a while watching the water move rapidly toward its rendezvous with Lake Okeechobee, just eight miles south. When it empties into the lake, it will dispatch the fertilizers and other chemicals it has accumulated from fields, lawns, and parking lots as far distant as the town of Kissimmee.

After much of the river is restored the canal from here on down to Lake Okeechobee will remain, but most of the polluted water will have been filtered out in the rejuvenated marshes upstream.

The Big "O"

From the bridge I continued east along **SR 70** through "God's Country"—so proclaimed several Bible-quoting signs along the highway. It was a picturesque drive with fine pastures. In many fields long rolls of harvested hay were protected for the winter by plastic wraps. I passed **NW 128th Avenue,** which, although still out in the country, was oriented toward the town of Okeechobee, the "Big O" according to local boosters. I had now passed more than a hundred numbered streets since I began noticing them out on Peavine Trail, and I had yet to enter metropolitan Okeechobee. It was quite a build-up for a town of barely over five thousand inhabitants. Finally, just after **SR 70** joined **US 98,** I entered the city limits.

As I drove toward the center of town along a spacious parkway, it was with great anticipation that I awaited the moment I would find First Avenue. But woe! After after crossing **Second Avenue,** I found that the next street was called **Parrott** in honor of the president of the Florida East Coast Railroad, whose branch line gave birth to the town. With the arrival of the railroad Okeechobee imagined it would become a great cattle metropolis, whose population would rival that of Chicago. This may account for the numbered streets extending so far into the country. The town also dreamed of becoming the capital of Florida, but it had to settle for being a county seat.

I located the courthouse at **NW 2nd Street** and **NW 3rd Avenue**. It was a pleasing structure with a classical façade and a pair of unusual exterior stairs. While walking the grounds I found a plaque commemorating a meeting held here in 1947. As a result of this meeting, a successful campaign was launched to have Congress authorize the diking and damming of the Kissimmee River that culminated in Canal 38. At last, the ranchers believed, they would no longer be subjected to the floods that periodically drowned their cattle and wrecked their pastures.

Although the object of my trip had been to explore the Kissimmee Prairie, I took a little time off to travel three miles south on **US 98** to Lake Okeechobee, where I strolled along the massive dike that runs around the lake. Then I drove five miles west along **SR 78** to the Okee-Tantie Recreation Area in order to see where Canal 38 emptied into Lake Okeechobee. This done, I returned to town, from where I drove a few miles north on US 98 to the Okeechobee Livestock Market.

The Sad Side of the Prairie

Since ranchers had instigated all the fuss that resulted in Canal 38, I decided to see just what the goal of the ranchers was. So I drove a few miles north on **US 98** to the Okeechobee Livestock Market. It consisted of an unimpressive, two-story auction house adjoined by a row of outdoor holding pens. I ascended the stairs to the second floor. Here was a gallery with several tiers of seats rising above a circular wooden wall that extended down to the ground-level auction pit.

The air was heavy and gamy, despite fans and air conditioning. Twenty-five or so ranchers were sitting in the gallery. Some wore Western hats. Many smoked cigars. Most looked a little grubby, but they could well have been millionaires. There was also an auctioneer and an assistant, who recorded the sales on a computer.

Then a gate at ground-level banged open and a bull stomped into the auction pit. Glued on his back was a tag with his number. He spun this way and that looking for something to gore, but there were only the pit walls, which he thumped for good measure. I heard him snort. I saw his muscles flex. I watched his hooves kick up the dirt. I had never been this close to an angry yet helpless beast. I felt sorry for him. He was meant to be on the wide open prairie.

The auctioneer began chanting into a microphone. To my unaccus-

I walked along the row of pens to the main building, which was a two-story affair with cattle facilities on the ground floor and offices and the auction area on the second.

tomed ears it sounded like some sort of primitive incantation: "Moneymoneymoney. . . ." When someone sitting around the pit gave a sign, such as a head-nod or hand-flick, the auctioneer inserted the price into the chant. If no other offers followed, the auctionaeer closed the sale by chanting the number of the bull and the number of the winning bidder, which the assistant entered in his computer. Then the exit door on the opposite side of the pit banged open. The bull charged through it and was gone. A moment later the entry door banged open and another confused bull stomped into the arena.

The Prairie's Destiny

I didn't remain in the auction building long—it was too oppressive. Reaching my car, I pulled onto **US 98** and headed north. The countryside settled about me like a comforting blanket of green and tan. The air was sweetened by grass burning somewhere. In the near distance a group of black and white milk cows stood placidly in the lowering sun. Beyond them I saw a ranch house dimly outlined in the smoky blue haze. It was all so tranquil.

But what I was crossing wasn't the true prairie; only a bahia imitation. Suddenly I wanted to see the wiregrass—the true prairie as it had been when buffaloes thundered across its unfettered expanse. I wanted to see a horizon that wouldn't quit. I wanted to experience nature's reality. I wanted to immerse myself in natural beauty.

What I wanted was to return to the Kissimmee Prairie Preserve.

5

Forests of the Spine

The Setting

*I*magine it is 100,000 B.C. A warm interval between the Ice Ages has come. The polar glaciers have melted and their water has flooded into the world's oceans causing them to rise several hundred feet above the present.

Picture peninsular Florida. The only land is a narrow string of sandy islands covered with the gnarled vegetation we know today as scrub. Waves break on the torrid shores, piling up dunes. A tropical wind whines through the twisted trees and bushes.

Then, ever so gradually, the last of the four Ice Ages returns. Glaciers again begin hoarding the water. The ocean retreats leaving the former islands as what geologists call the Sunderland Terrace, what geographers call the Lake Wales Ridge, but what we may call the Spine of Florida.

Getting There

I set out from the Kissimmee Prairie driving west on **US 98.** After crossing the Kissimmee River at Basinger, I reached the hamlet of Cornwell, location of the Riverwoods Field Lab from where the South Florida Water Management District supervises work on the river's restoration. A mile or so farther on I passed the Lykes Ranch, a huge spread that continues south for around thirty miles to Lake Okeechobee. Farther west I came to the Istokpoga Canal, a small cut through the flatlands that connects Lake Istokpoga with the Kissimmee River. Three miles farther west I came to **CR 621,** upon which I turned south.

Although CR 621 paralleled Lake Istokpoga for a dozen miles, road-planners managed to keep the lake just out of sight. Not long after the road turned west, the land changed from flat to gently undulating. This meant that I was passing from the Penholoway Terrace to the Spine of Florida.

Quickly the land became rougher. Scrubby oaks appeared. The road began to lead upward. A sign warned me of "limited distance sight." On my left I noticed a small lake cupped in a hollow twenty or so feet lower than the road. Soon I spotted the soaring observation tower that is the town of Lake Placid's trademark. At twenty-seven stories and resting on the Lake Wales Ridge, it was an impressive sight.

Then I emerged at the summit and turned south on **US 27.** Now I was atop the Sunderland Terrace.

I continued south on **US 27** a few miles to **SR 70,** where I turned west and descended part way down the Spine to **Old State Road 8,**

The intertwined branches of the scrub oaks were something out of a witch's nightmare.

which on many maps is **CR 17.** Here I turned south, heading for the Archbold Biological Station, where scientists investigate this ancient and rare scrub environment.

The Archbold Biological Station

Driving down **Old State Road 8,** a little-used highway through the scrub, I began to wonder what I was doing in this forlorn environment. The vegetation around me was grubby and disheveled, as if it were one of nature's dumping grounds for unwanted plants. The intertwined branches of the scrub oaks seemed like something out of a witch's nightmare. And beneath them was a frowning underbrush of bristling saw palmettos. Nonetheless, I had driven this far to visit the Archbold Biological Station, so I continued.

Upon reaching the station, I found it to consist mainly of a row of single-story buildings that resembled more a misplaced motel than a science facility. I drove to the office at the far end, where all visitors must check in.

Archbold is a privately-run research organization studying Florida's distinctive scrub on its five-thousand-acre preserve. The station utilizes a modest group of 1930s structures built to store furnishings for a mansion that was never constructed. Eventually the property was sold to Richard Archbold, scientist and explorer. Archbold added six cottages and founded the station. Although Archbold died in 1976, he left an endowment that is still an important source of funds.

Science in the Scrub

In order to understand the function of the Archbold Station, I spent some time paging through one of the biennial reports that the receptionist gave me. At various intervals over the years, fifty or so scientists had conducted projects here. They worked under federal, state, and private grants totaling nearly a million dollars. I wondered what was worth so much effort and money in this bleak-to-me place.

The report contained a list of scientific articles and books recently published by Archbold scientists. Reading it, I could see that there was a lot more to the scrub than I imagined. One researcher wrote an article on "Interspecific Interactions with Foraging Red-cockaded Woodpeckers." A second title described the "Defense by Foot Adhesion in a Beetle." The same author wrote on the "Use of a Fecal Thatch by a Beetle Larva." Another article was about the "Attempted Heterospecific Kleptoparasitism by Crested Caracaras of Ospreys." There was an article with the provocative title the "Benefits of Eating Conspecifics." It might have set me to thinking, if I knew what it meant.

Although most of the articles were too esoteric for an easygoing nature-lover like me, they showed how involved people can become when they are entranced by a subject. If pure science demands devotion and enthusiasm, there is apparently plenty of both at Archbold.

Getting in a Scrubby Mood

In addition to the literature furnished by the receptionist, there was a fine, nineteen-minute video that helped supplement my knowledge of the scrub. From it I learned that not only is the Florida scrub one of this planet's truly unique environments, but the Lake Wales Ridge is one of scrub's last major outposts. It extends up the center of Florida for a hun-

I stopped often on the trail and swept the sand pines and bushes with my binoculars in the hopes of locating a scrub-jay.

dred miles, with the Archbold Station near its southern terminus, yet it is rarely over ten miles wide. Not only is it a very small environmental unit, but much of it has been taken over by citrus groves. What remains has been broken into many segments, most of which are not self-sustaining. Many governmental and private organizations are trying to save the scrub by purchasing important parcels or by paying the owners to preserve them under conservation easements.

Hiking Through the Scrub

For most visitors Archbold's main attraction is its half-mile nature trail. So, after picking up a guide book, as well as a good assortment of ecological literature at the office, I set out on the trail.

One of the first things that impressed me was the sand. I cupped some in my hand and was attracted by its fineness and whiteness. The reason it was so fine was that only the lightest sand could be carried here by the winds. And it was so white because it was almost pure quartz, the dull powder of deteriorated seashells having been washed away.

Although the sand was beautiful, it was one reason that the scrub was such a harsh environment. Because the sand reached down more than one hundred feet, it conducted rainwater quickly out of range of most plants' roots. Furthermore, the sand contained no rich humus, for rains had carried it off. To add to the scrub's inhospitality, the soft sand was unable to support tall shade trees. This meant that only the toughest plants could survive the unrelenting sun of the torrid summers.

Most of the survivors have long tap roots reaching into the dampness far below. They also have a matting of shallow roots that catch the rainwater before it disappears. To protect these roots chemicals are often released that inhibit encroachment by other plants. The sand pines have evolved an astonishing system whereby the roots of one pine interweave and often actually graft with those of others to form a single unit able to obtain sustenance over considerable distances.

Crown Fires and Ground Fires

There are two types of fires that take place in the scrub, and they determine whether sand pines or scrub oaks are the dominant plants.

Crown fires occur only when a sufficient amount of flammable debris has accumulated to feed flames that burn with great intensity and reach up to the very crowns of the trees. This insures the success of sand pines. The reason is that their seeds are stored in waxy cones that remain on the trees year after year. A crown fire melts the wax that has sealed the seeds within the cones, causing the cones to open and the seeds to drop to the earth. After the fire has gone, they sprout.

On the other hand, ground fires occur when there is a smaller accumulation of debris. These low-burning flames destroy the pine seedlings, but not the faster-growing young scrub oaks.

Frequent fires promote scrub oaks and infrequent fires promote sand pines. A healthy scrub must have some areas devoted to each because different types of animals and subsidiary plants dwell in each. Thus there must be a delicate balance between the frequency and intensity of scrub fires. Archbold scientists are conducting prescribed burns to discover this relationship.

The Animals along the Scrub Trail

As I walked along the trail, I could see that the vegetation was restricted to relatively few plants. Besides the sand pines and scrub oaks, the other plants were mainly such bushes as gopher apples, silk bays, fetterbushes, and rusty lyonia. There was also a special type of scrub palmetto that was devoid of the rasping blades of the saw palmetto.

Since there was nothing really spectacular about the scrub plants, I spent a moment or two watching the ants. There were plenty of them—as a matter of fact the scrub boasts over a hundred ant species, which is the largest assortment in North America.

But what I was really looking for were the gopher tortoises, which have been called the keystone animals of the scrub. Their burrows descend ten feet into the sand, where it is cooler and more moist. The burrows can be as long as thirty feet. The tortoises, being amiable creatures, are contented to share their one-and-a-half-foot-wide tunnels with many small animals, including mice and snakes. Unfortunately, I didn't come upon any tortoises. Neither did I locate the opening to any tortoise burrow, although the guidebook said, somewhat mysteriously, that they can be found by taking certain nameless side trails.

Hunting for the Elusive Scrub-Jay

Even more frustrating was my failure to see any scrub-jays. Naturalists love this colorful blue and white bird that is almost a foot long. Scrub-jays are one of the few birds that are native only to Florida. They rarely leave the state's borders, for they nest only in their beloved scrub. And not just any old scrub—they insist on those with the tangled branches of the scrub oaks, whose acorns provide food over the winter. If sand pines begin replacing the scrub oaks, the jays are unable to survive. This habit of being so choosy has caused their numbers to diminish so severely that they are now on the federal threatened list.

Scrub-jays have an admirable lifestyle. For one thing they mate for life, which immediately puts them above the hordes of free-loving creatures. As the young birds mature, they help around the house, bringing food and serving as sentinels. And, in respect for their parents, they refrain from mating for as long as six years, which is very long in bird-time. This restricts the numbers of new chicks that might overburden the environment, since a scrub-jay family requires up to forty acres to sustain itself. Unfortunately, there are not many forty-acre oak scrubs left in Florida.

I stopped often on the trail and, with my binoculars, swept the trees and bushes in the hopes of locating a scrub-jay, but I found none. I guess that's why they're called threatened.

The Cat and the Butterfly

My own closest venture into research happened as I got into my car to leave. Nearby was a cat that was so still I thought it was a statue meant to scare mice. The cat was looking at something, but, when I followed its gaze, I saw only a pile of discarded plants, a few of which had small flowers. Then the cat went into a stalking position and began to move stealthily toward the garden trash. What was there? Only a swallowtail butterfly darting above the plants.

The cat stalked ever closer to the pile. Then she crouched, her legs taut, ready to spring. Still there was nothing there. Only the butterfly, which was clearly out of reach. But was it? Sometimes it dipped low. I realized that the cat was waiting expectantly for the butterfly's next dip.

Suddenly it happened. The swallowtail was within striking range. The cat leapt and swung its claw like an outfielder reaching for a fly ball. She came within a whisker of the butterfly, who rose rather nonchalantly, I thought, to a new height. Did the humble insect realize how close it had come to its final curtain? Did its miniature brain even know fear? Could it conceive of death? Would it care if it did? Here are questions for research.

As for the cat, she sat on her haunches and watched helplessly as the butterfly sailed away. I could imagine her uttering something to herself that might have been a curse. Do curses exist in a cat's panoply of emotions? Another query needing research.

With such questions playing in my mind, I took the road out of Archbold, passing through the scrub, watching for tortoises and scrub-jays and finding none.

The Honeybee Nemesis

Once back on **SR 70** I turned east. I passed several citrus processing plants as well as numerous citrus groves. These orange trees had been closely clipped to form easily harvested hedgelike rows. The scene represented such a vivid example of civilization shaping nature that I

These orange trees had been closely clipped to form easily harvested hedgelike rows.

stopped to take a photo.

Nearby were groups of beehives, for bees are vital citrus pollinators. The bees, too, were completely civilized, living in what amounted to factory towns as they diligently created honey for mankind. When the blooming season was over, the hives would be packed onto trucks and hauled off to new pollinating venues—maybe to apple orchards in Michigan or peach orchards in Georgia.

Recently the bees have been attacked by tiny mites that can kill an entire colony in a matter of days. These ruthless invaders are a serious menace, for honeybees are the major pollinators of many of our most important food crops. Although the bees are helpless against the mites, their human defenders are scurrying to discover a means to thwart the vicious bugs. One suggested line of counterattack involves trying to locate an even smaller predator that kills the mites. Ironic it would be if these saviors had mites of their own.

The Citrus Empire

In a mile I reached the top of the Lake Wales Ridge and headed north on **US 27.** Now I was really in citrus country, for these low hills are among the most favorable in the world for growing oranges. The trees almost smothered this ridge. The air was heavy with the almost intoxicating fragrance of orange blossoms. In many of the groves I saw field hands on ladders picking the bright fruit. Fork lifts then loaded the oranges onto large, open bin trucks that would haul them to the processing plants, most of which were farther north on the ridge.

There were almost no commercial establishments along this part of the highway, since the land was more valuable in citrus. Neither was there space for the sand pines and other scrub that had once claimed the ridge. These "junk plants," as one farmer called them, have been cleared, except in infertile areas not suitable for citrus. "Now the land furnishes a food that is both delicious and healthful," the farmer continued. "That's a durn sight better than the scrappy scrub with its bugs and mosquitoes!"

Just prior to reaching the town of Lake Placid I passed several round lakes. There are twenty-seven of these in the vicinity, some large and some small. They were formed when the limestone bedrock far below collapsed into one of the subterranean caverns that undermine much of Florida. These sinkhole lakes, scenic as they are, are harbingers of the distant future when all of Florida will have gradually disintegrated into the sea whence it came.

Lake Placid

In six miles I came to the turnoff to Lake Placid, a pretty town of less than two thousand people. I took a moment to drive down Interlake Boulevard, enhanced by the plantings and curb extensions of a recent streetscape. Along the way were almost a dozen of the nearly forty large murals that are Lake Placid's trademark. The murals continued for five blocks to Main Street, where there were more. Most depicted scenes or events of local significance.

Aside from the murals, Lake Placid is known for its 270-foot-high tower, which provides a stupendous view of the Lake Wales Ridge from its windy summit (reached by elevator) and for its extensive fields of caladiums, those low-growing plants with large, heart-shaped leaves colored with combinations of reds, pinks, greens, and whites. The town

The scene represented such a vivid example of civilization shaping nature that I stopped to take a photo.

accounts for a large percentage of the caladiums displayed around the world and even proclaims itself the "Caladium Capital of the World." A caladium festival is held each year at the end of summer. Since I travel only in the cooler months, I contented myself with viewing the caladium mural at the intersection of Interlake and Magnolia Streets.

Lake June in Winter

Back on **US 27,** I continued north for a mile and a half to the turnoff for a rather large lake with the tourist-enticing name "June in Winter." I stopped for a while beside the shore at Bishop Park, where there was a beach and a clubhouse for changing, but it was too cool to swim. I contented myself eating a sandwich beside the lake while watching kids on the swings and boaters on the water. I wondered why fishermen seem to never play on swings. It seems more enjoyable than sitting in a boat holding a rod on a hot day. But I'm not much different. Once I thought there was nothing better than the swaying motion of a swing and seeing my feet reach toward the treetops. But I haven't ridden a swing for years. What happens to us as adults? Where do the fun things of childhood go?

Atop Florida's Spine

US 27 for the next eight miles was a pleasureful ramble over the gently rolling landscape of Florida's spine. I pictured it as it was in the distant past when Atlantic waves broke on one side and Gulf of Mexico's waves on the other. Then the hills were crested by sea oats, not citrus. Pelicans skimmed the waves while terns and seagulls glided overhead and sanderlings darted along the seashore.

When I reached **SR 66,** just before Sebring, I turned west and drove through a wide patch of scrub oaks as I descended the ridge. In a few miles the land became fertile enough to support pines mixed with pastures and a few citrus groves. In six miles I came to **CR 635,** where a sign pointed north to Highlands Hammock State Park, at which I arrived a few minutes later.

Highlands Hammock State Park

The entry road was through a grove of loosely spaced pines underlain with saw palmettos. Wiregrass grew in the sunny openings close to the road. Ahead was a wall of deciduous trees that marked the beginning of the hammock. It was here that the toll booth was located. After paying the state park's entry fee, I continued on to the pair of former CCC buildings that are the tourist headquarters.

The CCC, or Civilian Conservation Corps, was part of President Franklin Roosevelt's nationwide efforts to combat the horrendous unemployment of the Great Depression. The purpose of the CCC camp that opened here in 1933 was to put otherwise jobless young men, most of whom were seventeen or eighteen years old, to work building the roads, trails, and boardwalks that would turn this dense forest into a park accessible to the general public. The camp held about two hundred youths who had volunteered for six-month tours at $30.00 a month, $25.00 of which was sent to their families.

The CCC recreation hall is now a museum commemorating life at the camp and the accomplishments of the young men who worked here. The former store, where the youths purchased whatever personal items they could afford on their princely $5.00 of monthly spending money, is the Hammock Inn, which sells snacks and souvenir gifts in a setting almost identical to that of seven decades ago.

Remembering a Miserable Era: The Great Depression

As I enjoyed a soda at the Inn, I thought about the 1930s. This period is often included in that fuzzy past that people refer to as "kinder and gentler years." But anyone who lived through the despair, the mass unemployment, and the soup kitchens of the Great Depression would certainly shake his or her head in disagreement. Just because an era existed long ago does not make it kinder or gentler. Is that what they'll say about our own era seventy years from now?

As I watched the cheery families milling about, I thought of the boys who once lingered in this very room, hot and sweaty, mosquito bites over their bodies, discouraged, far from home. They lived in crowded barracks, wore army uniforms, and were disciplined by tough army sergeants. They had to endure half a year of this at the Colossal College of Calluses, as they called the CCC. But, when this ordeal was over, most would sign up for another six months, for there was only misery and unemployment if they returned home.

With the advent of World War II, the camp was abandoned and the buildings were left to rot. However, as the years passed, the memories

Tall trees on both sides rose like the pillars of some great medieval hall.

mellowed. Five decades later the survivors, now men in their late sixties, formed the National Association of CCC Alumni. They donated their almost-forgotten memorabilia to establish the park museum where they and many others could recall those harsh yet satisfying days when the CCC workers were young and had transformed Highlands Hammock from an unfulfilled dream into a reality.

King Arthur and the Loop Drive

Across the small meadow between the Inn and the Museum a tram was loading passengers for the hour-long interpretive tour of the park. I might have taken it, if it had not been sold out since morning. It was just as well, for in my car, following the map and literature I was given at the entry booth, I could travel at my own pace along the three-mile Loop Drive that wended through the park. The road permitted access to eight of the park's nine trails, each of which featured a particularly interesting part of the forest. Most were circular and none would take more than thirty-five minutes.

The road itself was an experience. Tall trees on both sides rose like the pillars of some great medieval hall. I would not have been surprised to see King Arthur emerge from the shadows, a bear-skin cloak over his shoulders and the mighty sword, Excalibur, in his hand. In some places tree limbs reaching over the road resembled warriors' arms, with thick growths of resurrection ferns hanging like shaggy hair.

Of course it wasn't all this weird. The road led through a section where the land had been cleared to plant citrus. The farm had been abandoned for many years and now the trees had reverted to the wild. But they still bore oranges, and in the evenings white-tailed deer emerge to gorge on them. During the fruiting season many persons gather here to watch.

In some places tree limbs reaching over the road resembled warriors' arms, with thick growths of resurrection ferns hanging like shaggy hair.

Walking with the CCC: The Cypress Swamp Trail

I decided to hike the Cypress Swamp Trail, which is a pleasant stroll along a level boardwalk. The trail leads to Little Charlie Bowlegs Creek, which meanders along the park's western border where the Lake Wales Ridge fades into the Wicomico Terrace.

The ground beneath the boardwalk had a light film of water. Most of the trees early on were slim pond cypress growing close together. The larger bald cypress were mainly in the even wetter land along the creek. Many cypress had bromeliad air plants clinging to them. They'd soon be flowering. Although trees were everywhere, sunlight streamed across the boardwalk, for cypress shed their needles over the winter and the new needles were just now emerging. They gave the forest's upper levels a beautiful green haze.

Technically this area should not have been included in the hammock, since a hammock is defined as a compact grouping of broadleaf trees, such as oaks, growing on the drier areas above wetlands. A hammock excludes cypress as well as other conifers such as pines.

The trail passed over the creek, then paralleled it for a while before recrossing it. I paused to watch some of the long-legged water birds wading along the creek. A large tricolored heron was just upstream. Farther off a great egret stood out like a cameo against the dark forest. In the distance a trio of ibises appeared almost ghostly in the swamp's half-light. I could understand why the ancient Egyptians worshipped them for their mystical powers.

On the way back, I thought about the CCC boys. Although their original boardwalk has long since been replaced, I could imagine them laboring in the swamp. It was hard work at all times, but it must have been ever so much more difficult during the sweltering days of summer. The heat would have been unrelenting in this humid lowland. Even worse would have been the tormenting mosquitoes and the biting horseflies. The main defense was oil of citronella, a greasy liquid with an almost cloying odor almost as repellent to humans as to insects.

The Cement Oak

The swamp was interesting, but I had really come to see the hammock. So I drove to the trail marked "Big Oak." The central attraction here was a huge tree thirty-six feet in circumference. To many it was a symbol of strength, but that was only an illusion. Actually the tree was just a shell, for much of the heartwood had rotted out and only its replacement by reinforced concrete kept the weary old giant from falling to the ground.

Oddly, the living part of most tree trunks is only the three thin layers of green cells that encircle the trunk from the roots to the leaves. The outer layer of these cells, called the phloem, conducts the sugars manufactured by the leaves down to the roots. The inner layer, called the xylem, conducts water and nutrients from the roots up to the leaves. The center layer, called the cambium, manufactures the other two. Last year's xylem dies to become heartwood. The dead phloem becomes bark. Only the cambium stays alive in order to make more phloem and xylem for next year's growth. This explains why the Big Oak was still living even though so much of the heartwood was gone.

Into the Jungle: The Young Hammock Trail

I didn't pause long at the repaired oak, for the afternoon was wearing on and I had two more trails to take. The next was denoted the Young Hammock Trail. It sounded interesting, for it involved a battle between two forests—one predominately oaks and the other predominantly pines. This trail is the park's only one with informational signs along the route.

The first portion of the circular trail was through the oak hammock with which I was already familiar. The trees crowded in against the path, their branches overhanging it like a canopy, but their leaves were not so thick as to block out the light entirely. This permitted a palmetto understory as dense as a tropical rain forest.

As the path twisted through the labyrinth of vegetation, I felt cut off from humanity. The air was heavy and damp and smelled of procreation. I sensed that I was in the midst of a living Presence. I could feel it hovering over the mass of leaves and trunks and branches, even over the little ponds that nurtured incalculable multitudes of thriving organisms. All that lived here was part of this powerful thing called the Jungle. It was possessed of an insatiable urge to protect itself. I seemed to hear it warning me: "You are an intruder. Withdraw!"

How the Mighty Have Fallen: The Demise of the Mighty Ferns

But the sunshine slicing through the oaks was my friend. "Stay," it said, and, as I rounded a bend, I came upon a sunlit fern garden. Each frond

A large portion of the leaf was drenched in sunshine, which exposed an incredible array of shadings from dark jade to a green so intense it seemed to be composed entirely of sunlight.

As I rounded a bend, I came upon a fern garden. Each frond was a green lacework burnished with a golden veneer of sunlight.

was a green lacework burnished with a golden veneer. I sat on a log to enjoy the scene. Once the towering ancestors of these ferns had ruled the land. Masses of giant fern trees, broad and thick, covered entire continents. For millions of years they ruled, successive forests growing on top of the ones before until the accumulated weight turned them into coal.

Ferns reproduce by means of spores. I reached over to a fern and looked on the frond's lower surface. Each leaf was almost black with pinhead-size spore capsules that marched in double rows the length of the leaf. When the spores were ripe, they would be dispatched on the wind to find new homes. The spores were just single cells that depended on landing where there was an immediate food supply. This was a weakness, and when new plants evolved seeds—whose survival rate was far better, since they carried a food supply within them—the era of the ferns' dominance was over.

So here they were today, gentle little plants quivering in the light wind that wafted past my knees, clinging to the tiny space allotted them by the haughty oaks.

A Leaf is Complicated

I turned around on the log and discovered behind me the three-foot-wide fan of a saw palmetto. A large portion of the leaf was drenched in sunshine, which exposed an incredible array of shadings from dark jade to a green so intense it seemed to be composed entirely of sunlight. But leaves are far more complex than this.

I had studied leaves when, as a boy, I had borrowed my father's microscope and cross-cut the leaves of some backyard plants. Under the microscope I could see the individual cells. Those of the skin were very closely packed. Beneath the skin were four or five layers of elongated palisade cells. Within each were green globules of chlorophyll, for it was here that photosynthesis occurred—that amazing process whereby chlorophyll, stimulated by light, manufactures life-giving sugars from carbon dioxide and water.

Amid the palisade cells were leaf veins. Each vein had phloem cells that carried the sugars down to the roots for storage and xylem cells that conducted water and nourishment up from the roots. Located mainly in the underside of the skin were openings called stomata through which the leaf breathed in carbon dioxide from the outside atmosphere.

After the leaf used the carbon to help make its food, the unneeded oxygen was expelled through the stomata.

So here in Highlands Hammock oxygen was flowing out of each leaf—out of each tree—out of the total biomass of the forest in a great Niagara of fresh air. Had oxygen been been blue, I could have this seen massive torrent rising until it merged with the cyclonic weather systems circling the earth to eventually flow into the blood streams of humans and other animals around the world.

The Dreams of a Butterfly

Continuing on the pathway, I was fascinated by a swallowtail butterfly that was gliding and dipping among the vegetation. Sometimes she almost vanished into the shadows until only the markings on her wings were visible. Then she would dart into a sunbeam, making her dark wings sparkle. For a while she glided along beside me flashing her wings coquettishly. Suddenly she was gone.

I wondered if a butterfly had dreams. Surely a creature of such beauty must think about something more than just eating and mating. When she sleeps, does she dream of floating on fragrant summer breezes or of a forest's serene coolness? Of sipping nectar from golden goblets or being caressed by flower petals? Maybe she dreams of her caterpillar days, when she indulged in endless food orgies on tender leaf sprouts. Or, perhaps, of the placid time in her chrysalis, when she turned into liquid-softness and her essence drifted to the music of creation. Did she dream of these things? The ancient Greek word for butterfly was "psyche," which was also the word for soul. Was there something they knew that we don't?

Pines and Fire

I blinked as I realized I had been walking for ten minutes and had hardly noticed that my surroundings had radically changed. Almost all the oaks and most of the palmettos were gone. In their place were longleaf and slash pines and lots of open space in between them. This was no longer a jungle, but what is called a flatwood. These trees greatly differed from the bizarre sand pines I had encountered in the scrub, which reproduce only when they are consumed by the crown fires that release their seeds. The longleaf and slash pines evolved less flamboyant ways to survive, and even thrive, in the numerous fires that crackled through the forests before humans decided to restrict them.

I examined the bark of a longleaf pine. It was rough and I could peel away some of the scales with my fingers. When attacked by a fire, the scales may burn, but they will fall off, taking the flames with them. Thus the vital cambium layer beneath survives. Glancing up, I could see that the pine had shed its branches nearly to the top. This meant there was nothing for a low-level fire to attack.

Then I looked around the forest floor. Although it was mostly covered with ferns and low shrubs, I found a few longleaf seedlings. The youngest were in what is called the grass stage. They hardly resembled pines at all, for they hugged the ground in thick masses of needles up to a foot in length. These needles retained enough moisture to resist most ground fires. In addition, they had already established tap roots that went deep into the earth where they were below the fire line.

After the first year, the seedlings sprout fast. I found several that were as tall as I am, although they were probably only a half dozen years old. Their bark already had small scales and they had dropped most of the lower branches that were more liable to burn. The top was already above the range of a ground fire.

There is a big difference between the ground fires of a mature pine forest and the high-reaching, hot-burning crown fires of a scrub. The scrub's sandy soil lacks a ready fuel, but, once a rare fire gets started, the tough scrub wood burns hotly and fiercely. On the other hand, the floor of a mature pine forest is coated with dry pine needles which burst into flame at the slightest lightning strike. The frequency of these fires means that this fuel is limited, so the flames are only a few feet high and consume what fuel is available so quickly that they move on before damaging the pine trunks. However, the flames remain long enough to consume the oak seedlings and any underbrush that has sprouted since the last fire.

Reaching for the Sky

Walking along the path through the widely spaced sunlit pines was a relief after the almost overwhelming fecundity of the oak jungle. I found myself developing a distinct liking for the pines. They were no-nonsense fellows. They seemed to feel that trees had a mission: to reach to the sky. And they set out to accomplish it with no quibbling. The oaks, on the other hand, were indecisive whiners. They couldn't keep their branches from going first one direction, then another. "Oh, we can't do it," the oaks seemed to complain. Meanwhile the pines grew ever upwards, like knights seeking celestial rewards. In my mind I plucked King Arthur and his cohorts from the hammock and deposited them among the more amiable pines.

Friendly Fire This Isn't

It was with these thoughts that I came upon interpretive sign number 9. "The area around you," it said, "will eventually change because fire has been intentionally excluded from this section of the park. Many more oaks and hardwoods will appear and the pines will disappear."

Oh, woe! This was not right! Without human meddling, the pines

Walking along the path through the widely spaced sunlit pines was a relief after the almost overwhelming fecundity of the oak jungle.

would dominate. Yet, lacking fire, they were doomed. Even now I could see where the oaks, the palmettos, and the jungle's motley underbrush had spread. Their sunshine-hogging branches would shade the gallant seedling pines and the entire generation would be lost.

Then I came to sign number 10. "Dangerous Fuel: As fallen pine needles, branches and other debris build up on the forest floor, Park Rangers have to be concerned about wildfires. If fire swept this area during the dry season, many trees would be killed."

This is precisely why wild fires are needed. Without them, dead debris accumulates. The longer fires are put out, the greater the danger becomes. One day an unstoppable fire will explode here. It will not be the low-level, low-intensity ground fire that should come regularly. This will be a vicious crown fire, like the ones that devastated large areas of Florida a decade ago. These are virtual firestorms that reach up to the tops of trees and consume everything.

When it's over, the pines would have had the last laugh—except there will be none here to enjoy the party.

Glowing in the bronze sunshine, the statue called to me, "Remember us when you've gone."

Into the Fourth Dimension

The sun was low when I returned to my car. Before leaving the park, I decided to take another circuit on the **Loop Road.** It was that special pre-twilight hour when the sunlight changes and enhances everything it touches. Thus the vegetation on one side of the road glowed amber while that on the other side was immersed in ever-deepening purple. The scene was so different from my first time around that I felt I had entered a new dimension, one where physical objects were defined not only by their length, breadth, and width, but also by their place in time.

I drove past the citrus grove. In this new dimension the leaves seemed to expand and the fruit hung more brightly, making fine feasts for the deer that would soon be gathering about them. Then I drove by the entry to the Cypress Swamp Trail, knowing that the slanting saffron light was even now telling the birds along Little Charlie Bowlegs Creek to be off to their roosting sites.

Finally, I paused at the CCC buildings. The visitors had gone, releasing the phantoms of the Depression boys to roam as they willed. On the far side of the meadow the statue of a young worker glowed weirdly in the copper-tinted sunlight. It seemed to whisper, "Remember us when you've gone."

I will.

Part Two

'Tween Land and Sea

Introduction

The Geographic Regions of Southern Florida

The extreme southern portion of Florida is quite different from the rest of the state. In many ways it is almost as much a part of the sea as of the land. Rarely is the elevation more than a few feet above sea level. This means that the drainage is sluggish to almost nonexistent. Yet the movement of the water largely determines the nature of the vegetation. Where the water is almost stagnant but fresh, cypress swamps arise. Where the water is almost stagnant but brackish, there are salt marshes, grasses, and reeds. Where the water is brackish and subject to tidal influences, mangroves rule. Where the water is fresh and moves with a slow but steady flow, sawgrass dominates. Where the land is slightly above the perpetual wetness, pines trees thrive. And along the beaches, where waves and winds have thrown up sand, sea grapes and sea oats prosper.

Because extreme southern Florida is so low and so flat, it has not been subjected to the series of relict beaches that made ascending the Lake Wales Ridge, peninsular Florida's spine, so unusual. Although this spine largely vanishes just south of Lake Placid, a trace continues southward, where it may account for the natural division that bisects much of this part of Florida. On one side is the Western Slope—the tilt of the land discernible only by the westward flow of its rivers and streams. Here I planned to visit the Corkscrew Swamp, the Fakahatchee Strand, the Mangrove Tidelands, the Big Cypress Swamp, and miscellaneous salt marshes. All of these eco-units mingle and sometimes merge, especially during the heavy rains of late spring and summer and during autumn hurricane deluges.

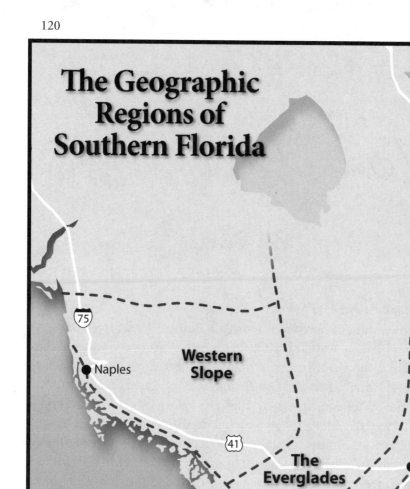

The Geographic Regions of Southern Florida

N

Western Slope

Naples

Atlantic Coastal Ridge

The Everglades

Miami

Mangrove Tidelands

Atlantic Ocean

Gulf of Mexico

Upper Keys

0 5 10 20
Miles

Eastward is the huge swath of the Everglades Slope. This slope, too, is not discernible to the naked eye. However, it is revealed by the flow of water through the dam at the Fortymile Bend on US 41 near where the Everglades meets the Western Slope. Although cattails are prolific along the roadside canals, where there is a richness of nutrients due mainly to runoffs from the large sugar plantations south of Lake Okeechobee, the vastness of the Everglades is chiefly the province of sawgrass, which dominates where the water is mostly free of nutrients.

The Atlantic Coastal Ridge defines the eastern limits of the Everglades. Although the ridge is not high, it stands out in many places by its growth of tall pines.

The Keys are a province all to themselves. The portion of the Keys that I intended to visit are projections of coral that grew when the Atlantic was higher. After the ocean level dropped, they were exposed to the air and died. Today a new coral reef is accumulating a few miles off-shore.

Transition

From Highlands Hammock State Park I returned to **US 27** and drove back south to **SR 70.** Proceeding west on **SR 70,** I descended the Lake Wales Ridge. As I continued west, I began to encounter the same series of terraces I had crossed when I ascended the spine, only in reverse order. I was once again in a prairie similar to that created by the Kissimmee River, but now the Peace River ruled. This river was original-ly called the Peas, probably from the same wild peas that gave the Kissimmee Valley's Peavine Railroad its name. The bones of mammoths and other Ice Age animals are often found along its banks.

At Arcadia, a cattle town similar in many ways to Okeechobee, I turned south onto **SR 31.** In about thirty miles I passed the entrance to the Babcock Ranch. At 91,000 acres, it is one of the largest spreads in south Florida.

For many years the Babcock family offered tours of the ranch, which included the famed Telegraph Swamp. But recently the ranch was put up for sale. The state wanted to purchase it, but funds were not available. Developers were eager for it, of course. While conservationists held their breath, a creative deal was worked out whereby a progressive developer bought the ranch, then deeded eighty percent of it back to the state for what many realtors consider a bargain price of $350,000,000. It was the largest environmental purchase in Florida history.

In return the developer received permission to erect a city of perhaps fifty thousand inhabitants on his remaining seventeen thousand acres. It was a win-win but also a lose-lose deal where compromise won.

At the time of this writing it is unknown just what sort of public access the state will allow on its land. Hopefully tours of Telegraph Swamp will be resumed. But, at the time I passed, the ranch was closed to the public.

When I reached **SR 78,** I turned west and in three miles reached **Interstate 75.** Driving south on I-75, in thirty-two miles I came to **Exit 111.** Here I turned east onto **Immokalee Road, CR 846,** and headed toward my first destination, Corkscrew Swamp, which lay fifteen miles ahead.

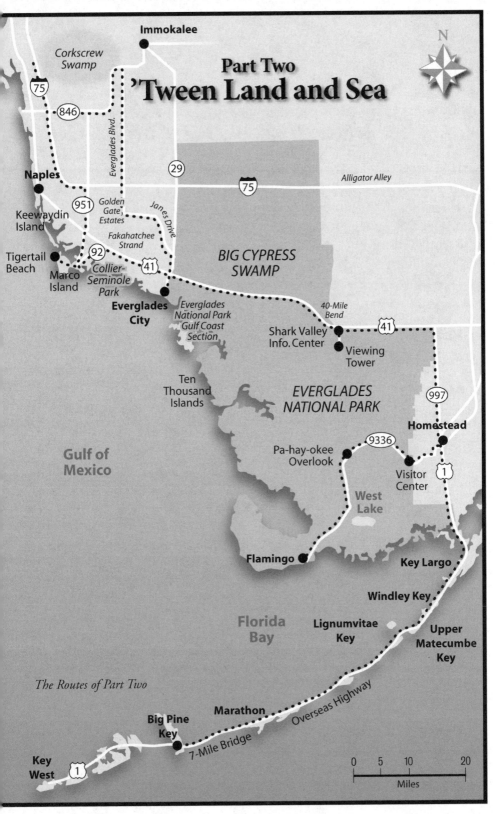

N

Immokalee

*Corkscrew
Swamp*

Part Two
'Tween Land and Sea

75

846

Naples

Everglades Blvd.

29

75

Alligator Alley

Keewaydin
Island

951

Golden
Gate,
Estates

Janes Drive

Tigertail
Beach

92

Fakahatchee
Strand

BIG CYPRESS
SWAMP

41

Marco
Island

Collier-
Seminole
Park

Everglades
City

*Everglades
National Park
Gulf Coast
Section*

40-Mile
Bend

Shark Valley
Info. Center

41

Viewing
Tower

Ten
Thousand
Islands

EVERGLADES
NATIONAL PARK

997

Homestead

Gulf of
Mexico

Pa-hay-okee
Overlook

9336

Visitor
Center

1

West
Lake

Flamingo

Key Largo

Windley Key

Florida
Bay

Lignumvitae
Key

Upper
Matecumbe
Key

The Routes of Part Two

Marathon

Overseas Highway

Big Pine
Key

Key
West

1

7-Mile Bridge

0   5   10   20

Miles

6

Swamp Worlds

The Setting

Swamps are an intricate brew of plants and animals that helps preserve the diversity of life needed for a healthy environment. Swamps also play an important role in Florida's aquatic system. Comprising ten percent of Florida's land surface, they are valuable in flood control, for they can retain water for long periods of time. In addition they filter the water that seeps into the underground aquifers.

Despite their value, swamps are vulnerable. Each is in a delicate balance, for if the water were a little deeper it would become a lake. And if the water were a little shallower, it would become a marsh. Although nature's adjustment is so precise that Florida's swamps have been around for thousands of years, mankind need only dig a few drainage canals and a swamp will disappear.

Swamps have gotten a lot of bad press. When people hear the word, they immediately conjure images of mosquitoes, alligators, and stagnant, scummy water. Much of this is true, for sloshing through a swamp is not the kind of recreation many people enjoy. One has to chose his or her swamp carefully. For me the main criterion was the presence of a boardwalk from which I could be *in* the swamp, but not *part* of it. Two of the best of these are the Corkscrew Swamp Sanctuary northeast of Naples and the Fakahatchee Strand State Preserve near Everglades City. I planned to visit both.

Getting There

Corkscrew Swamp is an irregular glob of wetness squiggling around an area about twenty miles wide and twenty-five miles long. Fed by rainwater, the flow oozes ever so slowly westward, finding, at last, a languid stream with the blatantly pompous title of Imperial River, down which it drifts to the Gulf of Mexico. It was the Imperial River's corkscrew shape that gave its name to the swamp, which has no cork trees nor any screws that are not manmade.

It was on a cool morning in mid-December that I turned off **I-75** at Exit 111 and headed east on **CR 846.** The Corkscrew Canal ran along the north side of the road. The region through which I was passing is destined for high density development in keeping with the Naples area's expansion, which is among the most rapid in the state. But for the moment it still had remnants of its rural past—businesses like Fogg's Nursery, Alligator Station, and a park called the Aviary of Naples.

The road became two lanes as it made an abrupt turn to skirt what early settlers called Big Corkscrew Island, which was a low rise amid the uninhabited wetlands. Today a growing subdivision called Orangetree is established at the junction of Oil Well Road. A half dozen miles east on Oil Well Road an entire new university called Ave Maria is being constructed. Financed by Thomas Monaghan, unbelievably wealthy from his Domino's Pizza chain, it will feature a mammoth church with an oratory ten stories high and will seat more than a thousand worshipers. Farther along **Immokalee Road** is a development known as Valencia Lakes. The Collier County University Extension, an IFAS extension of the University of Florida, is being built here.

It is not only human invaders who are attacking the pristine swampy wilderness. Melaleuca trees from Australia are spreading wildly. These trees, distinguished by their shaggy silver bark, are sometimes called "swamp eaters" for their propensity to soak up water. They formed a thick

forest on my left as I neared the Audubon Sanctuary.

After **Immokalee Road** made another abrupt turn to round the "island," I saw the sign to the Corkscrew Swamp and I turned in.

Corkscrew Swamp Sanctuary

Corkscrew Swamp is a precious oasis amid the exploding human and melaleuca populations. It boasts the largest stand of bald cypress in North America. The trees are so fine, in fact, that in the 1950s logging companies felt they just had to turn them into home siding and shingles, as they had nearly every other cypress in the state. This was prevented at the last moment when the Audubon Society, working with a coalition of other environmental organizations, purchased 2,880 choice Corkscrew Swamp acres. However, a further danger threatened soon thereafter as the Gulf American Corporation, a major developer, purchased a huge swath of wetland nearby and quickly proceeded to dig nearly two hundred miles of canals and build more than eight hundred miles of roads. Then the company began vigorously promoting its development as the Golden Gate Estates.

Audubon feared development of the Golden Gate Estates would imperil Corkscrew Swamp. Thus the Society set out to raise one million dollars to purchase four thousand more acres. But contributions lagged and it seemed the effort would fail. Only after the Society came up with the idea of selling numbered bird prints by well-known artists for one hundred dollars each did the fund drive succeed.

The "Crown Jewel"

Today the Corkscrew Swamp has been proclaimed "the crown jewel of Audubon's sanctuaries." I could see why as I entered the new Blair Center. The building was spacious, with a nature store that carried more books on birds, bugs, and critters in general than I knew existed. There was also a snack shop and a comfortable lounge displaying a few of the bird sketches that had insured the success of the fund raiser.

The highlight of the Blair Center was the Swamp Theatre. Here an innovative program is presented about life in the swamp every twenty minutes. Since there are no seats in this theater, I stood in the darkness and watched, just as I would in the swamp itself. As the "day" began, sunlight illuminated the various plants and animals, while a voice related facts about them. I heard thunder and saw rain. Eventually the sun set and in the blackness came sounds of croaking frogs, bellowing alligators, and other denizens of the nighttime.

Four Mini-Worlds

With the introductory program completed, I set out on the two-and-a-quarter mile, self-guided nature trail through the swamp itself. First, I purchased the Audubon's excellent two-dollar field guide. Then I paid the ten-dollar adult admission, a little perturbed with myself for not remembering my Audubon membership card, since then the fee would have been only five dollars.

Before I had walked very far I came to a display board with pictures of the birds that visitors had recently seen. Among them were wood ducks, purple gallinules, eastern towhees, brown thrashers, palm warblers, ibis, and wood storks. There were also some animals that caught my attention, such as bobcats, diamondback rattlesnakes, water moccasins, and, of course, good old Florida alligators.

"Swamp" is something a misnomer for the Corkscrew Sanctuary, for it is, in fact, a series of mini-worlds. First, the path crossed briefly through a flatwood forest composed of widely spaced slash pines and a groundcover of saw palmettos. Since these plants thrive in dry soil, when the land sloped almost imperceptibly into a more damp environment, the flatwood gave way abruptly to a wet prairie where thick cordgrass ran in a broad corridor to my right and left as far as I could see.

Because the soil from here on is usually wet, and often flooded, Audubon has built an elevated boardwalk that for the next two-and-a-half miles wends across the grassy prairie and on through the swamp. It is constructed of special decay-resistant wood from Brazil and should last longer than many of those who tread it. It is broad enough to permit dawdlers like me to do their dawdling while not interfering with those persons who believe briskness is a virtue.

The Glories of the Swamp

Where the land became watery the swamp began. It was surprising how quickly the plant life changed. There was almost no transition between the prairie grass and the pond cypress, which were so close together that

There was almost no transition between the prairie grass and the pond cypress, which were so close together that they appeared more as a wall than a grouping of trees.

they appeared more as a wall than a grouping of trees.

Although pond cypress are not giants, as are their cousins, the bald cypress, they can be nearly as impressive from their sheer numbers. Yet with sunlight playing over them, they did not seem overwhelming. Their trunks were relatively slim and their bark was light gray. From indentations in their trunks shaggy bromeliads grew. These air plants are not parasites and do the trees no harm. Instead, they get their nourishment from nutrients in the air and from the rainwater that collects in the bark cavities. In the early spring, modified leaves called bracts turn bright red, yellow, or ivory, decorating the swamps if they were small lanterns. At these times hummingbirds dart about the florescences, sucking the nectar as they pollinate the plants.

Pond cypress grow best in still water, and few natural environments I had seen were as still as this portion of the swamp. Actually it was not easy to see the water at all, what with the closeness of the trees and the broad pickerelweeds that sprouted between them. During most of the year pickerelweeds sport bluish-purple flowers that attract butterflies. But when I was there in December neither the flowers or the butterflies

From indentations in the trunks, shaggy bromeliads grew. In the early spring hummingbirds dart about the florescences.

had shown up.

As I continued on the boardwalk, a gray squirrel preceded me. He bounced along the wooden handrail that he obviously thought had been erected for especially for him. He didn't seem concerned that I was closely trailing him. Maybe he liked the human companionship, for every so often he stopped and waited for me to catch up. Finally, he sprang onto a convenient cypress and scrambled up the trunk, quickly reaching the top. Here, he nibbled on something delectable, while chattering away as if he were talking to me—and how do I know he wasn't? Then, tiring of a nonreceptive human, he bounded to another tree, then another. I watched him leaping across the rafters of the swamp. If only I could have joined him!

The Monarchs of the Swamp

After a moment enjoying the squirrel, I resumed my hike. I noticed that gradually the water became deeper and began to show a slight flow. I also noticed that the pond cypress were being replaced by bald cypress. These skyscrapers of the swamp had

massive trunks topped by foliage that almost snared the clouds. Usually this foliage is dense, but in the winter much of it is shed, so when I looked up, I saw patches of blue. It is this annual shedding that has given these cypress the name "bald." Their bases were surrounded by unusual conical growths called "knees" that hunched up a foot or so above the water. They are believed to give the trees support as well as help them breathe, since most of the time their roots are beneath the water.

Some bald cypress had strangler figs entangling their trunks. Each fig had begun as a seed dropped by a bird that became embedded in a bark crevice. Sprouting from the seed, the plant's vine grew upwards, while its root grew downwards, seeking water. For the root it was a race against time, and I had to sympathize with the figs, most of which died before water was reached. But once it was, the vine would continue growing until it reached the top of the cypress. Then the fig would spread over the crown and the tree would die. Thus, it's not the vine that strangles the cypress, but the blanket of leaves that smothers it.

As I was looking at a strangler fig, a lady nearby expressed shock and indignation. "Well!" she said to her friends, "I don't see why Audubon doesn't do something about those awful vines!"

"Oh, yes!" a companion agreed. "We should talk to somebody," another commented vigorously. They were all muttering as they walked away. I'm sure they burnt some ears when they returned to the Blair Center. But it wasn't necessary. The figs are susceptible to freezes, and when one comes along, as it does every few years, the figs die and the cypresses are saved. Mankind doesn't have to intervene. Nature knows what it's doing.

The Small Stuff

After the ladies left, it became very quiet. I stood alone on the board-walk marveling at the scene. Around me life's abundance was on display with an exuberance I had seldom seen.

In the placid water were a few late-blooming lilies. Their petals were brilliant white and even their reflections were as vivid as if they had been painted by Monet. Barely above the water's dark surface, the flowers' purity made me wonder how things so beautiful could emerge from such a murky liquid. But there they were.

Some bald cypress had strangler figs entangling their trunks.

Pickerelweed and arrowhead were stabbing upwards from the water with their spear-shaped leaves. Above them were pond apple trees, the fruit of which pleases raccoons and my friend, the squirrel, but tastes like turpentine to the more discriminating human palate. Overhead the lacy leaves of tall cypress created a shade so unusual that even the air seemed green. Bird calls echoed in the stillness as if though some great hall.

Ferns were everywhere, and in thirty varieties, according to the field guide. The most common were swamp ferns, with fronds up to four feet long. Even larger were the leather ferns, almost tree-size. The smallest were the water ferns, mere spots on the water's surface. Strap ferns sprouted from cypress trunks and cypress knees. Resurrection ferns were curled up on many tree limbs, their fronds waiting for the next rain to unfurl. Seldom have I seen so many different types of ferns. If each variety were playing a separate musical instrument, I would have heard a mighty symphony here.

As the boardwalk led me ever deeper into the swamp, I came to Lettuce Lake.

Lettuce Lake

As the boardwalk led me ever deeper into the swamp, I came to Lettuce Lake, which is actually a small pond too deep for bald cypress. The water was tea-colored with tannin from the leaves that had decayed in it. This gave it a surreal, reflective quality that caught every nuance of color and shadow from the trees and sky above. The lake received its name from the water lettuce plants that cover parts of it. Some persons regard water lettuce as noxious weeds, for they impede boating in certain rivers and lakes. Yet here they made a colorful, green display with the faint odor of watermelon. And their intricate root systems provided welcomed shelter for small fish, as well as camouflage for the alligators that often lurked amid the foliage.

Birds of the Swamp

Beside Lettuce Lake was a rain shelter with benches. It is a popular place for bird watchers. But no one was there when I arrived, so I had a chance to scrutinize the scene. Suddenly my eyes came to rest on a large bird perched on a branch just above the water. Its underside was whitish and it was crowned with a distinctive black cap topped with white head plumes. It was so utterly still that I wasn't sure that it wasn't a wooden statue—something to please the kids. So I tapped the wooden bench, hoping it would move. But the bird, or the whatever, did not so much as flick a feather. I clapped my hands, but it still did not respond. So I concluded it must be a statue and began looking at other objects. Yet, when I turned back, it had vanished. Later I learned this was a black-crowned night-heron. They feed mainly at dawn and at dusk, so I was lucky to be here at the right time. I wished the bird could have told me what he did during the long hours between breakfast and dinner.

But I didn't have to be lucky to sight many other birds. "Did you see that red-shouldered hawk?" asked a man who had sat down beside me. "It's right over there," he added, pointing to a cypress so distant that it could have been in Georgia. Then, seeing that I had only pocket-sized binoculars, he handed me glasses large enough to have spied an asteroid, had one been passing. Zingo! The hawk appeared, reddish shoulders and all. He was so close that he seemed to be staring right at me. I looked at his sharp talons and hoped he had just eaten.

Now an elderly man pushing a pleasant-looking lady in a wheel-chair stopped at the shelter. "Great birding place," he remarked to me and my new friend. "Yeah," we agreed. The elderly man took a tripod from the lady's lap and placed on it an expensive camera with a tele-scopic lens. My friend sidled up. "Mind if I look?" he asked, admiration in his voice. When the talk turned to the scientific refinements of bird photography, I bid them farewell and continued on my journey of discovery.

Camaraderie and Contemplation

As people passed me, I noticed that almost everyone had a friendly word. Sometimes it was to call my attention to an unusual bird: "Don't miss the anhinga drying its wings across the lake." But often it was as inconsequential as "Isn't it a wonderful morning for birding!" There was a camaraderie among us, even though we were complete strangers. After all, we were here for the same reason: to enjoy an up-close interchange with nature. There was a kind of reverence about this place. Small plaques attached to the hand rails reminded me that others before me had felt the same. "She Loved This Swamp," read one plaque dedicated to a woman named Lilla who died in 1975.

An alligator keeps one eye open as he watches for prey in Lettuce Lake.

Perhaps Lilla loved the swamp because it is a place for contemplation. There are few locations in Florida where a person can feel so detached from the work-a-day world. There was something about the swamp that brought a feeling that we are part of ongoing creation. It had a primordial quality. The tepid water and the profuse vegetation seemed to take me back to the Paleozoic Era—the time before man, before even the dinosaurs, flowering plants, or birds; a time when lizards, large-wing dragonflies, and other primitive creatures thrived in the thick fern forests. Some evolutionists believe there is a nook in our brains where memories of this era still exist. Is that why some of us are attracted to swampy places?

The Crazy World of Wood Storks

Corkscrew is well known among environmentalists for its colony of wood storks. These are big birds with wing spans of five feet. They reside in the tops of cypress trees in slap-dab nests of sticks, vines, leaves, Spanish moss, and whatever dribble-drabble they can scrounge from the swamp. Close up they are ugly, with a dark, featherless head something like that of a vulture. But in the air they are sheer fantasies. With great

Corkscrew Swamp is well known among environmental-ists for its colony of wood storks.

angel-white wings trimmed in black, they sometimes beguile onlookers with amazing dives, rolls, and turns. They can glide for long distances on thermal air flows and are said to fly up to sixty miles to secure food for their young. They migrate to Corkscrew in mid-December to lay their eggs and raise their young. When the young are mature enough to fend for themselves, the colony disperses, only to reappear once more the following winter.

The Bubble and I

For a while I let my attention drift back to the dark, placid water, which seemed almost as solid as asphalt. Yet, as I looked into it, a tiny bubble suddenly popped to the surface. And soon another. Where did they come from? Then I realized that plants give off oxygen as part of photo-synthesis. And after the bubbles burst, where did their little bit of air go? Maybe I breathed some into my lungs, and from there it had entered my bloodstream. If so, the swamp had become part of me. And maybe some of the carbon dioxide I exhaled had drifted to a fern—and the fern absorbed it and sent it down to its roots, and the roots used it to grow. If so, some small part of me had also become part of the swamp. We mingle with nature in many ways.

Water and Fire

For all the strength and power that swamps exude, they are just small pieces of Florida's intricate tapestry. In a way swamps are part of the sky, for they are largely dependent on rainwater for their existence. And the rain comes mostly from the Gulf and the Atlantic, so Florida swamps are created from the oceans too.

Yet, strangely, the water that creates a swamp can also kill it, not so much from flooding, as you might expect, but merely from being there. For, as the seasons pass, leaves drop into the water, where they sink to the bottom and decompose into muck. Year by year the muck could build up until the swamp depression is filled and water can no longer collect in it. If this should happen, the swamp would dry up. Then the cypress and ferns would die, to be replaced by marsh grasses.

Yet this has not happened, for most swamps have survived for thousands of years. How can this be? The reason is fire.

The idea of fire as a swamp savior seems incredible, but droughts do come. At these times the water vanishes for a few months or even longer. This allows the muck to dry. Then one spear of well-directed lightning sends flames springing forth. They race through the bottom land like lava. The ferns are consumed. The pond apples are consumed. The cypress bark sizzles. The birds fly off. Squirrels, raccoons, black bears, white-tailed deer, and other animals flee in terror. Dense smoke envelopes the area. The odor of burning wood permeates the air. Is this the end?

But after the fire burns itself out, much of the muck that was killing the swamp is gone. Rains eventually resume, and the swamp slowly refills. The cypress have survived, for, although their trunks are scarred, the leaves in the high crowns are unscathed. The ferns return, born from wind-blown spores. Then, from the wetness deep in the remaining muck, fish and crustaceans wiggle up into the fresh pools. As the water and plants repopulate the swamp, the birds and land animals migrate back.

The swamp has been reborn.

The Fakahatchee Strand State Preserve

Although the Corkscrew Swamp is impressive, it is merely a segment of the massive wetland that extends across much of the Western Slope. This wetland includes the Big Cypress Swamp, the mangrove fringe, and the Fakahatchee Strand, which mingles with the Corkscrew Swamp to the north. The Strand is a mostly forested, swampy channel almost twenty miles long and five miles wide through which some of the region's water drains slowly into the Gulf of Mexico.

To get to the Fakahatchee Strand, I took **CR 846** back to **I-75**, then followed it south for ten miles to **SR 951,** which is the road to Marco Island. Driving south on SR 951, in seven miles I came to **US 41, the Tamiami Trail,** upon which I turned southeast. The road passed through land that was originally an all but impenetrable jungle woven together by vines and bamboo. Not far beyond CR 92 I came to the Faka Union Canal, with which the notorious Gulf American Company planned to drain the huge area dubbed the Golden Gate Estates. But more of that later. Two miles farther on, as I rounded a curve known as the Big Cypress Bend, I came to the Fakahatchee Strand State Preserve. Because Fakahatchee is a preserve, it is in a more primitive condition than an ordinary state park. Thus there is no visitors center, only a Miccosukee Indian souvenir shop. The parking area is unpaved and the only restroom is a porta-potty.

Gators in a Ditch

Between the highway and the parking lot is a ditch. When I was there, it was the temporary home of a ten-foot female alligator and her brood of a dozen or so babies, all less than six inches long. Although a group of people had gathered along the ditch to watch the cute little gators paddle around the water, the female didn't seem to mind. She was on the lookout for the raccoons, wading birds, and snakes that would harm her babies. She surely would present a formidable challenge for these marauders. Nonetheless, one by one many of the babies will vanish down hungry gullets, including the gullets of other alligators. For many gators consider the small fry not so much offspring as savory snacks. "They'll gobble 'em up like popcorn," a naturalist once told me.

Boardwalk Beauty

The highlight of a visit to the Strand is the boardwalk reached from a sand path that skirts a walled-off Miccosukee village. Once on the

Wood Stork

boardwalk, I emerged into a setting of shadows and lush vegetation. The Seminoles called the swamp "fakahatchee" or "the hunting river" for the many animals that frequented it. In addition to alligators, these included squirrels, white-tailed deer, and river otters.

Strolling the boardwalk, I encountered brigades of ferns, many taller than my head. As I went ever deeper, the way grew dim as huge cypress devoured the sunlight. The air was a filled with the scent of growing things. In the spring and early summer the air can also be filled with biting insects. But, when I was there in mid-winter, only a few enjoyed lunch at my expense.

Although humans consider a swamp an undesirable place in which to live, many animals find it quite hospitable. For a while I watched a large wood stork strut slowly through the water searching for a meal. He held the tip of his beak open under the water, for wood storks don't spear their prey the way most wading birds do, but snap their beaks shut when a fish or tadpole touches it. I knew he'd find something, for the dark water was alive with fish—I could see them jumping. The stork was closely followed by a heron, prepared to snatch the stork's meal, when he found it. Watching them was a five-foot alligator lying on a log. Although gators can be very quick when they want to, they don't eat all that often, since they are cold-blooded and don't require food to build up their body heat. This complacent gator apparently preferred to let the sunshine caress his hide rather chase down a meal.

Soon I came to a slough where the boardwalk ended in an over-look. The slough was a dank depression where pickerelweeds and arrowheads mingled with low-growing pop ash and pond apple trees. When I was there, it was decorated with small, yellow flowers. An alligator slumbered on the far bank, ignoring a great egret across the pond. For a while a group of fourth grade children milled restlessly around the overlook. But, as it became clear that the gator was not going to chase the egret, the students grew unruly and their teacher herded them, and their nimbus of noise, back down the boardwalk. That left just a few of us to enjoy the silence.

My Sunny Friend

A swamp is a shadowy place—gloomy, some would say. So I was surprised when a dab of sunshine suddenly nestled like a kitten on my chest. It rested there for just a moment before it began prancing all around my shirt. Next it skipped to the boardwalk rail, where it twirled merrily. In a moment it jumped down into the swamp and spread itself like butter over a raft of duckweed. Duckweeds do not rate high on anyone's list of "must see" plants, and some persons simply dismiss them as pond scum. But, as if by magic, the sunny spot transformed them into a cluster of emeralds. Then the sun-sprite hopped over to a swamp lily, enhancing its white blossom to a purity you see only in photos of moon rocks.

I watched my bright chum frolic in the swamp until clouds sent him scampering home. He left me with a good feeling, for it is the minute, as much as the majestic, that makes a swamp beautiful.

You Can't Get Too Friendly with a Swamp

Despite many pleasant moments at Fakahatchee, I realized you can't get too friendly with a swamp, for there are few environments less accommodating to our species. We humans cannot live for any amount of time in a swamp. We are ungainly creatures with a distressing inability to remain wet for extended periods. And our exposed skin invites insect feasts. It is fun skimming over a swamp on a boardwalk. But a boardwalk is an alien thing—an artificial scaffold that strides the water on dead legs. Only when the boardwalk disintegrates and merges with the water is it part of the swamp. But, of course, we'd prefer to exit before that event.

Destruction Is Easy: Janes Scenic Drive

There's more to Fakahatchee than just the boardwalk, for the total preserve is the largest piece of land in the entire Florida park system. In order to see other parts of it, I continued east on **US 41** for a few miles to **SR 29** and the sign to Copeland. Upon turning north on SR 29, I drove through several miles of cattails and marsh grasses to **Janes Scenic Drive.** Following Janes Drive, I quickly passed through the village of Copeland, which was mainly a scattering of mobile homes. Reentering the Fakahatchee Strand Preserve, the road became sand, and that's the way it remained for the rest of its eleven-mile course. It led through a rather motley conglomeration of maples, palmettos, grasses, shrubs, and a few clusters of second-growth cypress. As for the original majestic cypress swamp, it was gone.

So what happened? The Lee Tidewater Cypress Company was what happened. In the 1950s Lee owned about two-thirds of the prime cypress land in the Fakahatchee, Big Cypress, and Corkscrew areas. In order to harvest the trees, the company dug canals to drain the water. Then rail lines were built. Soon thereafter loggers sent the massive trees crashing to earth. The hundred-foot-long trunks were reduced to thirty-two-foot segments, which were railroaded to the main loading depot at Copeland. From there long freight trains carried the wood to voracious sawmills in north Florida. Thirty-six thousand carloads of prime cypress came out of Fakahatchee. By then the only trees left were at the Strand, where, fortunately, the difficulty of draining this mucky channel made operations uneconomical.

Yesterday Is a Long Time in the Future
I experienced an odd feeling as I bounced along Janes (so-called) Scenic Drive, built on one of the old logging rail beds. The sun bore down with an intensity that only south Florida knows. The scrubby vegetation could offer little relief. Once this had been a shady cypress forest with

I experienced an odd feeling as I bounced along Janes (so-called) Scenic Drive, built on one of the old logging rail-beds.

ferns and swamp lilies and colorful water birds with broad wings. Now they were largely gone.

But the swamp is trying to regenerate itself. At a turnout I parked beside a stand of Florida royal palms, part of the largest natural grouping in the world. They were indeed royal, with erect, silvery trunks and elegant plumes of feathery green. Around them were moderately tall deciduous trees. But most of them were quick-growing maples, not elegant cypress. It will be a long time before the cypress will reclaim much of this forest. Perhaps it never will if the maples get too thick.

Several times I came upon birds hunting for meals in the ditch beside the road. Upon seeing my car, they would take off down the road ahead. They would fly low in order to avoid the effort needed to clear the trees, apparently assuming I would somehow go away and they could glide back to their roadside snack bars. I was driving slowly, for the constant potholes were effective speed controls. So we would go along—myself at twenty miles per hour and the birds at nineteen. At last they realized that I was an unrelenting pursuer. Then, with a squawks that sounded to me like bird curses, they rose above the tree tops and angrily flew off into the forest.

Despite the amusing birds, the royal palms, and the regenerating forest, Janes Scenic Drive was somber, for it was a vivid example of how we wiped out an entire environmental unit for the sake of roof shingles and home siding. Now the shingles and siding have rotted away and the primeval swamp that was once a storehouse of fresh water and alive with wildlife is gone. It wasn't a good trade.

The Moth Men: Picayune State Forest

After traveling eleven miles I came to a canal with a small dam over which the road crossed. This was the official end of Janes Scenic Drive as well as of the Fakahatchee Strand Preserve. It was also the beginning of the Picayune State Forest, although I found it a strange forest, since most of the trees were missing.

As I stood by the dam, I noticed a man on the other side of the road. A "hello" led to more conversation and shortly I learned that he and two friends were moth collectors. I don't know much about moths except they bonk themselves silly against lights. Yet somewhere I had read something about a moth called the luna. When I asked him if he had lunas in his collection, his face lit up as bright as a butterfly's wing. At last he could talk to someone from the general public about his hobby! I glanced across the dam, anxious to be on my way, but I really couldn't be rude.

"I'm down in Florida with two other collectors," he told me. "We've been camped here for a couple of days. This is the best collecting trip I've ever been on! Last night I got a Gaudy Sphinx! Come on, you have to see it!" Half his sentences ended in exclamation points.

He led me to his SUV where the Gaudy was fastened to a display board. It was a beautiful thing, mostly green with white markings. Its wings were four inches wide and had dark bands on them. The collector gazed fondly on the dead moth. "He must have been looking for flowers last night. To suck their nectar. I hated to kill him, but that's what collectors do." Then he reached into his car and pulled out some large display boards with many compartments. Each had a moth. "We're about the only active collectors around. The Smithsonian and other museums are happy to take our collections." He paused to be sure I was listening. "Did you know there are over eleven thousand moth species in North America?"

"No, I didn't."

"Well, there are. My favorite is *Cocyteaus antaeus*."

Now he was losing me. I began inching toward my car.

"You should read the book by Covelle. It's the classic on moths!"

"Yes, I really will," I mumbled, reaching my car at last.

"It's been great talking to you!" he said, shaking my hand as if he were getting water from an old-time pump.

I drove slowly over the dam. We waved. I looked at my wrist watch and noted that only fifteen minutes had passed. It seemed a lot longer.

Warning: Continue If You Dare

I had been advised to turn back when I reached what is now designated as the Picayune State Forest, but is more familiar to locals as the notorious South Golden Gate Estates. All that remains of this failed development is a deserted wilderness with aging dams, overgrown canals, and nameless roads that lead nowhere and upon which somebody is always lost. But to me it was a challenge. So I continued.

A Monument to Greed

The South Golden Gate Estates dates back to the 1960s, when the Gulf American Corporation shamelessly all but wrecked this huge wetland as it built canals to drain off the water. There were four main canals about two miles apart running north and south. They joined to form the broad Faka Union Canal (which I had crossed on US 41 earlier) to empty into the Gulf of Mexico. Then roads were built and the area divided into lots for sale. Most of the purchasers bought on the promises of hotshot salesmen who hyped colorful brochures that showed the development as it would be when it was built out. There were fine homes and manicured golf courses and fashionable shopping centers— all the amenities of a desirable community. But they were only drawings that soon vanished along with the salesmen who had ballyhooed them. Then the buyers were left with water-logged lots with no electrical or telephone lines, and not even sewers.

In all of Florida the South Golden Gate Estates was probably the biggest and most blatant example of irresponsible development. Gulf American not only never fulfilled its extravagant promises, but the property owners in this gooey wilderness were saddled with real estate taxes to pay for useless fire protection and for schools that didn't exist. Finally the State of Florida relieved them of their burden by purchasing

All that remains of this failed development is a deserted wilderness with aging dams, overgrown canals, and nameless roads that lead nowhere and upon which someone is always lost.

more than 22,000 lots—but for a fraction of their original, steeply inflated costs. It is now the Picayune State Forest, although it will probably be decades before there are trees of sufficient height to qualify as a true forest.

It would be gratifying to report that the unscrupulous persons who organized this gigantic fraud received their just punishment. But this is not the case. In 1969 Jack and Leonard Rosen, owners of Gulf American, unloaded their enterprise on an unsuspecting company named GAC. The Rosen brothers then walked away with millions in profits. GAC went bankrupt ten years later.

The Boulevard of Broken Dreams

I found driving through what had been the South Golden Gate Estates to be a strange experience. As **Janes Drive** crossed over the canal, it became **Stewart Boulevard,** although I had to take my map's word for it, since the road was unmarked. This canal is the first of the four that run for twenty-one miles north to drain the wetland that extends all the way to the Corkscrew Swamp. The state has plans to close most of these canals, which will enable the water system to be integrated with the Everglades. Then the area will revert to wetlands and gradually the forest will return.

Stewart Boulevard was paved and in surprisingly good shape— although to call this two-lane road through a scrubby wilderness a boulevard is stretching the imagination. It does have some stop signs, however. I paused at one out of habit, I guess, for I could have waited hours, if not days, for any cross traffic.

In a mile or so I passed over another canal, and a mile further on over a third. Just beyond was a stop sign. The cross street was **Everglades Boulevard**—unmarked, of course. It was designed to be the community's main street. I turned north (right) on it and for drove for seven miles through a dreary landscape of cabbage palms, saw palmettos, and miscellaneous junk bushes. Numerous sand roads branched off the "boulevard." From faded paint marks on the pavement I could see their names: 68th Street, 50th Street, etc. They must have sounded as if they were part of a thriving town to the persons who put down good money for lots on them. But they are rutted and deserted today.

South Golden Gate Estates ended where Everglades Boulevard

passed over Interstate 75, Alligator Alley. Because North Golden Gate Estates on the other side is on slightly higher ground, it has a sprinkling of homes, as well as those other marks of civilization, realtors' signs. Nearby is the town of Golden Gate, a thriving community of more than twenty thousand persons and not to be confused with the North and the South Golden Gate Estates.

Continuing north on Everglades Boulevard, in another few miles I reached **CR 846, Immokalee Road.** I had made a grand circuit, for the entrance to Audubon's Corkscrew Swamp Sanctuary was just three miles west.

7

Sunset Beaches

The Setting

*B*eaches on the Gulf of Mexico differ radically from those on the Atlantic. Atlantic beaches, particularly around the Sebastian Inlet, are favored by surfers who relish the large waves. There are many reasons for this pounding surf. One is that, because the ocean is wider and deeper than the Gulf, Atlantic storms stir up the water far into the depths, insuring that it may not calm before the next storm. Even a small hurricane will leave the ocean churning for a long time.

It's different on the Gulf of Mexico. Here the continental shelf reaches westward for more than a hundred miles. The relative shallowness of the water hinders lasting wave formation. While this eliminates the Gulf beaches for surfing, it makes for excellent swimming and boating. Furthermore, since the beaches face west, they offer some of the best sunsets in America.

Getting There

To reach the beaches, I took **SR 951** south from the **I-75 exit**. A few miles after passing US 41 I came to the Rookery Bay National Estuarine Research Reserve Environmental Learning Center. The Estuarine Reserve is a huge block of land and water that encompasses 110,000 acres along this portion of the Gulf coast. There are only twenty-seven such reserves in the United States. The Learning Center, which is in a new building, highlights the ecology of Rookery Bay, where I was heading. During my brief stopover I enjoyed the displays of the fish and ani-

To my right and to my left was an unspoiled beach, which, just like the Gulf, seemed to have no end.

mals that live in this low-lying area where the water is partly salt and partly fresh. There was also a fine ten-minute film.

Returning to **SR 951,** I crossed Henderson Creek, where I turned right on **Shell Island Road,** which would lead to the boat that would take me across Rookery Bay to Keewaydin Island with its secluded beach on the Gulf of Mexico.

Shell Island Road

I quickly learned the road wasn't called "shell" frivolously, for the shell surface contributed to a memorably bumpy ride. But it was scenic in its way, for it passed through slash pines, saw palmettos, wax myrtles, and Brazilian peppers—that hated exotic bush with red berries and a hankering to take over. In one area I noticed that a recent prescribed burn had consumed the myrtles and peppers. But, although the more desirable saw palmettos were badly scorched, green sprouts had already appeared. The trunks of the slash pines were blistered, but the trees' leafy tops were untouched. Obviously this had been a low-level ground fire, for frequent burnings had kept down the dry litter that might have produced a devastating crown fire that would have killed the pines.

Along the way I passed the shuttered building of the Briggs Nature

Shell Island Road ended at a small clearing beside Henderson Creek, where the excursion boat rested beside a rather narrow pier.

Center. In former years the Conservancy had an informative little museum here, behind which was an excellent self-guided boardwalk through various plant communities. But, when the far larger National Estuarine Learning Center opened across Henderson Creek, Briggs closed. The Learning Center is putting up a pedestrian bridge across the creek and is about to install its own trails. When this program is completed, word is that the Briggs boardwalk will be reopened and incorporated into the national system.

The farther I drove, the wetter the ground became. It must have grown saltier, too, for mangroves gradually replaced the pines until the land along the road was a snarl of prop roots and intertwined branches.

Across Rookery Bay

After four miles, **Shell Island Road** ended at a small clearing beside Henderson Creek, where an excursion boat operated by The Conservancy of Southwest Florida rested beside a rather narrow pier. I was greeted by a woman in tight jeans and a ready smile. Pointing me toward a porta-potty, she warned, "There're no restrooms on Keewaydin." That's why, I surmised, the excursion was for only two hours. I was also careful to bring several bottles of water, for neither was there fresh water on the island.

When a dozen persons were aboard, we shoved off down the creek and were soon in Rookery Bay. Seven of the passengers were chatty neighbor ladies from nearby Naples. They had brought their lunches and a couple bottles of wine, which they sipped judiciously, remembering the potty warning. They were here to collect Keewaydin's famed shells. Several had brought weighty books to identify their haul. Also aboard were three tourist couples, as well as a fashionable young mom in a broad-brim hat decorated with flowers. With her was her pre-teen daughter, who began scurrying about the boat taking pictures with her brand-new digital camera.

Our guide was a volunteer with The Conservancy of Southwest Florida, which is allied only informally with the national Nature Conservancy. We had hardly set out when she held up a life preserver and showed us how to put it on. "But don't be too concerned," she noted, "Rookery Bay is very shallow, so if the boat sinks, just pull your feet up and you'll be dry until help comes. I've got my trusty cell phone."

"So do we," came a chorus from the passengers.

The guide told us more about Rookery Bay. It's about two miles long and a half mile wide, and is fed by several creeks, of which Henderson is the largest. She said that, as we sailed north, the mainland was on our right and Halloway Island was on our left. Beyond Halloway, Rookery Bay connects with the Intracoastal Waterway, from which salty Gulf water mingles with fresh water from the creeks to turn Rookery into a brackish estuary.

We were passing a lot of small mangrove islands. "Habitats such as this are nurseries for two-thirds of the nation's commercial fish and shellfish," said the guide, quoting from the *Rookery Bay Field Guide*. "The bay is rich with oyster beds. Because the tide is low, some of the oyster beds are above the water." She paused while we noted the masses of shells and sea-stuff. "The coast for three dozen miles south from Naples is protected as part of the National Estuarine Research Reserve."

These facts were interesting, but I suspect that I was the only person listening, for the big event of the moment was the dolphins, which most persons were watching courtesy of the Conservancy's loaner binoculars. "Look!" one neighbor lady called. "They're tossing a fish between them as if it's a volleyball!" She laughed excitedly. But when no others saw them, she stopped, somewhat chagrined.

The Intracoastal Waterway

When we reached Rookery Bay's northern limit, we turned left, passed down a short channel, and emerged on the Intracoastal Waterway, which conducts boaters along the chain of barrier islands between Naples and the resort town of Marco Island fifteen miles south. I was surprised at the activity along the Waterway. Although it was mid-afternoon on a weekday, everything from simple motor boats to luxury cruisers were plying the waters. None were speeding for, as signs warned, this was a Manatee Zone where the speed limit was thirty miles per hour. There was a good deal of gaiety aboard the boats, and much hand waving as they passed us. I thought it odd that people from Naples wanted to party at Marco and people from Marco thought Naples would be more fun. If it was festive now, what would it be when they returned? Yet I didn't envy them—today was for enjoyment of quieter, more natural things. The kind of experiences that run deeper and linger longer.

Nearly Paradise: Keewaydin Island

After passing close to an osprey nest, where an alert mother and several little feathered heads watched us, we pull into the dock on Keewaydin. Nearby several other docks reached into the Intracoastal Waterway, for the island is ten percent privately owned. After it became part of the national reserve in 1978, restrictions were placed on further sales. As we disembarked, a pelican sitting imperiously on a dock post waited impatiently for us to leave. On shore an armadillo scrutinized us momentarily before vanishing into the underbrush.

Led by our guide, we filed along a path through the dense growth of brush and small trees that clothed this portion of the island. The ground was littered with limbs and leaves. In a moment we passed a ramshackle house sometimes occupied by Conservancy people when they monitor sea turtles' nests during the summer.

After a hike of barely five minutes, we reached the Gulf of Mexico. No plants grew on the brilliant white sand that belonged neither to the

We filed along a path through the dense growth of brush and small trees that clothed this portion of the island.

sea nor the land. The barrenness of the beach was somewhat of a shock, given the lushness of the vegetation through which I had just passed.

The guide told us we could roam the beach freely, but must be back in an hour. Then she marked the obscure entrance to the path with a multi-colored tube, and told us to be off. With that the Naples bunch headed up the beach and the others in the opposite direction. Everyone's head was down as they scrutinized the shore for shells. Terns and seagulls fluttered about them, but they didn't notice. Sanderlings scurried ahead of them, but they didn't notice. The sun highlighted some creampuff clouds, but they didn't notice. Shells, shells, shells were all that was on their minds. Soon everyone had wandered almost out of sight. Even the guide had disappeared.

I walked to where a tall Australian pine threw shade over the sand. Suppose, I thought, I spent the entire hour here. What could I discover in this little corner of nature?

An Hour of Little Things

So I sat beneath the tree. Before me the Gulf of Mexico extended as an unruffled turquoise plain merging with the misty blue sky somewhere beyond infinity. Behind me was a low dune topped by sea grapes, their flat, rounded leaves standing out against the bleached-ivory sand. To my right and to my left was an unspoiled beach, which, just like the Gulf, seemed to have no end. I reclined against the dune and breathed in the salt-flavored air. Ah!

As I lay there, I looked up into the branches of the tree above me. Environmentalists hate these Australian pines as exotics that out-compete native species. But other persons welcome them on barrier islands such as this where they are about the only shade trees salt-tolerant enough to survive. Their branches were beautiful up close. What appeared to be needles were actually tiny leaves wrapped tightly around jointed twigs, for the trees are not pines at all. Some of these "needles" that had broken from the tree and lay around me in graceful, foot-long arcs. I picked one up and could see each individual tightly-wound leaf. Also in the sand were many of the little globes that had held the tree's seeds.

"Junk" is Not Always Junk

I turned to regard the landscape beside me. There were a pair of dead logs, an exposed saw palmetto, and a few runners from the sea grapes on the low dune just beyond the high tide mark. It was a rather motley collection that most persons would dismiss as just junk. But I had vowed to explore my beach niche, so I gave it my full attention.

The logs were bleached and without bark, indicating they must have floated on the tides for many months. One of them, from its girth, must have come from a fairly large tree. I couldn't be sure what kind, but I'd guess it was from an Australian pine.

The saw palmetto was below the high water line, so I wondered how it had managed to keep from being either smothered by salt or swept away by the tides. Examining it closely, I discovered an unusual strategy: it was not rooted in the beach sand but its stalk bent parallel to the sand and extended for six feet into the tide-free dune. This was an ingenious solution to twin problems: first, the tidal water could not reach its roots and second, the sea grapes' dense shadows could not stunt its leaves. Thus the plant would eventually flower and produce the seeds of the next generation.

The sea grapes, for their part, also wanted to expand into the tidal zone. Their runners grasped the sand with tough and persistent fingers.

They would continue growing seaward until the tide nibbled off their fingers. Then they would retreat, to try again later. But they will never succeed in conquering the tide.

The Lives Beneath the Thicket

Then I heard a crackle from beneath the maze of gnarled sea grapes. What could penetrate this formidable growth? I lay on my stomach and peered into the thicket at sand level. Surprisingly the sand was smooth and covered with the footprints of many different animals. I couldn't see any of them, yet I had the feeling that several pairs of eyes were watching me.

What was there? A cotton rat? An opossum? A raccoon? I pictured them easing along the sand trails searching for food. The sea grapes would form a canopy as thick as that of an oak forest to a human. It was ideal protection from hawks, owls, and other airborne marauders. To the animals that lived here, this was not an inhospitable thicket. It was security. It was home.

Catastrophe

But how safe was it really? Viewing the fragile dune and listening to the

I heard a crackle and turned to see what had made the noise. Behind me was a four-foot-high sandy ridge capped by a maze of gnarled sea grapes.

rustle of the waves against the shore, I began to feel the flux of nature. A hurricane could strike any year. Then waves would crash across the island, carrying off the sea grapes and all the vegetation of the interior. If the storm surge were sufficiently violent, it could carry off Keewaydin itself.

Yet, after calm returned, Gulf currents would slowly redeposit the lost sand—if not here, someplace close by. Then a new island would form. The sea grapes and other plants would gradually take root. And in a few generations the animals would start their families. Eventually all would be as before.

Seashells

Although barrier islands like Keewaydin are impermanent affairs, the ocean and the sand and the creatures of the sea are almost eternal. The sand around me was replete with the shells of creatures that had lived in the oceans hundreds of millions of years ago—before, even, the continents as we know them existed.

I picked up some shells and brushed them off. They were not the fresh ones that my tour mates would gather closer to the water, but they had their own beauty. My pocket guide helped me identify them. One was a banded tulip, a slender shell with dark brown rings surrounded by whorls of bluish-green. Another was a cat's paw, a whitish shell with lengthwise folds that gave it an amazing resemblance to the paw of a kitten. A third was a lettered olive, a bright shell with a soft bluish tint.

I found a whole array of murexes, showy shells with prominent ridges decorated with parallel brown bands. And there were many coquinas—some yellowish, some rose-pink, some lavender. The three- and four-inch fragments of pen shells also pleased me, for they glowed like mother-of-pearl. Far less spectacular were the bryozoan remains, which, although they resembled heavily encrusted twigs, had actually been colonies of polyps similar to coral. Massive growths of bryozoans built up the plateau that became the lower Everglades. To my amazement, I even found a sand dollar, although how it arrived this far up the beach without breaking apart was a wonder. Also out of place were the long, slender red mangrove propagules. They must have originated in some calm backwater, been caught up in the tide, and cast ashore by the waves.

As I assembled my treasures on a piece of flat driftwood and prepared to take a photograph, they seemed to tell me their stories.

The shells around me were so numerous that I finally gave up trying to identify them. There was a lustrous jet-black one about an inch long and another that was almost pure white with small flecks of brown. There was a beautiful maroon fragment sprinkled with tiny globules of white . . . and another of rusty red. Some had ridges, some had spines, and some were as smooth as glass marbles. A few were whole, but most were broken.

As I assembled my treasures on a piece of flat driftwood and prepared to take their photograph, they seemed to tell me their stories. Some had lived tragic lives, for their shells had tiny holes in them where predators had drilled through. And there were the predators themselves, like the murexes. Many had grown fat feasting on their fellows. Others had died of starvation, for their shells were small. But some of those before me had lived full lives. They had found their mates and had helped reproduce their kind. Then they had died peacefully, having accomplished the mission for which they had been created. And they had left their shells as beautiful reminders that they had lived. That's more than most of us will be able to accomplish.

Thump, thump . . .

After taking the photo, I felt a strange mood come over me. The shells reached so far back in time it was almost scary to contemplate. Could it be possible that life had existed for so long? How can it all be gone in a flutter when the present seems so slow in passing? Suddenly it appeared that time had slowed, almost stopped. The branches of the Australian pine above me were utterly motionless. Ripples from the Gulf slipped up the shore so languidly it seemed as if they would forget to return. The water could have been made of pudding, for it created no sound. A lone pelican hovered in the heavy air, his wings barely moving. Farther out in the Gulf a sailboat, nearly lost in the soft haze, seemed permanently pasted on the brim of the horizon.

It was such an unusual sensation that I felt my heart to see if it was still beating. Its reassuring thump, thump was the only sensation indicating that time was passing. Thump, thump . . . a million sea creatures had been born and a million more had died. Thump, thump . . . uncountable specks of sap had flowed into the limbs above me and the limbs had grown infinitesimally longer. Thump, thump . . . the shadows had become a shade longer. Thump, thump . . . I was a little bit older. Thump, thump . . . although only a single minute had passed, the world was not quite the same as it had been.

Bo-or-ing?

As I was musing, the lady with the stylish flower hat and her energetic daughter returned from their walk on the beach. I could hardly believe the hour allotted us was almost over. Mrs. Style carried a large shopping bag almost overflowing with shells. Spotting me under the Australian pine, and seeking some shade herself, she strolled over.

"We've been doing a lot of walking!" she said, daintily dabbing her brow with a hanky that I knew must be delicately scented. "See the exquisite shells Daphne and I discovered."

The little girl bubbled with enthusiasm. "I can hardly wait to show my friends. Oh! They're going to be jealous!"

Mrs. Style asked to see what I had, so I showed her my meager collection of weather-worn shells. "I see you have some pretty things, too," she said in a tone that tried to, but couldn't, conceal the condescension. "Have you been right here the entire time?" she asked.

I nodded.

The girl couldn't believe it. "Gee!" she said. "You sure missed a lot!"

The two of them looked around and saw only the sand littered with debris from the tree, a line of sea wrack, and a bunch of seemingly half-dead bushes.

Then the girl pulled out her expensive camera. "Can I take your picture?" she asked. I had hardly agreed than I heard a click. With that, she darted off to shoot a much more interesting seagull that had landed nearby.

Now the rest of the group was gathering at the head of the path that led to the dock. I rose and said goodbye to my little sandy province. As I left, I imagined the girl showing the photos to her friends. "See this man?" she'd giggle. "He spent the whole time sitting under that one tree! Bo-or-ing!"

The Road to Marco Island

Upon returning to my car, I drove back down **Shell Island Road** to **SR 951,** where I turned south. My goal was the prized mud flats of Marco Island's Tigertail Beach. "Prized" and "mud flats" may seem hardly compatible, but to naturalists there's nothing wrong with a good field of sandy mud. Sure, mud isn't pretty. Sure, it's not suitable for picnic blankets. But if you don't reject it outright and show it some respect, a good mud flat will respond manyfold.

The road to Marco Island followed a route approximating that originally cut through the mangrove marsh for a rail line in the 1920s. Over many years the road was just two narrow lanes, but recently, as the area around it began attracting developers, it has been broadened to four. One of the earliest of the developers was the Deltona Corporation, which, in the 1960s and '70s, converted Marco from a virtually uninhabited sand and mangrove wilderness into a bustling vacation land of fashionable dwellings and scenic canals.

Much of the land on the east side of SR 951 is being developed as fast as financing is available. But almost all the area on the west side, from Henderson Creek to the Marco bridge, remains in its natural state as part of the National Estuarine Research Preserve.

Tigertail Beach

In a few miles the road ascended the bridge over the Marco River. Although I have been visiting this five-mile-long island for many years, the view from the bridge is always impressive, especially the long line of high-rise condos along Marco's trademark Crescent Beach. The towers end abruptly near the northern end of the island at Tigertail Beach Park, which the Deltona Company deeded to Collier County for public use.

To reach Tigertail, I continued on **SR 951** through the compact business district of this town of eighteen thousand persons and past Smokehouse Bay to **Kendall Drive.** Here I turned right, passing a series of short streets where the homes had docks on Clam Bay. Reaching **Hernando Drive,** I turned left and crossed over the channel that gives Clam Bay boaters access to the Gulf of Mexico and arrived at Tigertail Beach. Although sometimes during the tourist season beach parking can be difficult, it was now mid-afternoon and there were ample spaces. I walked past the open-air eating area where soft drinks and sandwiches can be purchased, and took the boardwalk leading to the beach.

Once on the boardwalk I paused to look south at Crescent Beach, which curved along the Gulf like the rim of a new moon. When the Deltona executives, led by Frank Mackle, came here on their initial inspection tour in 1962, there was no sign of habitation.

Once on the boardwalk, I paused to look south at Crescent Beach, which curved along the Gulf like the rim of a new moon.

"I fell in love with that island from the beginning," Mackle told me when I was gathering material for my book *The Last Paradise: The Building of Marco Island.* Some persons may ask, "If he loved it so much, why did he wreck it with all his buildings and canals?" Mackle, a genial and sincere man, would have answered that in developing Marco he was enabling many people, not just a few, to enjoy this bit of paradise.

The Mysterious Island

When Collier County created Tigertail Beach Park in the late 1960s, it fronted the Gulf for a half mile. Although it was an ample stretch of sand, no one could have imagined that a large, new portion would rather suddenly transform the beach into a popular place for nature aficionados.

The unexpected began as material dropped by Gulf currents created a sandbar a few hundred yards off shore. This sandbar gradually grew until it rose above the water. Soon it supported a fringe of sea oats and other low vegetation. Crabs and other sea animals made it their home. People would boat out to collect shells and watch the birds. Shells shaped like silver dollars were so plentiful that the thin strip was soon called Sand Dollar Island.

Year by year this mysterious island continued to grow. Eventually the southern end began curling toward the land. When I visited Tigertail in 1994, Sand Dollar Island's first tendril had reached the shore. There was concern that it would close off the beach and create a smelly lagoon.

By the following year Sand Dollar was firmly connected with Tigertail Beach and people could walk out on it from the mainland. The lagoon that many had dreaded was a reality. Yet the tidal flow kept the water circulating and the scent fresh. The same tides, along with the wind and rain, deposited sand and plant material into the lagoon, causing it to become ever shallower. Gradually the sand and organic detritus devolved into mud. In this manner the mud flats were created.

The Beach That Isn't

Continuing along the boardwalk, I crossed a sandy buffer zone where clumps of sea oats waved their seed-spires amid clusters of cordgrass. In places sand-sunflowers shone bright yellow. Closer to the beach, I passed long runners of railroad vines, which are related to morning glories. Although they bear large, purple flowers, I found none blooming.

The boardwalk ended at the beach. When the beach had been directly on the Gulf of Mexico, waves rolled in and swimmers frolicked in the water. Today it fronts only the shallow lagoon fringed on the west by Sand Dollar Island, with its low ruffle of greenery. Yet people still rent canvas cabanas, just as if this were a real beach. They can hear the waves breaking against Sand Dollar's far shore and can walk across the lagoon to enjoy the island when they desire. In addition, the kids enjoy paddling around the lagoon in rental canoes and kayaks.

The beach-goers are usually joined by gulls and terns, who have developed a craving for french fries and salted potato chips. Sometimes the gulls get very aggressive. I've seen a teenage girl who was carrying food from the snack area become so harassed by screaming gulls, some flying close to her face, that she threw her paper dinner plate to the birds and ran back to her family's cabana salvaging only a badly shaken-up Coke.

When beachgoers become weary of sunning, paddling, and shooing off the gulls, they can retire to the safety of the outdoor grill, whose penetrating fumes often waft over this part of the beach. The odors don't seem to disturb anyone. "What's a beach without burgers?" I heard a teenager call to a friend.

Off to the Mud Flats

But a beach without burgers is what I have come for over the years. Sometimes I walk south to where Sand Dollar Island joins the mainland. This provides an ideal habitat for such birds as egrets and herons. In places red and black mangroves are taking root, and, since it is prohibited to remove them, eventually there will be a small forest here.

However, today I turned north up the beach, leaving behind the cabanas and cloying fragrance of frying food. The tide was ebbing and large areas of sandy mud were emerging. The sun cast that strange, late afternoon light that is intense but carries little heat. Many persons were wandering along the shore, most in a quiet mood, savoring the tranquil, nonburger atmosphere. Quite a few had binoculars, for birds were everywhere.

"I wonder how close I can get to them." So saying, he moved slowly across the sandy mud.

Wings over the Lagoon

I stopped for a while to converse with a young man carrying a camera. He was from an Iowa farm and had never seen so many birds in such a setting. "They almost seem tame," he said. "I wonder how close I can get to them." So saying, he moved slowly across the sandy mud toward the open water. When the birds were only a few yards away, he raised his camera, causing the birds to become restless. As his shutter snapped, the nearest birds took off. Their alarm instantly spread to their neighbors, and they, too, fluttered up. This caused birds throughout this part of the lagoon to take to the air in an awesome cloud of feathers and squawks.

"Gee," the young man said, "I didn't know I'd create such a turmoil!"

But no harm was done and it was a pleasure to watch the birds circle over us. In another moment they descended, splashed to stops in the lagoon, and all was quiet once more.

After the young man left, I stood quite still and let the birds come to me. Soon a dowitcher hurried past. This was the first one I had ever seen. But I remembered reading that their heads bobbed like sewing machines. I recognized him instantly, although the last sewing machine I had seen was being used by my long-departed grandmother. How this little brown bird with a needle-beak half the size of his entire body could distinguish his prey quickly enough to direct his strike was a mystery to me. After some thought, I concluded he was just showing off and when no one was watching slowed down.

Next a plover came my way. He was another small brown bird, but he had a distinctive black ring around his neck. The plover was more methodical than the dowitcher, running in short bursts, then pausing to think it over before his next brief sprint. Not surprisingly, the dowitcher had missed a lot and the plover was picking up ample tidbits.

For a while I watched a snowy egret far out in the shallow water. His feathers, usually pure white, were sunshine-tinted with the palest of yellows, giving him a luster I had not seen in others. He shuffled his feet as he strutted through the water, thereby stirring up the fish that comprised his diet.

Large numbers of ibises also were active. Flying in for a landing, they were spectacular, with their large, white bodies and broad wings tipped with black. Their long legs permitted them to walk far out into the water, where they probed for crustaceans and frogs with their long, down-curved bills. Strangely, many ibises and egrets seemed to have formed a sort of symbiotic bond. For the ibises, moving through the water with their heads down could have been taken unawares by predators. But they were safe when accompanied by an egret lookout. Thus the ibises did not object when their companions sometimes snatched their catches. Obviously, they considered it the cost of doing business.

The Worm Woman

As I was observing the birds, a woman walked toward me. She had a trowel in her hand and her eyes on the sandy mud. When she was close, she suddenly stopped, bent down, and started digging. Since the unwritten nature-ramblers' code requires responding to questions by utter strangers, I walked over to her and asked with a smile, "Digging for gold?" It was a sad attempt at humor, but it's difficult to be witty on short notice.

No answer. She kept at it with her trowel.

I tried again. "Get to China yet?"

No answer.

Concluding that she was unfamiliar with the code, I turned to walk further up the beach.

"Wait," she grunted. "Here it is." She was as pleased as a fed sea gull. In her muddy hand was a thin tube about ten inches long. It looked like a tissue that could have enclosed a dirty cigar. "Ever seen a parchment worm?" she asked.

"No," I answered.

"Well you won't see it now," she chuckled. "It's inside." She brought the parchment close to my face so I could fully appreciate this ugly bit of flotsam. "The little creature in this tube started life floating in the Gulf. She spent a few weeks there as a larva, then came ashore with a high tide."

The Worm Woman paused, obviously waiting for me to respond. "That's interesting," I answered. I regarded that as noncommittal, but it was enough to put wind in her sails.

"Once ashore," she continued, "the little worm dug a burrow and coated it with the mucus that became this tube."

That was supposed to keep up my interest!

"The tube was U-shaped, with both ends sticking up just above the

She suddenly stopped, bent down, and started digging.

sand." The Worm Woman gazed at the mucus-tube with admiration. "The little worm gets her food by using paddle-like projections to draw water into her cozy tube-home. She eats the plankton in the water, then expels the waste out the other end. When it's time to reproduce, she expels her eggs the same way. The tide carries them off and the babies are born at sea. She never gets to see them." I detected sadness in her voice.

But she brightened quickly. "I'm going to take her home with me," she continued. "At night she'll glow with a lovely blue light!"

Enthusiastic as the lady was, I just couldn't work up an affection for the worm. It was almost beyond my imagination to conceive living one's entire life in a mucus sheath buried in the mud.

She was looking up and down the beach for more worms. "I found my parchment worm by the exposed tube ends," she continued. "Look over there. I see more evidence of worms! Maybe it's a plumed worm—they decorate the ends of their tubes with shell fragments. Their gills are the most luscious red. And I see some of the two-inch high mounds of acorn worms. You never know what you'll find beneath the mud's surface—there's all sort of thrilling life forms down there! Want to tag along?" Her eyes glowed with an enthusiasm that was almost erotic.

After I politely declined, she went on her merry way, enraptured by her Great Worm Hunt and forgetting about me almost instantly.

Niches

Resuming my walk, I became aware that the area around me was composed of several distinct zones.

The lagoon zone was home to wading birds.

Along the lagoon's shallows there was a zone of dark green matting where algae dominated. Algae are not appealing plants, for their uncontrolled growth in many Florida lakes has killed distressing numbers of fish and aquatic plants. But I acknowledge that I should pay algae more respect, for they manufacture more than ninety percent of the world's oxygen.

Closer to shore was the intertidal zone, pock-marked by worm mounds and small tidepools.

Beyond the reach of the tides was a fringe of sand. In this zone dwelt the fiddler crabs, which I intended to visit shortly.

And lastly there was the salt meadow behind the beach. Grasses, mangroves, and Australian pines thrived here, each occupying its own special sub-niche.

Sand Dollars

For the moment I was still intrigued by the intertidal zone, and every so often I came upon the four-inch-wide outline of a sand dollar buried just beneath the surface. Once I dug down with my fingers and pulled one out of the mud. He had five slits in his sandy shell through which he drew water to help him move through the mud. I knew the animal inside was alive, for his round shell was covered with minute hairlike fuzz that was almost as soft as velvet. If he were dead, the fuzz would have disintegrated, revealing the white shell beneath. I turned the sand dollar upside down. There was a small opening in the middle of the shell where the animal's jaws normally protruded, although he had withdrawn when he sensed this crisis. I set the sand dollar into a shallow excavation and covered him with his beloved slop. Leaving him happy, I moved on.

Bubbles

After a while I became entranced by prismatic sunlight playing on the bubbles that were scattered about the mud's surface. Each bubble, catching the light at a slightly different angle, reflected a particular color. I could hear the soft pops of bubbles bursting as they dried out. It was strange to be watching a sphere that seemed so substantial, then, without warning—poof! It was gone.

Life in a Tidepool

Across the flats, I could make out dozens of saucer-shaped indentations filled with water from the last high tide. Each was three feet or so across and about four inches deep. I squatted beside one. In it a school of quarter-inch minnows nibbled contentedly on strands of bright green algae. Beneath them a segmented, red worm wiggled nonchalantly across the bottom. On the edge rested several elongated, transparent jelly-blobs. I doubted they were alive until one moved ever so slightly. It had no arms or legs or even an area that looked like a head. Although many scientists surmise that life may have originated in similar ancient tidepools, it was difficult for me to conceive that these things and I had a common ancestor. Small wonder that creationists reject the concept of evolution.

When the minnows saw my form they darted to a far side of the pool, for anything overhead usually meant hungry birds. Then, when I raised my right arm to see what they would do, they rushed to the left. I waved my left arm and they flashed right. I began waving my arms rhythmically left, right, left, right. The fish responded correspondingly. I felt like Zeus leading an orchestra.

I sauntered over to another tidepool. Although it was the same size, there were no fish—not even one. Yet I could see no difference between the two. This one also had a juicy algae garden. I walked further on. About half the pools had fish and half didn't. What did the fish know that I didn't? Or maybe they just made their temporary homes in whatever pool was available as the tide receded. I wondered how many got stranded in the mud as the water vanished. The smart ones would find the depressions and would reproduce. So the less fit would be constantly weeded out. Evolution is a rough taskmaster.

In places black mangroves reached out over the sand. Each was accompanied by its usual miniature army of spiky projections that helped it breathe.

Along the Shore

The air had been still, but suddenly a fresh breeze drifted in from some hiding place up the beach. It made me want to do some serious walking. I moved back from the mud to where the sand was clean and firm. The lowering sun magnified every minor mound and delicate dimple, highlighting the unbelievably numerous bird footprints that peppered the sand as far as I could see.

As I strolled over the sand, I was surprised at how different the vegetation was back from the beach compared to that on Keewaydin Island. There were no sea grapes and few deciduous trees. Predominant here were marsh grasses. At the margin, where the sand met the meadow, were the reddish shoots of sea purslane, a sprawling, ground-hugging plant with scattered pink flowers shaped like miniature stars. In places black mangroves reached out over the sand. Each was accompanied by its usual miniature army of spike projections that helped it breathe. I had read that black mangroves have adapted to wet, salty environments by eliminating the excess salt through their leaves. To verify that, I ran my finger on the underside of a leaf then licked it. The salty taste told me that the leaf was doing its job.

The Skimmers and the Terns

Many of the birds that live in the wilds of Tigertail Beach make their nests on the ground, where they are hidden by the grass. Among them are plovers, gulls, terns, and skimmers. The skimmers are one of my favorite birds. Their top sides are black and their undersides white. But their most distinguishing marks are their bills, which are bright red with a strong tint of orange. They justly earn their name from their habit of flying so close to the water's surface they are almost part of the waves. When skimming, they dip the lower part of their bills into the water to scoop up the fish.

Noticing a large flock of skimmers and terns up the beach, I walked cautiously toward them, my camera ready. The closer I got, the more nervous the skimmers became. Nonetheless, I kept inching forward. When the skimmers could tolerate my intrusion no longer, they flew past me in a thrilling whir of black, white, and red, providing a photo opportunity for which I was actually ready. As for the terns, they gave a

When the skimmers could tolerate my intrusion no longer, they flew past me in a thrilling whir of black, white, and red.

figurative shrug, as if they wanted to tell the skimmers, "You've got to get used to these pesky folks. After all, it's the tourist season."

A Landscape in Flux

I continued up the beach to a point of land distinguished by a grove of Australian pines. These graceful trees may be slated for destruction as unwanted exotics, for I had seen many stumps in the meadow behind the shore.

Tigertail Beach terminated at the narrow channel that connects Clam Bay with the Gulf. At this point Sand Dollar Island to the west had dwindled to not much more than a low line of green fuzz. Since the tide had turned and water was flowing back into the lagoon, it was difficult to determine if a sandbar connected the island with the mainland. Currents from Clam Pass may prevent this. But, if Sand Dollar does reach the mainland, the lagoon will be closed. Then, as the water evaporates, the present lagoon will become a grassy marsh before gradually maturing into a mangrove forest. Some people will lament that the wading birds will vanish, but forest birds will replace them.

Of course, it could go the other way. As the climate warms and the polar ice continues to melt, the rising Gulf may not only destroy the lagoon, but Sand Dollar Island itself may vanish into the water whence it came.

Or, perhaps, both scenarios might occur: first the marsh, then the forest, and lastly the return of the Gulf. Evolving landscapes have many faces.

Fiddling on the Beach

I turned back along the damp sand. This was the domain of the fiddler crabs. Although each individual is barely an inch long, when massed in the hundreds, they seemed to give entire sections of the sand a reddish-orange pavement. Their eyes, being at the end of stalks, give them a comprehensive view of the beach, as well the ability to watch for predator birds above. When they saw me coming, they moved cautiously a short way down the beach. When I stopped, they stopped. When I moved again, they moved. It was almost like the minnows.

So I stood still, reasoning that the crabs, as with most animals, would not be alarmed by inaction. I was right. In a few moments they began ignoring me and returned to their normal activities. Much of this activity involved digging burrows, which can be a foot deep and have two entrances. I watched one little guy at work. He would emerge with a ball of sand, deposit it beside the opening, then disappear down the tunnel to emerge with another ball in a few moments. The digging went on constantly, for the stubborn, ground-level breeze kept blowing sand back into the hole almost as fast as the fiddler dug. The crab didn't seem to mind, and I do believe he was enjoying the exercise.

These burrows are vital in providing the crabs with relief from the blazing Florida sun, and they retire into their cool depths during the mid-day heat. But, even more importantly, the burrows afford them protection against predators. It was fun to see how, when a bird appeared, every fiddler dove into the closest burrow, whether it was his or another's. Often two or more fiddlers disappeared into the same burrow.

Oddly, the tunnels do not flood when the tide comes in. For at these times each fiddler secures his entrance with a ball of sand. Then he relaxes in his snug abode while the Gulf of Mexico rumbles over his roof.

Obtaining food was another major activity. For this the fiddlers scraped through the wet sand securing their meals of algae and decaying organic matter. When they were through, the sand was left in the form of balls that were whiter and smaller than the tunnel diggings.

Love Comes to the Fiddlers

I was privileged to be here during the spring courtship period. The males were strutting around each waving his oversized claw, which reminds many persons of a fiddle. The purpose is to attract the females as well as to warn off other males. They were pompous dandies, sometimes raising themselves as high as their little legs could take them and striking the air with their trophy claw, that mark of machismo, which the females don't have. Often they did this in sheer bravado even when there were no other crabs close by.

As for the females, they passed coyly among the males, checking them out. This caused the males to stomp their feet to get attention. The whole procedure was so reminiscent of human behavior that it was not too difficult for me to conceive that in some exceedingly distant past we two species may have had a common ancestor.

When a female crab had selected the most appealing of her suitors, she'd descend into the special bridal burrow he had dug in the hope of winning a mate. Since the female had the same plan, a union would soon be accomplished.

I consulted a reference book to complete the story. Two weeks after conception the female will emerge from the burrow and lay her eggs in the outgoing tide. The tide will carry them into the Gulf where, after hatching, the newborns will spend several weeks as larvae. When they are ready to return to the land, they will ride another high tide back to shore, where they will spend the rest of their year-and-a-half lives, unless cut short by a nasty bird. Incidentally, about two weeks after laying her eggs the female is ready for another wooing.

Señor Crab Man

Looking up from my observations, I noticed a figure far down the beach. He had a small shovel and a large, blue bucket. While I watched, he dug into the sand, quickly dropped to his knees, grabbed something, and tossed it into the bucket. As I walked toward him, he saw me and stopped, regarding me suspiciously. For a friendly salutation, I tried to think of something clever and at the same time disarming—something

He put the fiddler crab in the flat of his hand. Almost miraculously she didn't run away, and I got my shot.

better than I had used with the Worm Woman. When I was close enough, I asked "What are you digging for?" That was supposed to be clever?!

But the camera around my neck and beach book under my arm told him I was not a park official who might challenge his activities. So he opened the bucket lid. Inside were several dozen fiddler crabs—both male and female. They were surprisingly quiet, for, in the darkness of the bucket, they must have felt almost as safe as in their burrows.

"Are you going to eat them?" I asked.

The man chuckled. "No, no! I'm going to use them as bait when I go fishing in a little while."

Noting that he spoke with an accent, I looked at him more closely. He was short and wiry. His face was deeply tanned and crisscrossed with the lines of many seasons in the sun. His hair was jet black, but was receding and had many strands of white.

"Where do you fish?" I asked.

He waved his arms. "All over. Wherever there's a public fishing pier. But there's always too many people. Not like in the old country."

He paused, perhaps recalling memories of another land. Cuba, maybe. I was quiet. I'd let him go on if he wanted to. But he didn't.

"Can I take a photo?" I asked in a moment.

He pulled back. "Not of me."

"No, I want a close-up of a fiddler."

"Okay," he answered, plucking one from the bucket. I saw the pincer grasp his finger. "Ay!" he said, as he removed the claw. "They never break the skin, but they're uncomfortable."

He put the fiddler crab in the flat of his hand. Almost miraculously it didn't run away, and I got my shot. Then he tossed the crab back in the bucket and closed the lid. We talked for a while, until, almost abruptly, he picked up his bucket, said "*Adios, amigo,*" and began walking down the beach.

Watching the man go, I became aware of an elderly couple nearby. "They shouldn't let people dig up our beaches," the lady said to me. "You permit one do it and pretty soon there'll be dozens. Eventually there won't be a fiddler anywhere. Besides, I think it's illegal to take live animals from the park."

"Don't worry, Sweetie," the man remarked. "Somebody's going to report him. He won't be here many more times."

Everything they said was true. Yet what a pity that in some matters there's no room for compromise.

The Sunset Beach

The day was almost over by the time I returned to the bathing area. The cabanas had been hauled away and the odoriferous grills had been turned off. A rather large group of people stood facing west waiting for the sunset. Most were vacationing from northern climes where, at this time of year, they viewed sunsets from behind frosty windows. Here it was different. Florida's west coast is famous for the beauty of its sunsets. There's even a sunset ritual when people gather on the beaches to marvel at the colors.

The sunset ritual involves being quiet and respectful as the sun descends majestically into the Gulf. If the sun has done a good job coloring the sky, there is applause as the last scarlet ray puffs out. And so there was this evening. It was as if the sun were an actor who had just given a great performance.

That's Florida's sunset coast.

8

The Mysterious Mangroves

The Setting

Mangroves predominate along much of Florida's far southwest coast because of especially favorable conditions. The first is the warm climate. The second is the wide area of shallow water. And the third is the presence of freshwater streams that ooze down the Western Slope into the Gulf of Mexico to create a brackish mixture in which mangroves, but few other plants, can flourish.

Although they are far from beautiful, mangroves are valuable protectors of the land, for their tangled roots and wall of branches and leaves help break up the waves of the rough, erosive seas. Then, as the waves slip back into the Gulf, the mangroves' roots trap much of the debris that would otherwise be carried off. Some of this debris consists of sand and shells that help stabilize and add to the mangrove tidelands. Other debris is made up of leaves and other organic material that decomposes into the rich broth of nutrients that provides the basis for an intricate and important chain of life.

This chain of life begins with simple, single-celled plants and animals. Farther up the chain are shrimp that spend their early lives in the mangrove-sheltered waters, then migrate into the Gulf of Mexico, where they become one of the most valuable elements of the Gulf's commercial fishing industry. The chain ultimately provides essential suste-

cormorant

174

nance for such wading birds as cormorants, herons, and ibis.

Historically the mangroves reached all the way up Florida's coast to Tampa Bay, beyond which periodic freezes killed them. But humans had other uses for much of the sandy shores, so most of the mangroves all the way down to Naples had to go.

Getting There

From Tigertail Beach I returned to **CR 951,** which here is **Collier Boulevard,** Marco Island's main thoroughfare. It's quite an experience to drive south on **Collier** past the row of high condos worthy of Miami Beach. It's difficult to conceive that for endless centuries before the Deltona Company developed Marco in the 1960s and 70s this was a swampy tidewater island frequented only by the now-vanished Calusa tribe. But I can't knock Deltona, for I owned a time-share on the beach for several decades—and enjoyed it very much. Nonetheless, there are places for humans and places for nature, and I was always glad when I turned off **Collier Boulevard** onto **CR 92** and in a few miles reached the Marco River, where civilization abruptly ended.

The view from the lofty Goodland Bridge was so inspiring that I

To the north, south, and east there were only mangroves—countless numbers of them.

parked at the bridge's base and walked back up to the top. To the west was Marco Island, with its pricey homes along a network of man-made canals and its condo towers lining Crescent Beach. But to the north, south, and east there were only mangroves—countless numbers of them.

I returned to my car and headed northeast on **CR 92** through a mangrove swamp. The road had been constructed upon diggings from the canals on either side. It would have been nice if the canals and the accompanying road could have been designed by someone with a more artistic feeling who could have put in a few curves. But CR 92 cuts through the swamp with uncompromising straightness. Well, at least the primitive aspect has been maintained, for this area is part of state and national preserves.

In a few miles I reached **US 41, the Tamiami Trail.** Turning east, almost immediately I came to Collier-Seminole State Park, where motor launches take visitors on one-hour, up-close forays into the mysterious mangroves.

Another World: Collier-Seminole State Park

I boarded the tour boat at Collier-Seminole State Park and in a few moments we pulled into the Blackwater River and headed into the labyrinth of islands, sandbars, and mangrove tunnels known as the Ten Thousand Islands, which form a massive maze for a hundred miles along Florida's Gulf coast.

Almost as soon as the boat left the dock I knew I was entering a strange, chaotic world, a world utterly dominated by a single group of plants: mangroves. They were not sizable trees, as I had been led to believe, but more like densely foliated, overgrown bushes. Their prop roots were like long, thin claws that grasped the tidal muck with a firmness that only a hurricane could dislodge.

The mangroves quickly cut off any view of civilization. Within minutes the channel narrowed, then bent to the left, and then to the right. Mangrove roots snarled against the boat's sides and mangrove branches closed in overhead. We were in a two-dimensional mystery of length and width only, for height was lost in the topping of mangrove leaves. Gone, too, was any sense of direction, for there were no landmarks, only the everlasting mangroves with their everlasting sameness.

Almost as soon as the boat left the dock I knew I was in a strange, chaotic world.

The mangroves quickly cut off any view of civilization.

If the boat captain had fallen overboard, we'd have been there forever.

Where Red, Black, and White Make Green

About now the captain began his spiel. "There are three types of mangroves," he said, "the red, the black, and the white. Each has the ability to thrive in a salty environment. They look alike. They grow alike. But, sorry, folks, they're not alike. It would help if the red mangroves were actually red, but their leaves are as green as the others. They're the pioneers among the trio, appearing whenever brackish water is shallow enough to permit them to take hold. They're also the most common. Many persons call them ugly, for, although they can sometimes grow to impressive heights, out here they are low masses of snarled branches and tangled roots. You can identify them easily by their prop roots, which arch like long steel tubes from the trunks into the water. The roots are embedded in mud and covered with mollusk shells."

Although the roots looked tannish-gray to everyone in the boat, the guide assured us, with a grin, they were red.

Then he continued, "The next most common are the black mangroves. Their leaves are green, not black, but their trunks may be a half-shade darker than those of the red, whose leaves, as I've said, are not red but also green. The blacks usually grow in areas that are not as wet as the reds. For this reason they have no prop roots. Instead, they are surrounded by small growths protruding from the mud that look to me like hooded monks. They are believed to help them breathe.

"The white mangroves, of course, are green, not white," he went on, with a twinkle in his voice that I had not noticed before. "However, their leaves are a slightly lighter shade than those of the red or the black, which are also green, not red or black. The whites occupy slightly higher elevations than the others, although elevation in a mangrove swamp is hardly discernible. To me they are the most pleasing of the trio."

Two-footed Critters Are Not Welcome Here

The guide turned the boat into a narrow passage between two mangrove islands so we could see a red mangrove jungle up close. "I've lived around here for many years," he told us. "A couple of times I've had to stumble through a mess like this. I'd not recommend it! You struggle up to your knees in smelly muck. You're scraped by shells. There are more than twenty types of snakes around here and all of them swim and some are poisonous. Mangrove roots wrap around your ankles. You'd better get out before dark or you'll be trapped all night. And if you break your leg, God help you!"

He stopped the boat and gave us a while to contemplate what we saw. Before us was a worm's nest of intertwined branches and prop roots, the home of snakes and innumerable spider crabs. Brown water oozed between the roots. The leaves and branches intertwined in a low, almost suffocating canopy. From nearly every branch long drop-roots formed vertical bars. It was as if we were in a prison. By mid-spring the air would be filled with mosquitoes and biting bugs of every sort.

Raccoons Rush in where Wise Men Fear to Tread

Given the guide's experience, it was surprising to learn that a few four-footed mammals frequent the mangroves. Marsh rats are common, as are raccoons. Both are light enough to walk on the prop roots. The raccoons hunt for turtles' eggs, which they love. Of course, if they come upon a nest of birds eggs, they're not displeased. Baby alligators also suit their palate. But the raccoons are not at the top of the food chain, for bobcats also prowl the mangroves. Their food? Raccoons.

Before us was a worm's nest of intertwined branches and prop roots.

Time and the Tides

While the boat hovered beside the jungle, the guide told some mostly true tales about the Ten Thousand Islands. But I must admit my attention wandered. I didn't hear his voice so much as the soft hiss of the incoming tide. Strangely, in the midst of this tight little environment I experienced the sensation that far bigger things, even cosmic forces, were in control. As I watched the dark water swirling against the boat's hull, I realized that the surging tide was not moving on its own, but under the gravitational pull of the moon. I couldn't see this gravity; but it was there—a gigantic presence so potent that it could cause untold billions of gallons of water to rush toward it. Twice a day the tide floods in, sometimes raising the water level as much as six feet. It bathes the roots of the red mangroves, licks at the hooded monks around the black mangroves, and moistens the white mangroves, carrying with it the nutrients upon which the mangroves depend. So in a way the mangroves are creatures of the moon.

The onrushing tide is an unstoppable force. Sandbars that seem to be substantial disappear. New channels emerge where dry land had been a few hours earlier. As the moon cruises on, the tide slows and eventually pauses. The water becomes motionless, a perfect mirror of mangroves and sky, an aquatic masterpiece of jades and emeralds and turquoises and cobalts. There is hesitation, expectation, as when someone draws a deep breath. Then, gently at first, the water begins to retreat. The sound of the ebbing tide is low, almost imperceptible at first, but it grows as the flow increases. At its maximum the outgoing tide floods seaward, carrying leaves and sticks and even tree limbs. And, as the water level lowers, islands and sandbars reappear, sometimes stranding boaters who had not checked their tide charts.

The ceaseless ebb and flow of the tides are everything in the mangrove jungles. Time is different here. It does not pass; it constantly repeats itself with the tides. Night and day and even weather systems tend to be minor events. Hurricanes may come, and, although they can wipe out miles of mangroves, the plants quickly revive. In the long run the tides are what count.

Our boat hummed gently among the mysterious mangroves for an enchanted hour or so. The guide finally ran out of stories and we were left with the quiet that this unusual environment deserved.

The return trip went quickly, for we were being driven by the tide. The captain complained, however, for it was more difficult to steer with the tide than against it. "Get ready for a rough landing," he warned. But we glided smoothly to the dock.

The Lure of the Ten Thousand

As we disembarked, I noticed a very old man sitting on a bench watching us. Although his face was expressionless, there was something about him that caught my attention. So I sat down on the same bench. He seemed deep in a reverie, so I said nothing. But in a moment he spoke. Softly, as if to no one in particular, "Good day for fishing."

"Are you going out?" I asked.

"Nope. Not today. Not tomorrow." He was silent for a moment, then continued. "I used to fish every day. That was when I had a cabin on one of the islands. I rented it from the Colliers. Wasn't much, but I loved it." He leaned forward as if he were trying to see down the Blackwater River and across Chokoloskee Bay.

"That was in the nineteen-twenties and thirties. I was a young buck. I knew every fishing spot in this part of the islands. Had me a nice business as a guide. Magazine writers would line up for me to take 'em out so they could learn my secrets.

"Them was good times. You could sail for hours and not see anyone 'cept some commercial fishermen. Thunderstorms? What's a little rain! Mosquitoes? You get used to 'em. Beached on a sandbar at low tide? Just get out and push. Lost in the endless islands? Never, I always knew where I was going and where I'd been. This was my country!"

"Would you go back to your island if you could?" I asked.

"In a coot's eyelash I would. But I can't. When the national park was formed, rangers burned the cabin down. Said it was their policy to return the islands to nature. It's over. All over!"

He became contemplative, so I nodded to him and left.

Controlling the Urge to Canoe

Oddly, after my brief talk with the old fisherman I had an urge to return to the mangroves. On the excursion boat we had passed a few canoers gliding almost effortlessly over the calm water. It seemed like a great way to get really personal with the scenery. Finding that they rented canoes at the park for just a few dollars per hour, I walked down to where the canoes were stored. I had with me *Day Paddling Florida's 10,000 Islands* by Jeff Ripple. This book includes canoeing on the Blackwater River.

Ripple, who is one of my favorite nature writer/photographers, makes it sound almost idyllic. Channel markers keep the most amateur paddler on course. Supposedly there's virtually no chance of getting lost, for everyone must file a route plan with the ranger before leaving. Yet, when I spoke to a ranger, he was not quite so sanguine. "Take rain gear, for thunderstorms can come up very quickly and there's no shelter on the river. Be sure to consult the table of tides we'll furnish you, for if you get caught in an ebb tide, you might get stuck on a sandbar. If you're not back by closing, we'll have to call in a helicopter to locate you. That will be at your expense."

I decided to forgo my canoe excursion.

Mangroves on the March

Instead of canoeing, I took the Royal Palm Hammock Trail. It was described in park literature as a pleasant circular path through a variety of trees that could be strolled in less than an hour. This fit my criteria

The land turned mushy and now I was back in the mangrove world, with its interlacing limbs and tangles of prop roots.

for "easygoing," so I set out on the southern portion of the trail. The only thing that could have been difficult were the mosquitoes. But I had a can of insect repellent, which must have made me smell horrible to the bugs, for they steered shy once they got a whiff of me. However, it was otherwise with hikers, for loaning them the can gave me great popularity on the trail.

The hammock was a densely forested limestone platform slightly higher than the mangrove area. The trees were an unusual mixture of those found in the subtropics and of those found further north. Interpretive signs along the way pointed out the more unusual subtropical trees. Among them were gumbo-limbos, with their reddish, peeling bark, much like a tourist's sunburned skin. Others were white stopper trees. A sign noted that they are also known as skunk trees from the odor of their leaves when crushed. I mashed a leaf and didn't smell anything, but maybe it was disguised by my mosquito spray.

Along the trail I came upon a sign saying that Hurricane Donna had flattened this hammock in 1960 and since that time no group of trees has had time to establish its dominance. Peering into the dark, lush growth around me, I realized that every plant was fighting for the limited light available. It was a silent, but deadly, war for survival. Leaves were being created, branches were growing, trunks were expanding. When the leaves of one tree thrived, the leaves of another might be shaded. If the shaded tree could not reach the sunshine, it would be stunted and would produce fewer seeds. Gradually those trees would be replaced by the successful ones. Eventually what is called a "climax forest" of just a few species would take over.

The path crossed a small bridge, beyond which the land turned mushy and a boardwalk began. Although I hadn't noticed any change in elevation, a sign informed me that the elevation had just gone down six inches. Now I was back in the mangrove world with its interlacing limbs and tangle of prop roots There was more humidity. And more frustrated mosquitoes buzzing over my head. Just six inches made such a difference!

The forest ended suddenly at an observation platform overlooking a wide marsh. What appeared to be cordgrass rose in thick, greenish-tan bunches. Yet among them were young mangrove bushes. This was not an ordinary mixture of plants, for where there are grasses, there almost always are fires, and fires kill mangroves. What this peculiar landscape told me was that humans must have repressed the fires and that, accordingly, the grass was being replaced by mangroves. If, however, fires are once again left to pursue their natural courses, the mangroves will burn out and grasses will reign. I'll return in a few years to see which plant won. Until then I'll just have to live with the suspense.

Royalty on the Trail

As I returned on the northern portion of the loop trail, I passed through the grove of royal palms that gave the trail its name. Mature royal palms, such as these, are indeed regal, with their smooth, straight trunks glinting in gun-barrel gray. Some of the trees were up to a hundred feet in height with trunks up to three feet in diameter. Although royal palms are favored for street plantings, they are rarities in the wild. As a matter of fact, there are only two other locations in Florida where they grow wild, one of them being the small grove I came upon earlier in the Fakahatchee Strand.

The Gulf Coast Section of Everglades National Park

Returning to my car, I drove back to the **Tamiami Trail** and turned right. I followed the road for fifteen miles, passing Fakahatchee Strand, to **SR 29,** upon which I turned south. In five miles I arrived at the quaint little town of Everglades City, distinguished by its ornate Greek Revival administrative center that was the court house in the glory days when Everglades City, not Naples, ruled Collier County. Everglades City's lofty, if temporary, position was due to the fact that it was Barron Collier's headquarters when he was constructing the southwestern portion of the Tamiami Trail in the late 1920s.

Continuing on **SR 29,** in a mile or so I reached the Gulf coast section of Everglades National Park. The park's name is misleading, for many people come here expecting to view the famed River of Grass. They are disappointed, even shocked, when the sightseeing boat heads into mangroves. Since that was what I wanted, I purchased a ticket for another excursion into the tidelands.

Among the Mangroves Once More in Everglades National Park

The boat had an upper deck that provided a more sweeping view than

Wherever there was free sand and calm water, so there would be mangroves.

the vessel at the state park. But the view was also less intimate—there always seems to be a trade-off. We headed west on the Barron River, named for, and probably by, Barron Collier. The river had been Collier's main supply route.

Almost immediately we passed the little airport where President Harry Truman landed in 1947 to dedicate the Everglades National Park. In a few more miles the river emptied into Chokoloskee Bay, which is seven miles long, two miles across, and a few humble feet deep. It separates the mangroves on the mainland from those that are part of the Ten Thousand Islands.

An Afternoon in the Life of an Osprey Family

Chokoloskee Bay's shallowness gave its water an olive-green tint. Pelicans sped close to the surface hunting for fish. I think one had a wingspan of close to eight feet. We passed a couple of low, sandy islands that had apparently formed around channel dredgings by the Army Corps of Engineers. Mangroves were taking over these islands, for wherever there was free sand and calm water, so there would be mangroves.

Our channel was delineated by markers set in the water. Although boaters thought they were to guide their craft, ospreys knew they were really for nest-building. The osprey nests were messy affairs of randomly assembled sticks and general debris. But they evidently hold together sufficiently for them to raise their young.

Ospreys have grown accustomed to the tour boats, and only glare at them as they rumble past. That is, unless the captain decides to please his passengers with a loop around the nest, as mine did. Thereupon the mama osprey sitting on the nest raised up and cussed something awful, which fortunately sounded like a tire screech to me. I noted her vicious beak, curved like a meat hook, and was not sorry when we moved on. Later we saw the male osprey winging home with a black snake in his talons.

"Watch this," the captain said. "Over there's an eagle's nest. He's likely to pop out and bully the snake away from the osprey." We waited for the drama to unfold. But the eagle was a no-show—either he was not home or or he was daydreaming. So the lucky osprey family was going to enjoy fresh snake for dinner.

As we proceeded across the bay, we came to schools of redfish and silver mullet feeding on the incoming tide. This had attracted a group of hungry dolphins, who were leaping and frolicking as they gorged on the fish. Everyone on board began taking photographs. The captain, a young man hardly into his thirties, became almost as excited as his passengers. So he turned the boat to follow the dolphins. As a result, we did an incredible series of zig-zags and figure-eights and generally had a lot of fun.

Lost in the Mangrove Labyrinth

Eventually we reached the far side of Chokoloskee Bay and entered the Ten Thousand Islands. Surrounded by mangroves, we passengers were instantly lost—it was impossible to differentiate between the islands. All were the same low, flat elevation. All were almost smothered by the same intertwined mangrove jungles. When the boat rounded one island, more islands appeared, all absolutely identical to the one behind us. There was no variation to indicate where we were, only an endless repetition of these tiny mangrove islands. Channels ran off in every direction. Nearly every one would dead-end in some island-clogged lagoon. Even if we had had compasses, they would have been of no aid, for the direction was meaningless when every channel was endlessly serpentine.

Nearly everyone who goes boating in the mangrove mystery has become lost at one time or another. "There are three states of being lost," wrote Jono Miller in *The Book of the Everglades*, "the first, challenging; the second, annoying; and the third, potentially terrifying." And there was the experience of Harold Lanigan: "I had been fishing in the Ten Thousand Islands many times with a guide," he told me. "So I thought my wife and I could go out without him. But I was lost almost right away. There were no landmarks. I had a radio and a good map, but I still didn't know where I was. I just kept trying the channels until I chanced on the right one. I was just plain lucky."

The Wilderness Waterway
The captain loved to joke around. "I have a wonderful surprise for you folks," he said. "I've decided to let you experience the mangroves the way few people do. We're going to sail the Wilderness Waterway down to Florida Bay. It's ninety-nine miles of narrow channels. Sometimes overhanging branches create leafy tunnels where even canoes get stuck, But I'm sure we can make it. On the route we'll pass Lostmans Bay. When night comes, we'll go ashore at Camp Lonesome. I hope you've brought plenty of bug repellent.

"It will be a challenging, week-long trip. But I have an ample supply of panic flares, just in case we need help from a passing boat—if there is any. When it's over, you'll really know the mangrove world."

He paused while the passengers murmured among themselves. Some felt he was nutty enough to do it.

"Only kidding," he said at last. "Now let's head home."

He turned the boat in a slow circle. "Gosh, I hope I remember how to get out of here. You know it won't be long until night. And when it's dark out here, it's really dark. I mean black! Even worse, the tide is turning. Soon the channels that were open when we came will turn into mud bars. If I make a wrong turn, we'll be stranded. Maybe I should have replaced those burnt-out floodlights." We knew he was joking, but were still relieved when we reemerged into Chokoloskee Bay. Just don't ask me how he found the way.

Memories of Chokoloskee

Having now gone on two excursions around Chokoloskee Bay, I decided that, as long as I was so close to the village of Chokoloskee, I would take the **SR 29 causeway** and actually see what the village looked like. Not only was the name intriguing, but I had with me the memoirs of Loren "Totch" Brown, who had grown up in Chokoloskee and spent most of his life cruising the bay and the Ten Thousand Islands.

When Totch was born in 1920, Chokoloskee was an island and would remain with no land connection for nearly four decades longer. It was covered by mangroves and only the massive Calusa oyster shell midden that left the island above most storm surges made it habitable long term. Wild animals also found it habitable. Panthers frequented the island and rattlesnakes were so common that at least one citizen fashioned their fangs into toothpicks. Mosquitoes were everywhere in such throngs that, during the season, smelly smudge pots had to be kept burning from dusk to dawn.

Most of the inhabitants made their living fishing, but there were plenty of less wholesome occupations. Plume hunters shot egrets and other birds almost at will. During Prohibition, Totch and his father joined others in distilling moonshine. Rumrunners frequented many of the islands. Later, when dope became profitable, Totch and his buddies used their speedy fishing boats to bring in large loads of marijuana from Colombia.

With more than its share of crooks, the Ten Thousand Islands became notorious for its murders. One of the desperadoes, Ed Watson, was finally killed in a gun battle beside Ted Smallwood's store.

As I drove the causeway to Chokoloskee, I was surprised that, although it had been constructed across open water, the mangroves were now so dense on both sides of the road that the bay was hardly visible. I found the modern hamlet of Chokoloskee, with less than five hundred persons, a dull place, now that all the ruffians were gone. But Ted Smallwood's general store sitting beside the bay made the trip worthwhile. The store had changed little from the days of Totch Brown, but now it has not only made the National Register of Historic Places, but has become a fascinating museum of frontier life on the mangrove coast.

As I stood on the landing beside the store, I tried to imagine Ed Watson's boat heading this way. Watson was armed to the teeth, as were the men lining the landing. A volley was fired and, when the gun smoke cleared, Watson lay bleeding and quite dead. Meanwhile, beyond the landing the tide continued to flow, the mangroves continued to thrive, and Chokoloskee Bay was unruffled, affected not at all by man's petty conflicts.

The Mysteries of the Mangrove World

Looking out on the bay and the mangrove islands beyond, I began to sum up my feelings about this weird world, so different from any of the other environments I had encountered. I had the sensation of impermanence. This was a twilight world, not totally water nor totally land. It was yesterday, when the ocean was releasing its grasp on the land. And it was tomorrow, when the land is succumbing once more to the ocean. There was a restless eternity here—just as some islands were being destroyed and new ones created, so various life-forms are being destroyed and new ones created. Perhaps some of these new life-forms will be too beautiful, too complex, too revolutionary for our narrow minds to even conceive. Perhaps these forms will lead to the next level in the evolutionary flow of life. Perhaps they are out there even now, waiting for mankind to have had its day, waiting for mankind to return to dust—or to vanish into the stars as it fulfills its own mystic destiny.

9

Roaming the Everglades

The Setting

The middle section of Everglades National Park consists mainly of the twenty-mile-wide sheet of fresh water known as the Shark River Slough. This slough has traditionally been fed by rainfall as well as by sources as distant as the Kissimmee River and Lake Okeechobee. The Shark River Slough makes its way ever so gradually down the Everglades Slope, which is a forty-mile-long dip in the underlying limestone, ending in the Gulf of Mexico. This moving film of water is ideal for sawgrass

Getting There

To reach the Everglades from the west on **US 41 (the Tamiami Trail)**, I had to travel through the Big Cypress Swamp, the last of the ill-drained lands of the Western Slope. Big Cypress is forty miles of damp beauty composed of salt marshes, grassy wetlands, and cypress strands.

Big Cypress Swamp began where US 41 crossed SR 29 (the road to Everglades City). Almost immediately I passed Wooten's, an old-time attraction offering airboat and swamp buggy tours into the hinterland. Just beyond was Ochopee, once a small settlement serving an extensive tomato farm. Although the farm has vanished, the post office remains. Almost as tiny as an outhouse, it is America's smallest postal facility.

Three miles beyond Ochopee I stopped at the H. P. Williams Roadside Park, where a good-sized boardwalk ran along the canal that connects the Turner River with the interior. The canal was built in the

This is a dangerous venture, for hungry gators can run faster than humans.

late 1950s by developers who planned to drain this portion of the swamp. Some persons had ventured beyond the safety of the boardwalk to stand at the river's edge for closeup photos of alligators. However, that's a dangerous enterprise, for hungry gators can run faster than humans over short distances. Among their favorite foods are cute little dogs and human toddlers.

This portion of the Tamiami Trail is sometimes frequented by panthers. Florida panthers are an endangered species, of which only about ninety remain. Their main problem is loss of territory due to human encroachment. It would have been even worse had the gigantic jetport planned for 1968 been built. Fear of its construction was a central reason for the establishment of the Big Cypress National Preserve six years later.

Beyond the Turner River I passed through a wide, freshwater prairie. Maidencane grew rank and shaggy along the roadside while, beyond, the infertile, rocky land was dotted with dwarf cypress—short, thin trees, even though they may be more than a hundred years old. Where the land was ever so slightly higher pine trees grew.

Paralleling the highway was the canal from which rocks were

blasted to make the Tamiami Trail's roadbed. From the roadside I saw an otter in the water. He was black and sleek, and almost invisible as he glided through the liquid leaving no wake.

At intervals along the road, I passed through a strand, which is a ridge of trees that has crowded into one of the long, narrow depressions made by lethargic streams draining the interior swamps into the Gulf.

At one of these strands I came to a boarded-up old building known as the Monroe Station. In the 1930s, when the Tamiami Trail was a scary, infrequently traveled gash in the wilderness, establishments like this, and one that's vanished at the Turner River, were placed each ten miles to provide fuel and sustenance to needy motorists. In addition, motorcycle patrols from here would cruise the Trail on the lookout for stranded travelers.

Beyond Monroe Station I encountered a beautiful ribbon of large trees known as the Gannet Strand. Past this strand the grasslands begin to be decorated with cypress domes, which are mounds of cypress growing in a near-circular depression filled with water. A few miles farther on I came to the Big Cypress National Preserve's Visitor Center. I joined a group of spectators watching nearly a dozen alligators lounging in the canal between the building and the road. The center featured exhibits, literature, and a fifteen-minute movie on the beauties of the park. Of special interest was a mounted panther killed by an auto a few years back.

Past the Visitors Center cypress settled in. A couple of miles farther on I came to the Big Cypress Gallery where Clyde Butcher displays his renowned black-and-white, oversized photographs of Florida landscapes.

Continuing east, the I passed a few Miccosukee Indian villages. Far from being tourist attractions, these villages are walled off for privacy.

At the Fortymile Bend the cypress abruptly end. Here the Tie Back Canal, also known as Levee 28, funnels the Shark River Slough to a large dam that regulates the water's flow south into the lower Everglades.

It was here early one morning that I began a fascinating day roaming the Everglades.

Dawn in the Everglades at Fortymile Bend

The sun had not yet cleared the horizon as I stopped on the shoulder of the Tamiami Trail. The sky was oleander-pink. A bird sang vigorously in the distance. Then another called back. On either side of the road was a limitless vista of sawgrass. Puffs of wind floated across this vast prairie, causing the grass to bend before it, then allowing it to swing upward after it passed. The breezes came in many groups, each advancing at its own pace, none in a hurry, but each graceful and forever on the move. The grass, for its part, accepted the wind-dancers; after all, it had known them for centuries. It bowed and swung to the silent rhythm as if it, too, were a dancer. I drew in my breath to listen more intently. And gradually I heard the hushed duet of the wind and the grass.

An entire day lay before me. A fresh, newborn day. A day that had never existed before in the history of the world. And would never exist again. This day would offer me new experiences. It would bring into my life new people. This day would provide me the opportunity to see life in a slightly different way. I could learn. I could grow. This day was here for me to use as I chose. I vowed to use it well.

One of the largest of the dams controlling the Everglades' water flow is at Fortymile Bend.

The Shark River Slough

The Everglades' water flow is regulated by a series of canals and dams. One of the largest of these dams is at Fortymile Bend. It has six gates which can be controlled individually or collectively. On the north side of the dam the water was placid, almost pensive, as it awaited human orders to be on the move. On the south side the water churned eagerly through the one gate that was open.

In the long centuries before it was caged the water flowed as it willed, not as some technician decreed. Today, when gauges indicate the allotted amount has gone through the gates, they are closed. The churning diminishes and the water lies quietly behind the dam awaiting the next human summons.

But few things are as simple as they seem. Although the main object of the dam is to insure a proper flow of water to satisfy the sawgrass, another aim is to protect endangered animals such as the Cape Sable Seaside Sparrow, for whom high water during nesting time can prove disastrous. Thus at these critical times the flow is restricted.

However, this means that the water often floods back into the land north of the Tamiami Trail, location of the Miccosukee Reservation. Not only does this cause hardships for the Indians, but it is deleterious

I paused to admire a solitary palmetto rising above the boundless sawgrass like the headdress of some lost Seminole brave.

to the snail kite, another endangered bird. Thus the Miccosukees are suing the U.S. Fish and Wildlife Department under the Endangered Species Act to reverse the policy and open the gates wider.

The Mystery of the Sawgrass

Leaving the knotty controversy to experts, I resumed traveling east along the highway that was now dusted with early morning saffron. I paused to admire a solitary palmetto rising above the boundless sawgrass like the headdress of some lost Seminole brave. How did the palmetto end up here, I wondered? And where were its companions? If the location was good enough for one palmetto, why wasn't it good enough for two, or three, or a whole forest of them?

Another mystery was the sawgrass, which is not a grass at all, but a fierce, wild sedge. I wondered if this graceful green plant, so picturesque from afar, could really cut like a saw? If I could believe Hugh Willoughby, who poled a boat through this part of the Everglades in 1897, this was the case. "What makes this grass so formidable and much to be dreaded," he wrote, "is the saw-like edge with which it is armed on three sides. If you get a blade between your hand and the pole, it will cut you to the bone with a jagged gash that takes long to heal." Doubting this plant was really that sharp, I walked to a stand of sawgrass and ran my finger up the blade. It was smooth as milkweed. Ha! Then I moved my finger gently down the blade. But not very far, for the sharp teeth bit maliciously into my skin. I quickly concluded, in agreement with Willoughby, that sawgrass is not people-friendly.

Building the Tamiami Trail

Construction of the Tamiami Trail through this scowling, sawgrass wilderness was more than a remarkable feat. It was almost a miracle. It took thirteen years to complete this miraculous road that ran from Tampa to Miami. In many places the roadbed had to be formed from rocks blasted out of the underlying limestone. To do this derricks on floating platforms drilled holes into the rock. Then dynamite sticks in waterproof casings were placed in the holes and exploded. Next a dredge with a large bucket lifted the rock fragments out of the water and deposited them on one side to form the roadbed. Finally the road was graded and shaped into a thoroughfare nineteen feet wide.

The workmen lived in bunkhouses on wheels that were moved forward as each section of the road was completed. They suffered through the heat, the humidity, the mosquitoes, and the rancid food. When the Tamiami Trail was finally completed in 1928, a huge celebration was held at Everglades City. No one was concerned at the time that the Everglades portion of the Trail formed what was in effect a twenty-five-mile earthen wall separating the lower Everglades from its water source to the north.

Flying the Glades

One of my objectives in coming to the Everglades was to take an airboat over the sawgrass. An airboat is a bizarre contraption invented in 1933 by a couple of guys having trouble hunting up frogs to sell to restaurants because their motor boat's propeller was always getting tangled in the sawgrass. So they came up with the idea of attaching an airplane propeller to an automobile engine and letting the air push their boat over the grass. It worked splendidly. But because their minds were on frog legs, they did not bother patenting their invention and thereby let a fortune slip through their fingers.

The captain turned off the Tamiami canal and into the mass of sawgrass. Then he opened up the throttle!

There were many outfits along the Tamiami Trail offering airboat rides. The boats came in many sizes, but I wanted a small one for a more personal experience. I found one with an Indian captain who didn't disappoint me. Once we half dozen passengers had paid our fares, the captain started the engine. With that the large propeller, almost as tall as myself, roared into action. Then the captain, occupying a seat that was four or five feet above the passengers, flipped the pair of broad rudders that directed the propeller wind and we were off.

The captain went slowly at first. A pair of ducks paddled leisurely out of our way. The canal water gurgled gently against the hull. I leaned back and folded my hands against the back of my head, stifling a yawn. But when the captain turned off the Tamiami canal and into the mass of sawgrass, he opened the throttle! The boat leaped into forward and I thought I heard the captain give an enthusiastic whoop. A wall of air smacked me in the face so abruptly that I almost lost my sunglasses. The ducks took flight. The sawgrass was flattened as we swept over it, but it bent back up after we passed. Ahead there was nothing except sawgrass and a sky brimming with blue. Both land and sky had a limitless quality I had seldom experienced before. If there is such a thing as infinity, I believe I saw it from the seat of that Miccosukee airboat.

Part way through our pell-mell flight we stopped at a forested island where there was a replica of an ancient Miccosukee camp. It consisted of a pair of thatched-roof, open-sided shelters called chickees. One chickee was for cooking and the other for living and sleeping. Entire Miccosukee villages once looked like this. The primitive chickees afforded no protection against mosquitoes, snakes, or other undesirables. As I stood there in the hovering humidity, I had an inkling how difficult life in the Everglades must have been for the Miccosukees forced by the Seminole Wars into such an environment.

Drying the Everglades

After my airboat flight, I felt an added affection for the awesome expanse of sawgrass. Its very immensity made it seem indestructible. But such is not the case.

The completion of the Tamiami Trail in 1928 was not the only attack on the Everglades. This water-soaked mire had long been viewed as an unwanted obstruction to the march of civilization. At the beginning of the twentieth century, with the state entering an era of explosive growth, Florida expansionists felt that the time had come to convert much of the Everglades from a useless wetland into productive farms. This meant eliminating the Lake Okeechobee overflows, a major source of the Shark River Slough. Thus by 1940 the lake had been not only encircled by an earthen dike thirty-four feet high, but four major canals diverted the lake water into either the Atlantic Ocean or the Gulf of Mexico. With Okeechobee now under control, United States Sugar and other companies began converting significant portions of the upper Everglades into agricultural plantations.

Lady with a Mission

As it became clear that the Everglades was under stress, some persons grew concerned. One of these was Marjory Stoneman Douglas, a middle-aged newspaper writer whose father happened to be owner of the influential *Miami Herald*. When Douglas was assigned to write an article about the Miami River, her investigation included the Miami Canal. The canal led her to examine Lake Okeechobee. And Okeechobee conducted her to the Everglades. Slowly the article expanded into a major treatise, then into a book. In 1947, after four years of intensive research, her book came out. Entitled *The Everglades: River of Grass*, it received national attention.

Douglas contended that the earth had plenty of farmland, but there was only one Everglades. It was unique. Nowhere else on earth is there such a fortuitous combination of subtropical flat land with a porous limestone base fed by flooding fresh water from a massive system that extended for hundreds of miles. Douglas' book conveyed her enthusiasm for the wonder and beauty of the Everglades. "The miracle of the light," she wrote, "pours over the green and brown expanse of sawgrass and of water, shining and slow-moving below, the grass and the water, that is the meaning and the central fact of the Everglades of Florida."

Shark Valley Tram Ride: Everglades National Park

So it was that, with Douglas' book in hand, I turned off the Tamiami Trail into Everglades National Park on the Shark Valley Loop Road. Here I boarded the sightseeing tram for one of the first tours of the day. The two-hour trip was down the valley of the Shark River Slough, that foot-deep,

Outstanding were the great egrets, majestic white birds more than three feet tall.

twenty-mile-wide dip in the underlying limestone—a dip so gentle that it drops only a few inches each mile. Far too wide and shallow to be a true river, this is "slough," pronounced for some reason "slew." There are no sharks, but there are plenty of alligators.

At this hour not all the seats were taken—that would happen later in the day. The tour was billed as a fun excursion, and that's just what it was. Even the raspy-voiced guide conveyed a feeling of enjoyment. And why shouldn't he? After all, this was the height of the season with near-perfect temperatures, loads of sunshine, and virtually no bugs.

The tram moved slowly along a road originally built to accommodate oil drilling equipment, for 1940s field studies indicated there might be petroleum down below. We stopped before a pond, a gift from the oil company, which excavated it to secure the limestone that formed the base of the road. During the dry season—winter to early spring—fish gravitate to ponds like this where they became easy pickings for wading birds, who congregate around the ponds in great numbers. They were here today.

What diversity! Outstanding were the great egrets: majestic white birds more than three feet tall. And there were a couple of anhingas with their blackish wings extended to dry in the sun. Floating on the water were purple gallinules. At this distance they were not outstanding birds, for their colors were subdued shades of deep violet—that is, except for their bright red bills. They did not have the slender grace of the egrets nor the eye-catching silhouette of the anhingas. There were also stilts and snowy egrets and storks and roseate spoonbills and . . . the guide kept riddling off ever more.

The birds were simply so numerous that I decided to watch the mass rather than the individuals. I discovered that there was a mini-society here, although the birds were of many species. When a new bird landed with a splash, the others made room without much fuss. Nearly every bird went about his own business unconcerned about his neighbor. Egrets kept busily poking the water with their spearlike bills. Anhingas continued diving beneath the surface to chase fish, and, when they surfaced, they tossed their catch in the air, then caught it head down for ease of swallowing. Gallinules paddled happily about as if they had no worldly cares. Roseate spoonbills wagged their heads contentedly as they swept the water for food. There appeared to be a group feeling, a live and let live attitude. The congregation was enjoying the warm pond, fair weather, and lots of wiggly little fish. If birds dream of paradise, this must be what it looks like.

The Lady and the Tower

The tram ended at a densely forested hammock on land slightly higher and drier than the surrounding wetlands. In the 1940s this particular tree-island was the site of oil drilling. Now it is occupied by a fifty-foot-high tower offering a spectacular view of the Everglades.

I ascended the tower's circular ramp slowly, for I wanted to sip the view, not take it down in a single gulp. Halfway up I paused to read from Marjory Douglas' description of the Everglades: "Nothing anywhere else is like them: their vast glittering openness, wider than the enormous visible round of the horizon. . . ." It was true, the glades reached out like an immense saucer decorated with designs of grassy green and gold that actually glowed in the morning sunshine.

I continued upward, then paused again. I had never seen the sky so all-encompassing. It was an azure-tinted semi-sphere of infinite size surrounding the earth. And within it the air moved with a brisk, flowing

The tower offered a spectacular view of the Everglades.

motion. Douglas before me, experiencing the same sensation, had written about "the racing free saltiness and sweetness of the massive winds, under the dazzling blue heights of space."

At last, almost with reluctance, I reached the summit. Before me stretched the Everglades, blissfully barren of human structures—no roads, no dwellings, no strip malls. From this height the surrounding plain looked as soft as an Oriental tapestry. There were so many variations of a theme in green! Green with a tint of straw. Green blended with bronze. Green almost the color of pewter. Chartreuse, the most delicate of all. And accenting this overwhelming green masterpiece were bright clusters of emerald bay heads, willow heads, and oak hammocks. My reaction may have been overly poetic. If so, blame it on the altitude, for five stories is a dizzy height in a flat world. But Douglas, too, waxed poetic: "The line they make," she wrote, " is an edge of velvet against the infinite blue, the blue-and-white, the clear fine primrose yellow, the burning brass and crimson, the molten silver, the deepening hyacinth sky."

I paused in the hammock to watch a five-foot-long alligator ambling slowly along a dirt footpath.

Gator Getaway

Walking back to the tram, I paused in the hammock to watch a five-foot alligator ambling slowly along a dirt path. He had no concern about me, being more used to humans than I was to gators. But I was curious. Did he have a important destination? Had he been forced from his water hole by some larger gator? Or was he just out for a stroll on this fine day? In any event he was heading my way, and by the time he was only a few feet distant, I was beginning to consider a strategic retreat. Then he turned abruptly off the footpath and onto a trail I had not noticed. It was overhung with vegetation and so narrow that the gator's shoulders brushed the leaves as he passed. It was well-worn, for gators have their own network of pathways between water holes. He vanished quickly into the underbrush, off on a mission I'll never learn.

The Keepers of the Everglades

On the return journey, the guide, speaking with what seemed to be a slight Texas accent, concentrated on alligators. He was fascinated by them, calling them "The Keepers of the Glades." Almost all the animals here, he told us, depended in some way on the excavations the gators make in the muck with their powerful snouts and tails. These holes are five or more feet deep in order to get below the water table so the gator

can spend the dry season in wet comfort. Other creatures also find refuge in and around the gator holes. There is a surprising harmony among the raccoons, turtles, snakes, and otters that take up temporary residence here. Fish, too, find their way to the holes, and they attract birds. The gator tolerates them all, for he can go for months without eating during the winter.

Over the years trees and shrubs take root in the dirt piled around the gator hole. They form thick thickets called "heads." If bay trees are the primary plants, it is a bay head; if coco plums, it is a coco head; if cabbage palms, it is a cabbage head. I noticed these heads everywhere as mounds of dark green amid the lighter sawgrass. They remain for years after the gator is gone.

The Bellowing Season

"Alligator bellowing announces the April through May mating season," the guide told us. "A bellow is something one never forgets. It is deep and rough, and speaks of power. It's also a warning: 'If you're another male, stay out of my territory. If you're a pretty female, you're welcome.'"

The Everglades is a mosaic of sawgrass interspersed with hammocks, many of which define former gator holes.

Males will fight each other at these times, usually until one drives the other away. But sometimes it's to the death. "I've noticed that gator," said the guide, pointing to a particularly large alligator, "each of the last four years with a dead gator nearby that he must have killed in combat. I just wish I could have seen it!" The guide stopped the tram while he must have been picturing to himself the gator battles. We had no choice to wait until he was through.

Love among the Gators
Finally the guide started the tram. Click went the microphone: "Although gators have thumbnail-sized brains, they know how to court. The ritual can encompass several days of ecstasy. They stroke each other. They rub bellies beneath the water. Then they mate. When the thrill is gone, each goes off separately to find new joy with other partners."

Keeping Nature in Balance
"Once a female feels motherhood approaching," the guide continued, "she builds a nest of mud around six feet wide and three feet high on the bank of a pond. Next she digs a cavity in the top of the nest into which she lays about fifty eggs. Then she covers them with mud and vegetation and relies on the sun and the heat of the decaying plants to keep the eggs warm. Oddly, the sex of the developing eggs depends the temperature of their position in the nest. Where it's hotter the eggs will develop into males; where its cooler they will be females. After about two months, many of the eggs begin to hatch. Those that don't, the mother gently cracks open with her teeth to help the little ones emerge. The mother not only guides the babies to water, but she sticks around for a couple of years to protect them from predators. Among these predators are raccoons, wading birds, snakes, large fish, and even other gators."

"I'm sure the mother alligator does a good job protecting her young," said an elderly woman near me.

"Sorry," the guide answered. "I remember a female alligator whose fifty young had just hatched. Each time I drove past she had fewer. At the end of the first season, there were only seven. At the end of the second year there were only three. Surprising, isn't it." There were some moans and lots of sympathetic remarks concerning the awful snuffing out of the helpless babies and the assumed grief of the mother. Then there was silence. Wisely, the guide held his comments.

Meanwhile I was doing a little figuring. A female gator will lay fifty eggs yearly during each of her thirty reproductive years. If none of the young died, a total of 1,500 individuals would develop into mature alligators. I guessed that there were around one hundred female gators within a radius of several miles. If each created 1,500 new gators before she died, in thirty years there would be 150,000 gators here. The Everglades would be paved with them! But, of course, long before that the Everglades would have been destroyed and most of the gators would have died of starvation. Nature's way was best. But I didn't try to tell that to the elderly lady.

Man-Eating Alligators?

Since the guide was quiet most of the way back, I had time to recollect facts and experiences I had read about alligators.

It's said there are well over a million alligators in Florida. And their numbers are growing, for they are a protected species. They are fond of sleeping under cars in parking lots. They also love swimming pools. One gator was found lounging in a living room, having entered through the dog door.

Some gators have been turned into pets. One man raised a gator that he named Gwendolyn. She hung around his refrigerator awaiting handouts and even slept in his bed! She enjoyed playing with a toy football and bellowing while he played his favorite rock songs. Although it was a sweet relationship, the neighbors felt uneasy when Gwen began wandering through their backyards. State trappers were called and Gwen was hauled away. Her owner hired a lawyer and got her back.

But persons who think gators are harmless are deluding themselves. One article recounted an experiment with alligators' jaw-power. Whereas a shark bites with 330 pounds of pressure and a lion with 940, a gator can chomp down with nearly 3,000 pounds. Gators have bitten through aluminum boat hulls as well as tough fiberglass. They can flatten truck tires.

Their jaws exert a force that probably exceeds that of any other animal on earth.

And alligators can be dangerous. At a lakefront park in Mount Dora the city alligator control officer just happened to arrive as a gator was moving stealthily through tall grass toward a toddler splashing in the shallows. Although the toddler's mother, as well as other park patrons, were nearby, gators are so swift that this one would have had the infant in his jaws and off into the lake before the mother could have gotten help. However, the officer splashed into the water between the gator and the child, startling the gator, who fled. Other toddlers have not been so fortunate.

As for human adults, gators have little interest in them. The problem is that, whereas gators can chomp, they can't chew. Thus they must swallow their prey whole. Humans are just too bony and angular, what with all those arms and legs sticking out. When a human swimmer is attacked, the gator almost always releases him. But "almost always" is not the same as "always" and it seems that almost every year there is a fatality or two.

The Spirit of the Everglades

The sun was high as I resumed my eastward journey on the **Tamiami Trail.** When I reached the place where the Tamiami Trail made a slight bend six miles east of Shark Valley, I turned onto a side road and passed over a one-gate control dam and up to the top of the levee. On my right were a series of columns commemorating the 110 persons who lost their lives in the crash of a ValuJet airliner in May 1996. Looking north toward where the jet went down, I saw a limitless expanse of quivering sawgrass. The air was quiet except for insect rasping. The crash site was five miles ahead.

After the crash, an attempt was made to recover the bodies. A single dirt road running on the top of a levee led to the site. As the search team waded through the soupy water, the stench of rotting bodies all but choked them. Meanwhile the sharp blades of the head-high sawgrass ripped at their polyethylene suits. The sun broiled down and the humidity approached one hundred percent. Late in the afternoon, monstrous thunder clouds rumbled over them and lightning stabbed dangerously close by. Then, on the fringes, the workers saw the alligators leering at them. And there were snakes, far more dangerous, that they couldn't see.

They felt that there was something elemental out there. Something that humans had never tamed. Something humans could never tame. "There is nothing fragile about the endangered Everglades," one worker commented. "It is an indomitable, unyielding enemy." They had encountered what the Indians called the Spirit of the Everglades.

Standing among the somber pillars of the crash monument, I, too, sensed a powerful essence hovering over the area. It was not exactly hostile, but it was aggressively protective of the Everglades. I sensed that mankind was not welcome here. That the grasslands with all its plants and animals wanted to be left alone. Wanted the dikes and dams to be gone. Wanted the road removed. Wanted the airboats and autos with their fumes and rasping motors to disappear.

I drove back to the highway. I loved the Everglades. But I wanted to be gone before nightfall.

Levees and Dams

East of the ValuJet Memorial the scenic portion of the **Tamiami Trail** ended, for from this point on a levee blocked the view to the north and junk trees screened out the view to the south. The levee is part of a misguided project of the Army Corps of Engineers in the 1940s and '50s. Eventually a total of 1,000 miles of levees were erected, accompanied by another 1,000 miles of canals, 150 dams, and 16 major pumping stations. In this manner the essential sheet-flow water upon which the Everglades depended was restricted.

The Corps' policies horrified Marjory Stoneman Douglas, who wrote that the army men knew and cared little about the true nature of the Everglades. Their goal, according to Douglas, appeared to be to rid the Everglades of its water so it could be put to agricultural use as quickly as possible. In that the Corps was partly successful, for the portion of the Everglades closest to Lake Okeechobee was soon converted into extensive sugar cane fields. The cane required tons of fertilizer, much of which was eventually carried by rainwater into the rest of the Everglades. Under these altered growing conditions, the sawgrass began to be replaced by cattails.

But matters changed as the environmental movement gathered momentum in the 1970s and 1980s. In 1994 Florida passed the

Everglades Forever Act, which called on the sugar growers to clean up the runoff water that drained into the Everglades. But that wasn't enough and six years later the U.S. Congress decided that the entire Everglades plumbing system need overhauling. Thus a law was passed whereby the federal and state governments would share in a massive program estimated to cost more than $8 billion over twenty years. Plans are to utilize a series of reservoirs to store water during the rainy season and release it into the Everglades during the dry season. To insure a sheet flow, 250 miles of levees and canals will be removed, including the levee that runs along the eastern portion the Tamiami Trail. In addition, this section of the highway will be elevated and a series of low bridges will installed to insure an unimpeded water flow.

Miccosukee Madness

I continued driving east on the **Tamiami Trail.** At the corner of **SR 997** I came to a ten-story gambling casino and hotel. It belongs to the Miccosukees, who evidently are able to temper their desire for Everglades' restoration with their need for tribal income. It's difficult to blame them, for they have lived close to poverty for so long. Although I

The sawgrass had been replaced by an overpowering wall of trees. They were the hated melaleuca.

had a delicious lunch at the casino, the interplay of canned music, of amber and lavender neon lights, of bright green carpeting accented in red, black, and yellow, and of a thousand pull-tab slot machines left me feeling I was in Las Vegas, not in the Everglades.

The Terminators

From the Miccosukee pleasure palace, I turned south on **SR 997.** My route would take me down the eastern edge of the Glades for twenty-two miles to Homestead/Florida City, from where SR 9336 would lead me to the main portion of Everglades National Park.

By now it was mid-afternoon. The sun was high and hot. Although the Everglades were on my right, the sawgrass had been replaced by an overpowering wall of trees with shaggy gray bark and greenish-silver leaves. They were melaleuca, hated by environmentalists, who often refer to them as the Everglades Terminators. They had been first imported from overseas as decorative trees. As such they became quite popular. Then in the 1930s, when their ability to soak up huge quantities of water was realized, they were planted in the Everglades to help dry it out. They spread with a vengeance and are now turning ever-increasing areas of sawgrass into melaleuca forests.

Melaleuca might well be as great a danger to the Everglades as the water problem. Yet the $8 billion program to restore the Everglades has made little provision for eliminating these rapidly spreading trees.

Another tree regarded as unwanted are the Australian pines. As distinguished from melaleucas, these trees are tall and majestic. I came upon some fine specimens five or so miles after turning onto SR 997. The ancestors of these trees were brought to America from Australia because they were about the only tall shade trees able to grow in south Florida's sandy soil. With their wispy branches towering above the flatlands, they give me pleasure whenever I see them. But environmentalists view them as hateful invaders that crowd out native vegetation. Furthermore, they claim these trees topple in high winds and thus present a physical danger. But Hurricane Andrew, one of the state's fiercest storms, passed this way in 1992 and these Australian pines still stand.

Was Sawgrass—Is Tomatoes

Still on **SR 997,** I passed Kendall Drive (SR 94), beyond which the

These vegetable fields are a sore point with environmentalists, who resent that they have usurped Everglades land.

Everglades eastern fringe has been turned into agricultural land. I passed signs telling me where I could purchase any variety of landscaping plants. They didn't tempt me half as much as the sign "pick your own strawberries."

As I approached Homestead, I expected the worst, for I had been through the town just after it had been devastated by Hurricane Andrew. All that was left then were piles of wood, broken glass, scattered personal items, and bare, cement platforms where buildings once stood. Today it's a rebuilt and growing town of 35,000.

Passing through Homestead, I turned west on **SR 9336,** which leads to the main section of Everglades National Park, which includes Lone Pine Key and Flamingo. After driving a couple of miles past small homes, I reached fields rich with tomatoes, beans, corn, avocados, and squash. They are important to Florida's economy, for up to a third of the state's winter produce comes from the Homestead area.

I stopped to examine the soil. It was brownish and sandy and looked like nothing the roots of a pampered vegetable would enjoy. But with fertilizer and proper watering, it supports truck gardens on a vast scale. Irrigation comes from pumps scattered about the fields. When I was driving past, they were shooting thick streams of water in arcs that I estimated to be forty feet high. These water jets are big and powerful. I can attest to that, for a particularly malicious one blasted over my car, shaking it down to the seat springs and dousing my windshield with such a Niagara that I almost drove into a ditch.

In many areas teams of workers, mainly Mexicans, were laboring in the fields. They were bending low, for whatever they were picking lay close to the ground. Nearby were large platform trucks onto which they were loading the harvest. A short distance away were the dilapidated buses that brought them. The sun had been bearing down upon them during most of the day, for there was no shade. It was tough work that most Americans are reluctant to take. It's said that without these foreign workers, it would be difficult, if not impossible, to bring in the crop.

At one location I paused to take a photo. The workers were a good distance away and no one seemed to notice me. But, as I adjusted my camera, one of the women raised up and looked my way. Then she waved. I waved back. We had communicated across the steamy fields and across an almost impossible cultural and linguistic gulf. Two people who didn't know each other, who would never know each other, had said "hello." I got in my air-conditioned car and she bent down once more, the torrid sun on her back. But, as I drove off, she waved good-bye. And I waved in return. For all its brevity, our encounter was rewarding. I wish her health and plenty of shade.

These fields are a sore point with environmentalists, who resent that they not only have usurped Everglades' land, but their irrigation pumps divert precious water from the remaining Everglades. I passed over a major canal from which some of this irrigation water is taken. It links up with the canal along the Tamiami Trail and flows south to empty into Barnes Sound off of Key Largo.

Back in the Glades: Coe Visitor Center

crappie

After proceeding eight miles on **SR 9336,** I came to a slight rise topped by pines. This was the Atlantic Coastal Ridge. Extending northward for fifty-five miles, it forms the rim of the Everglades. It originated as a sand bar when the ocean was higher eight thousand years ago. Just beyond, I came to the Ernest F. Coe Visitor Center. Ernest Coe is often called the "Father of Everglades Park," for he was instrumental in having Congress set aside the initial Federal land. When the original legislation was passed in 1934, it was snidely referred to as the "alligator and snake swamp act." The Coe Center is a spacious building with some fine exhibits. One was a replica of an alligator hole. It was ten feet or so in diameter and four feet deep. Around it was saw-grass, and in it were representative fish, such as blue gills, largemouth bass, and Florida gar.

While I contemplated the pool, a man and woman close by started arguing. Ordinarily I find family disputes uninteresting, but this was different.

"It's a crime," the woman said, "the money they're going to spend trying to preserve the Everglades. Eight billion dollars over twenty years! And they aren't even sure it will work! What a waste."

"You're way wrong," the man retorted. "It's well worth it. The Glades is a national treasure."

"I'll tell you what a national treasure is," the woman replied warmly. "It's our children. Do you know what we could do with eight billion dollars? That's four hundred million dollars each year. For that we could raise the annual salaries of ten thousand teachers by ten thousand dollars a year and still have plenty left to build schools and for other worthy projects."

"Sure, you'd like that, you're a teacher. But, just because we'd don't spend the eight billion dollars on the Everglades, doesn't mean it would be given to teachers. Besides, there's a diversity of plant and animals in the Glades that's vital to humans. And how about the beauty of the thousands of birds that frequent the area?"

"I know all that. But they could get much the same effect for a lot less money if they tried to save just a few hundred thousand acres, not one and a half million!"

As the pair began moving away, it became harder to eavesdrop.

The man objected. "It's all one immense ecological unit. You can't save just a portion."

"Sez you! Here's what should be done . . ."

It was frustrating. I was going to miss the best part. I was tempted to follow along. Maybe ask them to argue a little louder so I could hear.

But I had to content myself merely watching them head toward the parking area, their arms waving ever more wildly. Yet, when they reached their car, the woman smiled as the man opened the door for her. Then he gave her a kiss. The car engine started and they drove off.

On the Road Again

Leaving the Coe Center, I continued down **Main Park Road** that would ultimately end thirty-eight miles ahead at Flamingo on the Bay of Florida. In a couple of miles I came to the turnoff to Royal Palm, location of the Gumbo Limbo and Anhinga trails. Because the Gumbo Limbo Trail is on the Atlantic Coastal Ridge, the land is slightly higher and drier than the main part of the Everglades. For this reason gumbo-limbo and other tall trees as well as an understory of ferns and other hammock plants can grow on it. On the other hand, the Anhinga Trail leads through a sawgrass marsh, where alligators and turtles often glide through the water and herons, egrets, and, of course, anhingas frequent the area along the shore. Each trail takes about a half hour. But I had walked them before, and the lowering sun told me that I must be on my way.

In the winter the dwarf cypress lose most of their needles and stand like skeletons awaiting bodies.

The Hundred-year-old Dwarfs in Long Pine Key

Quickly I came to Long Pine Key, a slight elevation where pines grew. These trees were thin and scrappy, for the larger ones had been destroyed by Hurricane Andrew. Beneath them was a carpet of thick grass more pleasing to me than the pines.

Beyond Long Pine Key **Main Park Road,** which had been running due west, began to turn gently southward. At Rock Reef Pass the road made a virtually invisible descent to sawgrass country, barely three feet above sea level. It offered a better view of the sawgrass than from much of the Tamiami Trail, for there was no levee to obscure the scenery. Neither were there barriers of bushes and low trees lining the roadside ditch. An added bonus was the lack of traffic.

I was traveling now along the fringe of the Shark River Slough where the water had very slow circulation. For this reason dwarf cypress grew sporadically amid the sawgrass. But, because there is almost no nutrition in the underlying limestone, their growth rate is so minimal that a hundred-year-old dwarf might be barely ten feet high. In the winter they lose their needles and stand like skeletons awaiting bodies. Even after needles flesh them out, they maintain a spectral quality. However, they are plucky little trees and I could not help admiring them.

Pa-hay-okee, the "Grassy Waters" Overlook

Just beyond Rock Reef Pass I turned on the short access road to the Pa-hay-okee Overlook. I parked in the lot and started on the boardwalk across the sawgrass. It was hot, even though it was late in the afternoon. It was also dry, and had been for some time. The only open water lay in the limestone crevasses. I leaned over the wooden rail to peer down into one of these little ponds. Agile water bugs scooted over the surface, leaving not even a ripple. Their dark backs shown brightly in the sunshine. Flying insects also enjoyed the crevasse as they skimmed over the water, dropping their abdomens as they laid their eggs. It would have been a good place for mosquito larvae to thrive, except for the patrolling squadrons of hungry minnows anticipating a feast of immature mosquitoes. This pond, inconsequential to me, was a treasured larder for them. For the minnows were at the top of the food chain in this Lilliput world.

Continuing on the boardwalk, I reached a hardwood hammock, where willows, cypress, pond apples, and wax myrtle made it cool. Here

The sky was so immense that for a moment it seemed as if I could feel the whirl of the earth's rotation.

I climbed the observation tower. It was not especially tall and hammock plants obscured the view on three sides. But to the north stretched an awesome expanse of sawgrass.

Alone on the tower, I had a strange sensation. The sky was so immense that for a moment it seemed as if I could feel the whirl of the earth's rotation. I clutched the tower's railing to keep from being spun off into space. If I released my hold, I'd be adrift in the solar wind. I'd become a cosmic voyager, whirling amid the planets and stars. Some would call this experience absurd. Perhaps it was. But the Everglades can do that to you.

Python Pete

The strange mood continued as I walked back through the haunted sawgrass. The Everglades was strangely quiet. But it was swarming with creatures that I could neither hear nor see. I was reminded of a recent news item about the unwanted pets that have been dumped off in the Everglades. Most of them die, but some do not. Among these are Burmese pythons. Some of these snakes have grown to lengths of twenty feet. They like to lie across pathways to sun themselves.

I began to watch carefully where I stepped. Pythons kill by wrapping their prey in a death embrace. Their jaws are large enough to envelop a basketball. And their bites, while not poisonous, can be quite painful. Even alligators leave them alone.

About the only animal that is not afraid of these invaders is a small beagle named Python Pete. Trained to recognize their scent, the small dog bounds joyfully across the sawgrass sniffing them out. When one is located, rangers dispose of it. There are not many of these snakes, but Python Pete is very good at his job, and park officials are hoping that he and his fellows will help eliminate them all.

The Mangrove Empire

Returning to the car, I resumed my drive. The sawgrass continued until I passed the sign to Mahogany Hammock. Then mangrove trees appeared—a few at first and ever more the further I drove. Soon the sawgrass was gone; replaced by a dense mangrove forest. The mangroves meant that the fresh water from the north had been made brackish by salt water from Florida Bay to the south. Although I was still in the Everglades National Park, it was not exactly the Everglades one usually pictures.

The mangrove-sawgrass battle is ongoing. One day, some say, the mangroves will displace the sawgrass entirely in the lower Everglades. For, as the earth warms and the glaciers melt, the oceans will rise. Then salt water will penetrate ever further inland. Certain scientists estimate that a third of the Everglades will either be solid mangroves or part of Florida Bay by 2050.

Another appealing mangrove vista was Mrazek Pond.

But after another geological period, the Ice Age may return. Then the sea will retreat, the mangroves recede, and the sawgrass will flourish once more. There's a constant ebb and flow to the earth cycles over which humans have no control. Time and Change roll on forever.

The farther I drove, the more humid and heavy the air became. There was a not-unpleasant smell of fecundity. Although this was a swamp, there was none of the usual swamp vegetation, like bald cypress or ferns. For mangroves were the only plants able to handle the brackish conditions.

I passed several mangrove-enclosed lakes, some ideal for canoeing and kayaking. One was near Noble Hammock, where a short canoe trail led to Hells Bay. Several miles farther on I came to West Lake, a rather good-sized body of water along which there was a half-mile boardwalk. Another appealing mangrove vista was Mrazek Pond. Finally I crossed a narrow bridge and entered the park settlement of Flamingo.

Flamingo

I didn't know what to expect from a settlement called Flamingo. I knew that a flamingo is a beautiful bird with a graceful neck and wings the color of sunsets. So by association I expected something more from the settlement than just a motel-like row of lodgings, a screened swimming pool, and a few other park buildings looking out on Florida Bay. As for flamingos, they are no-shows at the settlement honoring their name.

I guess it doesn't pay the Park Service to put a lot of money into Flamingo, since during much of the year the place is almost deserted. The reason is the mosquitoes. During the warm months they are so horrendous that the few visitors wear long pants and long-sleeved shirts and soak themselves in insect repellent. Yet, oddly, the park's sundries store does not stock mosquito repellent, for a bizarre quirk in the regulations forbids the sale within the park! Instead it sells hats draped with mosquito netting.

However, the mosquitoes were not bad when I was there in early April. I didn't use repellent and could go for several minutes without a bite.

The Murder of Guy Bradley

I did not have a lot of time to spend at Flamingo, for the day was almost over. So I didn't stop at the restaurant, even though it had a nice view of Florida Bay. However, I did manage to visit the small but interesting museum. I also paused for reflection at the monument to Guy Bradley, a little-known hero.

The National Audubon Society hired Bradley in 1905 to serve as game warden in the Florida Bay area. His job was to enforce the Florida law that forbade the hunting of such birds as egrets, ibis, and spoonbills for their plumes. These plumes at that time were quite the fashion for ladies' hats. The hunters were very efficient at killing birds. One hunter bragged he and his crew had killed eleven thousand in a single season. Such was the carnage that plume birds were on the verge of being wiped out in the Everglades and other areas.

As a youngster Bradley had been a plume hunter himself. But now, at the age of thirty-five, he had been revolted by the slaughter and eagerly accepted his role as game warden. He lived in Flamingo, and when he heard the sound of gunfire he strapped on his pistol and set out in his small boat. When he confronted the hunters, one shot him dead. The murderer claimed self-defense and a grand jury refused to indict him.

Newspapers across the nation were filled with the shocking news. Then the aroused public began condemning women who wore plumes. When this happened the fad was no longer fashionable and the bird slaughter stopped. Thus Guy Bradley accomplished more in death than he probably could have in life.

Mirages

My main purpose in coming to Flamingo was to see Florida Bay, the centerpiece of the park resort. On a map Florida Bay looks impressive. It runs all the way from Key Largo on the east to Cape Sable on the west, a total of thirty-five miles. It is embroidered with innumerable miniature keys with names that run from the whimsical, like Topsy and Dead Terrapin, to the silly, like Dump. The average depth of the bay is only four or five feet, so shallow that hurricanes can blow the water clear out of it. Due to the lack of depth, boaters must be very careful, particularly during low tide. A good map with the location of the channels and banks is essential. Knowledge of the banks is so important that even the minor ones have names. Someone in a fit of humor named one bank

The entire scene appeared as fragile as a pastel painting on a silken veil.

First National, and it stuck.

Although the park offers sightseeing cruises in the bay (as well as through the back country), it was too late in the day for them. So I walked across the meadow and stood on the shore. Articles I had read assured me that I'd view great bird congregations here. Egrets and white herons and black-necked stilts would be hunting for tidbits in the tide-lands. Overhead ospreys would soar. And from somewhere I'd hear the unmistakable call of a bald eagle.

But that's at low tide when wide mud flats are exposed. At high tide all I saw was a limitless expanse of sunset-tinted liquid. I watched a private boat leave the marina and glide quietly across the placid water, passing a solitary mangrove on its left and heading toward other mangrove islands shimmering in the distance like unsubstantial mirages. There was about the bay an air of unreality. It seemed to have no boundaries, extending across my line of vision from an eastern horizon with no beginning to a western horizon with no ending. Above, a birdless sky was draped with shapeless, wispy clouds. The entire scene appeared as fragile as a pastel painting on a silken veil: tenuous and insubstantial. I felt that with the slightest wind-puff the entire seascape would blow away like smoke.

As I watched, the leading edge of the sun reached the horizon, hovered there for a moment, then dipped into the bay, casting a crimson glow that spread over the water like magician's dye. A moment later the sun was gone.

My day in the Everglades was over.

10

Adrift in the Keys

The Setting

From the Everglades the long and wide limestone platform upon which Florida is located curves gently southwest on a course that takes it more than a hundred miles out into the Gulf of Mexico. But on its eastern side, the platform ends precipitously at the Atlantic depths. Along this eastern edge of the platform, ocean currents combined with the warm water of the platform's shallows created the ideal environment for the growth of a great coral reef.

Getting There

From Homestead/Florida City I headed south on **US 1.** During the twenty-one miles to Key Largo, I enjoyed long vistas of salt marshes and mangrove tidelands. Once on Key Largo, I followed **US 1** southwest and in four miles arrived at John Pennekamp Coral Reef State Park.

Off to the Reef

The smell of the sea floated over the Pennekamp marina even though the Atlantic was a mile or so distant. I boarded a two-decker sightseeing boat that soon set out for the great coral reef seven miles from shore. This reef extends for two hundred miles from Miami's Biscayne Bay, along the Keys, and into the Caribbean. But before reaching it, we had to pass through the dense mangrove forest that dominates this portion of the Key Largo coast. The tangled mangrove branches and prop roots formed a jungle that was almost impenetrable.

The smell of the sea floated over the marina.

The waterway down which we traveled was murky, muddy, and curvy. One bend was so sharp that the captain sounded a warning horn to unseen boaters coming in the other direction. When I took the same trip a number of years ago, there was no such warning and we surprised a young lady sunbathing in topless splendor on the deck of her boat. With no cover-up handy, she simply nodded as if she were at a garden party while we cruised slowly by. She deserved the applause we gave her.

Blue Freedom

Just as it seemed we must creep through the mangroves forever, I heard the rumble of ocean waves and the call of sea birds. Then we emerged into the wild freedom of the Atlantic. The water was dark blue over which small waves crested as white as cake frosting. With the boat rocking gently, a crew member announced that motion-sickness pills were available for those who were prone to seasickness. He warned that we were still in the protected part of the channel and the rocking might increase when we reached open water. No one took the pills and no one became sick.

The waterway down which we traveled was murky, muddy, and curvy before we emerged into the wild freedom of the Atlantic.

We passed several small islands composed of channel dredgings. They were alive with birds. As the boat picked up speed, foam hurried along the hull and watery mounds of blueberries and cream rose in the boat's wake.

An unusual exhilaration came over me. It was as if I had broken some invisible cord that bound me to the land with its fenced yards and paved streets. Out on the water there were no restrictions. The boat could go wherever the captain turned the rudder. It made its own path, and, when it had passed, the pathway dissolved and the ocean was as before. There were no trees to snarl the wind. It, too, could pass freely. Yes, the freedom of the sea was appealing.

Everyone on board was in a good mood. "If you sit on this side," a crewman told us, "you may get spray from a rogue wave." No one moved, and, when the spray came we all laughed and waited for the next. After all, the sun was warm and the breeze fresh. And it was a pleasure to lick your lips and taste the saltiness.

After traveling for around a half hour, I noticed there were splotches of lighter water amid the dark blue. We had reached the coral reef.

Divers' boats, scattered here and there, were tied up to mooring buoys installed by the authorities so the boaters wouldn't drop anchor and injure the coral, as many had done over the years.

Now our boat slowed and the captain announced that the viewing ports were ready. We descended to the lower deck and seated ourselves along a rather narrow shaft that extended down to glass panels in the boat's hull. Our legs dangled along the side of the shaft. There below us was a completely alien landscape. As I took out my binoculars to draw the panorama closer, I heard a youngster near me whisper to his mother, "Why is that man looking for birds under the water?" I'd have loved to have heard her answer.

Mountains of the Deep

The binoculars worked magic. The dangling feet disappeared and I was suddenly transported into an entirely different environment. Before me was a forest, but not one like I had ever seen. There were sea plumes, as supple as feather dusters. There were sea fans, delicate as Belgian lace, with veins of bright purple. Scattered about were sea anemones, reddish lumps in the daylight, but, I was told, when they opened at night their massed tentacles would be almost scarlet. And there were dense masses of sea rods and sea whips. All these plantlike animal colonies swayed to invisible ocean swells with a rhythm that was almost hypnotic.

As the boat ran slowly along the reef, corals came into view. Some were the large, rounded blocks with coiled grooves and ridges of brain coral. Nearby were massive star corals, some green, some brown— miniature mountains up to ten feet high. And there were the seven-foot-high bony antlers of the impressive staghorn and elkhorn corals.

Suddenly the corals gave way to a sandy valley. The sun cast long, deep blue shadows over the flat expanse. I could almost picture pioneer wagon trains wending westward through such scenery.

Coral's Strange Saga

Now the guide began telling us about corals. They are actually colonies of tiny animals called polyps. Theses polyps are very soft creatures composed of just an outer and an inner layer of cells that have formed themselves into a hollow stalk. This stalk is topped by an array of tentacles which, after stinging the microscopic plankton floating past, conduct them into the stalk, where they are digested. The polyps themselves would be prey for about every other denizen of the sea if it were not for their casing of tough, limy material. This casing forms the permanent part of the coral.

Although coral polyps were among the earliest multicelled animals to evolve, they discovered the art of reproducing sexually. When the time comes, some polyps produce sperm and others eggs. The fertilized egg becomes a free-swimming animal. After a short time the polyp swims to the bottom seeking someplace to anchor. If it finds a suitable, hard surface, it attaches itself and quickly constructs a hard limy casing. From then on, the polyp reproduces asexually by budding. The buds break from the parent, become new polyps, and begin budding themselves. In this manner a large block of coral may be derived from just a single parent.

But each polyp is very small, so the coral formation grows slowly. One estimate is that a reef rises just sixteen feet in one thousand years. The Florida reef took seven thousand years to achieve its current level.

The guide was such a fountain of facts that I felt drenched. So I let my attention wander back to the reef itself.

The Citizens of the Reef

Fish were everywhere. I saw foot-long angelfish with their yellowish, winglike fins and speckled bodies. There were sergeant majors with pale bluish sides and distinctive black vertical bars. And damselfish sporting bright yellow tails and dark brown bodies. There were schools of bronze grunts, pretty despite their name. And platoons of parrotfish, the males shades of blue or green, the females silver with black-edged scales.

There were larger fish, too, such as the rust-colored, two-and-a-half-foot grouper that lumbered past. And hovering in the darkness at the edge of my vision was a barracuda, streamlined as a torpedo, nearly three feet long, his protruding lower jaw exposing his vicious teeth. The guide said she often saw sharks and sea turtles on the reef, but we encountered none that day.

Just Driftin'

The captain cut the engine and let the boat slide along the reef. As I ran my binoculars over the watery scene below, I realized I had emerged into a geologic age when the earth was young and life had not yet left the protective seas from where it had first evolved. I was drawn to this exotic landscape. So I let my mind descend through the water to merge with world beneath me . . .

The boat drifted over a school of parrotfish. I joined them. The mood was festive: we were off for a picnic. Our goal was a rocky coral ledge. Coral was one of our favorite foods and we knew this ledge was good eating, since we'd been there before. Soon we were all crunching away. It wasn't that the actual coral tasted so good. It was the algae and polyps attached to it. I tried to imagine how algae and polyps tasted— maybe like lobster salad. I wanted more, but the boat drifted on.

Now I was amid a group of sponges. I picked out a large loggerhead sponge and descended into the central opening. Ahead of me was a maze of tunnels, each lined by polyps with gyrating tentacles by which they snared some of the plankton being drawn into the interior. But the polyps were not alone. Although they had created the spongy material that they called home, a great number of minute pistol shrimp, sea worms, and other critters had moved in—so many, in fact, that it was almost like a house party. But I had not been invited, and the fierce current, impelled by special polyps with whiplike flagella, hurried me through the winding chambers and out the back side of the sponge. It was so much fun that I decided to return for another ride, but the boat drifted on.

A massive brain coral hove into view. It was almost bizarre, as if someone's scalp had been peeled off. Yet it was nonthreatening, so I floated down and settled next to one of the polyps. In my fantasy it talked to me—it was part of a brain coral, after all. "You tell me," the polyp said, "that there is a wide world out there. I know, for in an earlier form I swam through the Great Liquid. I was young then, seeking a home. So I was happy when I found this comfortable place. I built my home here, and here I will stay until I die. Then, although my body will disintegrate, the walls of my chamber will remain to support the dwelling of other polyps."

"But wouldn't you like to see the beauty around you?" I asked.

"No," the polyp answered. "I can savor the ocean as it flows over me carrying food. Beauty is living a fulfilled life. That is what I'm doing. I want nothing else."

The boat drifted on, past a platoon of parrotfish that swam quickly across my line of vision. Were they my former group? I wanted to ask, but they moved on toward a destination I would never know.

Past more sponges. Were there house parties going on?

Past another barracuda.

Oddly, I was beginning to feel I was no stranger. These animals were becoming, if not friends, certainly acquaintances.

Suddenly my reverie was broken. "We're heading back," the captain's voice boomed over the intercom. The boat throbbed as the motor came on. Bubbles sped over the glass and the reef vanished. I raised my eyes from the binoculars and blinked as the topside world materialized around me. Everything seemed so stark. The metal was so hard. The paint was so bright. The air was acrid with engine fumes. The sky had turned dark with storm clouds. There was a sharpness around me that had not been there before.

I yearned to return to the soft, watery world of the reef.

The Way to Windley

The living coral reef off the Florida coast is relatively new, geologically speaking. But there was another coral reef that thrived in the warm, clear waters one hundred thousand years earlier until the ocean level dropped and the polyps died. This dead coral reef makes up the upper Florida Keys. The composition of this ancient reef is exposed in exquisite detail at the old quarry on Windley Key, seventeen miles down US 1 from Pennekamp.

So leaving Key Largo, I headed southwest on **US 1.** Tavernier was the next key in the chain of islands that continues for nearly ninety more miles down to Key West. The name, Tavernier, had a pleasing sound even though it comes from the Spanish word for horsefly.

Next I passed through Plantation Key, named for the pineapple farm once located here. This key is separated from Windley by a narrow channel called Snake Creek. Crossing the bridge, at **mile marker 85.5** I turned onto the short entry road that lead to the Windley Key Fossil Reef Geological State Park. First I went to the Environmental Education Center, where I examined some of the excellent exhibits. The center was named in honor of Alison Fahrer, who lead the community effort that saved the site just before a 156-unit condo complex was slated

The grooved coral stood in a row like something the Mayas might have sculpted to immortalize their kings.

to go up. Then, after purchasing a booklet entitled "Trail and History Guide," I set out to explore the quarry.

Life in a Wall

The quarry is wide and long, but only about eight feet deep. It is encompassed by a coral wall that reminded me of some partially excavated, timeworn fortress. About the grounds were large coral blocks that could have been the overturned stelae.

I walked to a part of the quarry where tree-shadows swayed, ghostlike, across the immobile coral rocks. They had been grooved by an old cutting machine, causing them to resemble something the Mayas might have sculpted to immortalize their kings. But the limestone relayed its own immortal stories. Aside from the corals were the fossilized shells of other sea animals, among them barnacles, mussels, and clams. These small creatures had bored thin tunnels into the coral. Here they made their homes—and left the holes to remind us that they, too, had passed this way.

I strolled to another part of the quarry where one of the grooves

One of the grooves provided support for a small tree. I wondered if it sensed how limited its life would be.

provided support for a small tree. I patted the tree's trunk. It was silly, but I had to admire its fortitude in this hostile environment. I wondered if it sensed how limited its life would be. I guess it's best not to be able to see the future.

Henry Flagler

Also passing this way was a gentleman named Henry Flagler. It was he who left us this remarkable quarry. Here his workers hacked out the large coral blocks that provided the bed for his Overseas Railroad, which opened between Miami and Key West in 1912.

The mining was done by burly labor gangs imported from sources as diverse as the waterfront dives of New York City and the rum gardens of the Caribbean. They sweated in the unrelenting sunshine as they were tormented by mosquitoes and biting bugs of every kind. Their water was sometimes bad, for almost all had to be imported from the mainland and stored in cisterns. Driving them forward was Henry Flagler, a weak old man with failing eyesight, a frail body, and only a few years to live.

Flagler purchased the Windley site in 1908 for less than $900.00. Even after the railroad was blown away in 1935 by one of the fiercest hurricanes ever to hit the Atlantic coast, Windley was mined for coral until the 1960s. These stones, often polished to a luster, now face many public buildings and at least one church.

A Chilling Monument

Continuing down **US 1**, I found that Windley quickly merged with Upper Matecumbe Key. In a mile I came to another old quarry. But what a difference. This has been flooded with seawater and converted into a tourist attraction called Theater of the Sea. There are continuous shows featuring dolphins and other marine mammals. Although Theater of the Sea is a popular destination for families with kids, it was not what I was looking for. So I drove on.

There is nothing much to remember about Matecumbe—nothing except the unusual monument to the people who died here during the Labor Day hurricane of 1935.

I found the monument in a small park beside US 1. It was surrounded by palms waltzing serenely in gentle breezes that strayed in from the nearby Atlantic. Approaching the monument, I was not impressed by its stylized carving of trees bending in the wind. Nor did the fossils embedded within the Windley coral impress me. It all seemed so peaceful. Just another monument.

But then I read the plaque informing me that the cremated remains of approximately three hundred people lie in the tiled crypt in front of the monument. Suddenly I felt a rush of wind and the lash of rain. I was back at that horrible night in September. A crowd of frightened workers and their families was huddled at the railroad station. They had been assured that the train dispatched from Miami would take them to safety. But it was growing dark and the train had not arrived. They didn't know it had been delayed for an hour and a half at Snake Creek while it was untangled from a loose cable. Meanwhile the wind grew stronger and Atlantic breakers crashed ever closer. The people became frantic, for the island was only seven feet above sea level.

At last the train appeared out of the driving wind and rain. By now seawater was already cascading over the tracks. It was so dark and the rain so fierce that the train overshot the station. Precious time elapsed

The cremated remains of approximately three hundred people lie in the tiled crypt in front of the monument.

while the engineer backed up to the station. Then people hustled onto passenger cars that were shaking violently. As the engineer pulled the throttle and the train started, a tremendous tidal wave nearly two stories high roared in from the Atlantic. People screamed as the wall of water smashed against the cars, overturning them and hurling everyone into the raging surf.

The next day hundreds of bodies were found floating on the ocean swells. More had vanished beneath the sea. Graves could not be dug in the tough coral bedrock, so the dead were burned in great funeral pyres. Two years later their common ashes were interred in the crypt, where they remain today.

As I stood before the monument, the warm day suddenly became chilly. I returned to my car and drove off, carrying with me uneasy memories.

A Paintbrush and Flamingoes

I left Upper Matecumbe on a bridge that reached out across the aquamarine-colored water that is so distinctive of the Keys. I paused at Indian Key Fill, a platform-island composed of channel dredgings. Looking east, I could make out the low, green form of Indian Key. It was here that John James Audubon spent seven days with Jacob Housman during the artist's epic voyage about the Keys on a small navy cutter in 1832. The islands were virtually uninhabited, aside from Key West. The shores were thick with mangroves, and, inland, hardwood hammocks ruled. Birds were everywhere, so numerous that when the crew sought fresh food, all they had to do was shoot a cannon to kill scores of birds. Audubon does not seem to be have been overly repelled by the practice, since the birds were so plentiful.

"I felt for a moment," he wrote "as if the birds would raise me from the ground so thick were they all around. . . . Their cries were indeed deafening. . . ." The highlight of his entire journey occurred one day, when "far away to seaward we spied a flock of Flamingoes. . . . Ah! Reader, could you but know the emotions that then agitated my breast! I thought I had now reached the height of all my expectations, for my voyage to the Floridas was undertaken in a great measure for the purpose of studying these lovely birds in their own beautiful islands."

Although modern visitors may take boats out to Indian Key, which is a state park, they probably won't see flamingos, for they are quite rare in Florida except in zoos and as plastic lawn decorations.

Ancient Florida

Scanning the water west from Indian Key Fill, I made out the island of Lignumvitae. From the distance of several miles it had the appearance of a thin, blue brush-line smudge. Because Lignumvitae is the highest point in the keys, "soaring" eighteen feet above sea level, it can support a hardwood hammock surpassing even that on Windley Key, which is several feet lower. This hammock is the last unspoiled virgin forest in the Keys. It was saved from developers in 1971, when it was turned into

When the pelicans were sated, they strutted along the pier or camped out on boat decks, daring any human to dispute that this was pelican territory.

Florida's first fully protected botanical site. No one is allowed into this forest unless accompanied by a state ranger—and, even then, visitors must stay on the single path that circles through a small portion of the key. One-hour walking tours are conducted twice daily. The only access to Lignumvitae Key is by private boat or on the launch from Robbie's Boat Rentals. Robbie's is not much more than a palmetto shack, a wooden pier, and a few docking stalls. But for seekers of Florida in its primeval dress, it seems an appropriate place from which to embark.

Robbie's Roost

I found Robbie's just beyond Indian Key Fill near **mile marker 77.5** on Lower Matecumbe Key. While waiting for the launch, I strolled onto the pier to watch an attendant toss herrings to a school of ravenous tarpons. These silver-backed game fish were about five feet long and as quick as harpoons. Even so, they were often left hungry by the more aggressive pelicans that dove fearlessly into their midst to snatch herrings from the tarpons' very jaws. When the pelicans were sated, they strutted along the pier or camped out on boat decks, daring any human to dispute that this wasn't pelican territory. Only the egrets, who were also pier-strutters, challenged that claim.

When the boat was ready, six of us climbed aboard and soon we were plowing through wavelets glistening with a thousand chips of turquoise. Overhead fair-weather clouds rode the wind like ocean foam. Once more the exhilaration of open water came upon me to such an extent that I was hardly aware that we had arrived at Lignumvitae until the boat's engine slowed and the arms of the pier began to enclose us. It had taken only ten minutes.

Lignumvitae Key

The pier was very long, for Florida Bay is shallow and it takes a distance to get to deeper water. A park ranger was there to greet us. He wore a broad-brimmed hat from which mosquito netting hung down over his face and neck. I had been warned about the bugs, so I had on long pants and a long-sleeved shirt. Then, upon landing, I doused my face with so much insect repellent that I felt I had taken a shower in it. Most of the others did the same. Those that didn't reported later that there were no mosquitoes out this morning. So it goes.

We walked up a low mound to the sturdy coral home of William Matheson, who once owned this island. Although Matheson was smart enough to have invented the dye for blue jeans, this house was a mistake. It was too hot and buggy, so he rarely spent time here. We were given a tour of the house, about which I found nothing special. Thus I was happy when the guide led us off into the jungle.

Immediately I felt the sensation of being in a strange environment. There were no oaks or hickories or maples, and few of the other plants with which I was familiar. Instead, the trees bore names that could have been invented for an old Tarzan movie: cat's claw, milbark, boxleaf stopper, fishfuddle. And, of course, lignum vitae. These trees are from the tropics. They don't really belong here. Their seeds snuck ashore on ocean currents and in the digestive tracts of migratory birds.

As the path extended deeper into the hammock's shadowy interior, the thick, green foliage muffled sounds until there was an eerie silence. I grew aware of the faint, musky scent of tropical vegetation. The still, humid air became heavier; became almost liquid. I leaned against a tree and let my companions continue down the path. Within a few seconds they had vanished, and in a half second more the hammock had devoured their chatter. So I was alone in the jungle, as free as the yellow-tipped swallowtail butterfly that floated across my line of vision

An Interlude with a Tree Snail

On a nearby tree were candy-striped Liguus tree snails. Their shells were about two inches long and each had variations of colors from vivid yellows and greens to more subdued browns and blues. They are native to a few keys and some hammocks in the Everglades. Once almost decimated by collectors, these beautiful little creatures have now been listed as "Species of Special Concern" by the Florida Fish and Wildlife Conservation Commission.

The snails slid forward slowly on the tree limbs as they feasted on fungi and lichens. I watched one closely. He had two pairs of stalked eyes. With the short ones he analyzed the twig over which he advanced. I could see that he had a pleasant experience waiting, for a short distance ahead, but beyond his feeble sight, was another candy snail who I felt sure would want to mate with my handsome friend. Was the snail ahead male or female? It didn't matter, for these snails have organs of both sexes. Each also has a miniature heart that will surely pump a little faster as his miniature nervous system informs her or him of the coming union. Ah, love.

Meanwhile my snail was waving his other pair of eyes—those at the end of long stalks—toward me. Each eye could distinguish movement and variations of light, but little else. I poked my head closer to the snail to give him a better view. What did these eyes reveal about my nose? Did the snail imagine it might be something to eat? Did he feel it might be dangerous? Or was he just amused that something could look so bizarre? I began to wonder what was the snail's conception of the universe as revealed through his primitive eyes? All he knew was that he was on a woody rod and there were vague shapes and shades of light around him. But it was all he had to know.

Then I heard the guide call, "You can't eat him, he's protected." I raised my head and we laughed. So I rejoined the group. And it was well that I did, for one really needs an expert to identify what he is seeing on this unusual island.

Strangers on the Shore

The most important of these strange trees to identify is, naturally, the lignum vitae. I expected showy masses of this blue-flowering tree—after all the entire key was named for it. Instead, the lignum vitae were low, inconspicuous, and rare. They are rare because once they were the ingredients of a popular drug used in the treatment of syphilis. Hence their popular name: "tree of life." These unusual trees had another characteristic that was unfortunate for their happy existence. Their wood was so

It was pleasure enough just to walk along a path paved with leaves, softened by humus, and arched by slender gumbo-limbo trees.

hard that it was also invaluable in making objects from ship propellers to bowling balls and even false teeth.

Far more spectacular were the gumbo-limbo trees, outstanding with their reddish, peeling bark. Named by West Indian workers, "gumbo" was the word for slave and "limbo" referred to the sticky sap which, when applied to a branch, would cause a bird to stick. The slave would then collect the bird and either cook it as a delicacy or, if it were colorful, cage it as a pet.

Another significant tree was the poisonwood, pleasing to the eye with its orange-tan trunk but causing serious rash upon contact.

The guide riddled off the names of more plants until it sounded as if he were talking in a foreign tongue. I suppose he could have gone on almost indefinitely, since upwards of two hundred West Indian species thrive here. But I let the words brush past me, for it was pleasure enough just to walk along a path paved with leaves, softened by humus, and arched by slender gumbo-limbo trees.

There's Only One First Time

From Lignumvitae I resumed my trip southwest on **US 1.** I've traveled this route many times over the years, but there was only one first time. I was on leave from the navy and was driving from New Jersey to Key West. I had heard about the Overseas Highway, constructed on the foundations of Henry Flagler's wrecked railroad, and wanted to see it. In those days there was no Pennekamp Park and no Windley Key fossil display. The Theater of the Sea had recently opened, but the vegetation around it was so new that most persons simply parked at the side of the road to watch the show. I recalled that the bridges were so narrow that two cars could hardly pass. Between Key Largo and Lower Matecumbe these bridges were lined with fishermen. I don't remember whether I was more concerned that I'd get a fish hook in the face or that I'd smash into another car.

The memories continued as the road broke out onto the mile-long Channel Five Bridge. The Atlantic Ocean was rocking on my left and Florida Bay shimmered with luscious shades of blues and greens on my right. Sea breezes blew furiously through my side window. Next I descended onto Long Key, which, when I first visited it, consisted of coconut palms and a few buildings dilapidated enough to have been left over from the days of railroad construction. Then I was on the Long Key Bridge, which had been featured as the railroad's logo. It spanned more than two miles of open water—two beautiful, aqua-tinted miles; two miles of lapping waves and sea birds coasting in the wind.

I came to earth at Grassy Key and quickly reached Key Vaca, site of the settlement of Marathon. Construction of the Overseas Railroad had halted here for four years while Flagler and his sweating crews tackled the great expanse of water between Marathon and Bahia Honda Key. Meanwhile at the adjacent Knights Key Flagler built a railroad terminal and docks for the steamships that would carry his wealthy guests to international playgrounds at Havana, Cuba. Although these facilities are long gone, they were still there when I first arrived. I had wandered among the fishing boats, talking to the crews. One sailor gave me a half-dried-out sea horse. I wrapped his little tail around my car mirror and kept him as a boon companion for as long as I owned my old Hudson, which was far longer than I expected.

Now the Seven Mile Bridge awaited me. On my initial trip there was a single span across the open water, with no parallel bridge, as there is today. Just a narrow cement ribbon and a fabulous expanse of open water on both sides. Flagler's trains took a half hour to cross this bridge, for they only went 15 mph, wary of the wind gusts. I took nearly that long, for there wasn't much traffic and I didn't want the experience to end.

Next was Bahia Honda Key. Years ago it was almost deserted, and I stopped to swim at the gorgeous beach before setting out on the Bahia Honda Bridge. The original railroad structure was a girder box-bridge. When it was incorporated into the highway, the road was simply laid directly on top of the girders. This added height gave it a spectacular elevation found nowhere else in the Keys. For me, ascending that old bridge created the sensation that I was motoring right up toward heaven. It was an experience I'll never forget. Nor will I ever have it again, for, after a replacement bridge was completed, a section of the old bridge was removed to make it impassible. The current bridge is four-lane, flat, and generally a far more comfortable drive. But it no longer leads toward heaven.

From the Bahia Honda Bridge I entered Big Pine Key. With that the spectacular portion of my drive was over, for the islands from here to Key West were no longer the thin crests of an ancient coral reef, but were instead squat, broad island-pads composed of a limestone-sand mixture called oolite. They were covered by slash pine, with sprinklings of cactus and extensive stands of mangroves along the shores.

The Dear Deer of Big Pine Key

My purpose in coming to Big Pine Key was to see the famed Key deer. These deer are dainty animals seldom much more than two-and-a-half feet high. At birth a fawn will weigh less than four pounds. Even at maturity a male will be under seventy-five pounds and a female under sixty-five. These deer exist nowhere else on earth. Their ancestors were full-sized deer that migrated to the Keys on the land bridge that existed when the ocean was lower during the Glacial Age. After the ocean rose, the deer were not only cut off from the mainland, but their environment was restricted to the small bits of land encompassed by the Keys. With a limited food supply, the smaller deer were more likely to survive. So they were the ones that reproduced. Thus the deer size became smaller century by century. It is a classic example of Darwin's survival of the fittest. In this manner an entirely new subspecies of deer was created.

Because they are protected animals, the deer have grown accustomed to humans and walk up to them without fear. They are so friendly and cuddly that many persons are overwhelmed with the desire to feed them. When the government established a $250 fine for such actions, some Big Pine residents began inviting the deer into their

It was then that I saw the doe's big eyes looking at me.

homes for secret banquets. But this lack of fear almost brought the deer's demise. Motorists could not avoid hitting them. At one time their population fell to barely fifty. Experts were concerned that they would soon become extinct.

In 1957 the National Key Deer Refuge was established on Big Pine Key. Now the deer population has rebounded to more than six hundred, so many, in fact, that they are almost nuisances as they gobble up prime garden plants. There are so many that there is fear that Big Pine is too small to support such numbers—and, yet, they keep growing. The surpluses can be placed on other keys, but they will eventually overpopulate these islands too. Nature did not intend for a species to exist without predators.

But that is a problem I will gladly pass on to others. I came to Big Pine just to see the lovable little deer.

Two Eyes in the Night

I arrived at Big Pine Key toward evening, which, along with early morning, is the best time to see the Key deer. During the day I had been admiring cumulus clouds piled up on the western horizon like platters of ice cream parfaits. But by the time I crossed the Bahia Honda Bridge the parfaits were melting into rain clouds. They seemed far enough off to not pose a problem—and, besides, they were putting on a pleasing show with lightning dancing about their billowing tops.

By the time I arrived at the **mile marker 30** stop light and turned right on **Key Deer Boulevard** the lightning was almost overhead and thunder was playing a resounding bass drum. Then a light shower began. As I neared the Deer Refuge parking lot the showers turned into heavy rain. Quickly thereafter the heavy rain turned into a deluge. I kept on. Then it really got bad. I've never seen such a torrent. It was as if someone had put the entire Atlantic Ocean into a plastic bag and dumped it right on me. All I could see was water. I couldn't even make out the edge of the road. The only thing I could do was stop and pray that some fool didn't ram into me.

Suddenly the torrent unaccountably let up. It was then that I saw the doe's big eyes looking at me. They did not blink, nor did the rest of her delicate body stir. She just stood there. Unafraid. Curious. Our eyes met. It seemed that I could almost see into her soul. And she into mine.

A long moment passed. Then she ambled out of my headlights' range and vanished.

So that was my total encounter with a Key deer—twenty seconds. But it was a deep experience; a quality experience. And it was enough . . . for now.

Bibliography

Adams, Amy W. et. al. *The Indian River Lagoon Comprehensive Conservation & Management Plan.* Indian River Lagoon National Estuary Program: Melbourne, FL, 1996.

Alden, Peter, et al. *National Audubon Society Field Guide to Florida.* New York: Knopf, 1998.

Angel, Heather and Pat Wolseley. *The Water Naturalist.* New York: Facts on File, 1982.

Baker, Richard H. and Juanita N. Baker. *Reflections of Blue Cypress, Photographs, History and Poems of the Headwater Lake of the St. Johns River.* Vero Beach, FL: Pelican Island Audubon Society, 2003.

Bell, C. Ritchie and Bryan J. Taylor. *Florida Wild Flowers and Roadside Plants.* Chapel Hill: Laurel Hill Press, 1982 & 1992.

Belleville, Bill. *River of Lakes, A Journey on Florida's St. Johns River.* Athens, GA: Univesity of Georgia Press, 2000.

Brown, Loren G. "Totch" *Totch, A Life in the Everglades.* Gainesville: University of Florida Press, 1993.

Cerulean, Susan, ed. *The Book of the Everglades.* Minneapolis: Milkweed, 2002.

de Golia, Jack. *Everglades: The Story Behind the Scenery.* KC Publications, 1978 & 2003.

Douglas, Marjory Stoneman. *The Everglades: River of Grass, 50th Anniversary Edition.* Sarasota, FL: Pineapple Press, 1997.

Head, Clarence M. *The Face of Florida.* Dubuque, IA: Kendall/Hunt, 1984 & 1987.

Healy, Henry G. *Terraces and Shorelines of Florida.* Tallahassee: Florida Bureau of Geology, 1975. Map Series 71

Hinchcliff, Ginger. *Rookery Bay Field Guide.* Naples, FL: Rookery Bay National Estuarine Research Reserve, 2004.

Hoffmeister, John Edward. *Land From the Sea: The Geologic Story of South Florida.* Coral Gables: University of Miami Press, 1974.

Indian River Lagoon National Estuary Program Quarterly Newsletters. Melbourne, FL.

Katz, Cathie. *The Nature of Florida's Beaches.* Melbourne, FL.: Atlantic Press, 1998.

Lane, Ed, ed. *Florida's Geological History and Geological Resources.* Florida Geological Survey, Special Publication No. 35. Tallahassee: Florida Geological Survey, 1994.

Levin, Ted. *Liquid Land: A Journey Through the Florida Everglades.* Athens, GA: University of Georgia Press, 2003.

Maehr, David and Herbert W. Kale. *Florida's Birds, 2nd Edition.* Sarasota, FL: Pineapple Press, 2005.

Martin, Mal, compiled by. *Steamboat Days of Geneva, Florida: Traveling on the St. Johns from Lake Monroe to Lake Washington.* Geneva, FL: Geneva Historical & Genealogical Society, Inc., 2003.

Molloy, Johnny. *A Paddler's Guide to Everglades National Park.* Gainesville: University of Florida Press, 2000.

Morris, Allen. *Florida Place Names.* Sarasota, FL: Pineapple Press, 1995.

Myers, Ronald L. and John J. Ewel, ed. *Ecosystems of Florida.* Orlando: University of Central Florida Press,1990.

Parks, Pat. *The Railroad That Died at Sea.* Key West: Langley Press, 1968 & 1990.

Perry, John and Jane Greverus. *The Nature of Florida.* Athens, GA: University of Georgia Press, 1998.

Peterson, Roger Tory. *A Field Guide to Birds.* Boston: Houghton Mifflin, 1980.

Proby, Kathryn Hall. *Audubon in Florida,* with Selections from the Writings of John James Audubon. Coral Gables: University of Miami Press, 1981.

Randazzo, Anthony F. and Douglas S. Jones, ed. *The Geology of Florida.* Gainesville: University Press of Florida, 1997.

Ripple, Jeff. *Big Cypress Swamp and the Ten Thousand Islands.* Columbia, SC: University of South Carolina Press, 1992.

Ripple, Jeff. *Day Paddling, Florida's 10,000 Islands and the Big Cypress Swamp.* Woodstock, VT: Backcountry Guides,2003.

Ripple, Jeff. *Florida, The Natural Wonders.* Stillwater, MN: Voyageur Press, 1997.

Ripple, Jeff. *The Florida Keys, The Natural Wonders of an Island Paradise.* Stillwater, MN: Voyageur Press, 1995.

Ruppert, Edward E. and Richard S. Fox. *Seashore Animals of the Southeast*. Columbia, SC: University of South Carolina Press,1988.

Scott, Thomas M. *A Geological Overview of Florida*. Open File Report No. 50. Tallahassee: Florida Geological Survey, 1992.

Smith, Patrick D. *A Land Remembered*. Sarasota, FL: Pineapple Press, 1984.

St. Johns River Water Management. District. *Recreational Guide to District Lands*. Palatka, FL: St. Johns River Water Management. District, 2001.

Tebeau, Charlton W. *Florida's Last Frontier, The History of Collier County*. Miami: University of Miami Press, 1957 and 1966.

Tebeau. Charlton W. *The Story of the Chokoloskee Bay Country*. Florida Flair Books: Miami, 1976.

Voss, Gilbert L. *Coral Reefs of Florida*. Sarasota, FL: Pineapple Press, 1988.

Voss, Gilbert L. *Seashore Life of Florida and the Caribbean*. Miami: Banyan Books, 1976

Waitley, Douglas. *The Best Backroads of Florida, Volume 2, Coasts, Glades, and Groves*. Sarasota, FL: Pineapple Press, 2001

Waitley, Douglas. *The Last Paradise, The Building of Marco Island*. Marco Island, FL: Marco Island Eagle, 1999.

Walden, Fred. *Dictionary of Trees*. St. Petersburg, FL: Great Outdoors Publishing, 1963.

Walker, Steven L. and Matti Majorin. *Everglades, Wondrous River of Life*. Charlottesville, VA: Elan Publishing, 1992.

Whitney, Ellie, D. Bruce Means, and Anne Rudloe. *Priceless Florida: Natural Ecosystems and Native Species.* Sarasota, FL: Pineapple Press, 2004.

Williams, Joy. *The Florida Keys: A History & Guide.* New York: Random House, 1987 & 2000.

Williams, Winston. *Florida's Fabulous Trees.* Tampa: World Publications, 2000.

Willoughby, Hugh. *Across the Everglades.* Port Salerno, FL: Florida Classics Library, 1898 and 1992

Windhorn, Stan and Wright Langley. *Yesterday's Florida Keys.* Key West: Langley Press, 1974.

Works Projects Administration. *WPA Guide to Florida: the Federal Writers' Project Guide to 1930s Florida.* New York: Pantheon, 1984.

Zim, Herbert S. *A Guide to Everglades National Park and the Nearby Florida Keys.* New York: Golden Books, 1960 (1992 edition).

Zim, Herbert S. and Lester Ingle. *Seashores: A Guide to Animals and Plants Along the Beaches.* Golden Press: New York, 1989.

Credits

Photos

U.S. Fish and Wildlife
  pages 5, 31, 238

Scott Shook
  pages 134, 135, 199

All others are by the author.

Maps

All maps by Jennifer Borresen

Index

If you enjoyed reading this book, here are some other Pineapple Press titles you might enjoy as well. To request our complete catalog or to place an order, write to Pineapple Press, P.O. Box 3889, Sarasota, Florida 34230, or call 1-800-PINEAPL (746-3275). Or visit our website at www.pineapplepress.com.

Best Backroads of Florida by Douglas Waitley. Each volume in this series offers several well-planned day trips through some of Florida's least-known towns and little-traveled byways. You will glimpse a gentler Florida and learn lots about its history. **Volume 1** The Heartland (south of Jacksonville to north of Tampa) (pb). **Volume 2** Coasts, Glades, and Groves (South Florida) (pb). **Volume 3** Beaches and Hills (North and Northwest Florida) (pb).

Florida History from the Highways by Douglas Waitley. Discover Florida, with its unique geography and exciting history—from ancient gold to modern real estate speculation—by journeying along its highways. You'll travel through changing times and landscapes and emerge filled with new appreciation for what has made Florida the colorful place it is today. (pb)

Historical Traveler's Guide to Florida 2nd Edition by Eliot Kleinberg. From Fort Pickens in the Panhandle to Fort Jefferson in the ocean 40 miles beyond Key West, historical travelers will find many adventures waiting for them in Florida. In this new updated edition the author presents 74 of his favorites—17 of them are new to this edition, and the rest have been completely updated. (pb)

Exploring Wild South Florida by Susan D. Jewell. The new third edition includes over 40 new natural areas and covers Broward, Collier, Dade, Hendry, Lee, Monroe, and Palm Beach Counties. (pb)

Florida's Finest Inns and Bed & Breakfasts by Bruce Hunt. From warm and cozy country bed & breakfasts to elegant and historic hotels, author Bruce Hunt has composed the definitive guide to Florida's most quaint, romantic, and often eclectic lodgings. With photos and charming pen-and-ink drawings by the author. (pb)

Visiting Small-Town Florida Revised Edition by Bruce Hunt now covers the whole state in one volume. From Carrabelle to Bokeelia, Two Egg to Fernandina, these out-of-the-way but fascinating destinations are well worth a side trip or weekend excursion. (pb)

Florida Magnificent Wilderness by James Valentine and D. Bruce Means. A visual journey through some of the most precious wild areas in the state, presenting the breathtaking beauty preserved in state lands, parks, and natural areas. Valentine has used his camera to record environmental art images of the state's remote wilderness places. Dr. D. Bruce Means has written the detailed captions and main text, "Florida's Rich Biodiversity." Each section of the book has an introduction written by a highly respected Florida writer and conservationist. (hb)

Florida's Birds, 2ⁿᵈ Edition: A Field Guide and Reference by David S. Maehr and Herbert W. Kale II. Illustrated by Karl Karalus. Now with color throughout, this new edition includes 30 new species accounts. Each bird is illustrated 3 times—with the species account, in the index listing, and on a plate with similar species to aid in identification. Sections on bird study, feeding, and habitats; threatened and endangered species; exotic species; and bird conservation. (pb)

Priceless Florida by Ellie Whitney, Bruce Means, and Anne Rudloe. An extensive guide (432 pages, 800 color photos) to the incomparable ecological riches of this unique region, presented in a way that will appeal to young and old, laypersons and scientists. Complete with maps, charts, species lists. (hb & pb)

The Everglades: River of Grass, 50th Anniversary Edition by Marjory Stoneman Douglas. This is the treasured classic of nature writing that captured attention all over the world and launched the fight to save the Everglades. The 50th Anniversary Edition includes an update on the events in the Glades in the last decade. (hb)

Common Coastal Birds of Florida and the Caribbean by David W. Nellis. This comprehensive guide reveals 72 of the most common birds found along the coasts of Florida and the islands to the south. Includes abundant information on each bird's nesting, feeding, mating, and migrating habits, as well as more than 250 color photos that show many features of these birds never before so fully illustrated. (hb & pb)

Over Key West and the Florida Keys by Charles Feil. A gorgeous album featuring aerial photographs of islands large and small, glistening waters, and serene communities. Captions provide bits of Keys history. (hb)